**BOCCONI
UNIVERSITY
PRESS**

Emiliano Finocchi

DISRUPTING INTERNATIONALIZATION

A Redefinition with Market Pareidolia

Foreword by **Alessandro Terzulli**

Cover: Cristina Bernasconi, Milan

Copyright © 2025 Bocconi University Press
EGEA S.p.A.

EGEA S.p.A.
Via Salasco, 5 - 20136 Milano
Tel. 02/5836.5751 – Fax 02/5836.5753
egea.edizioni@unibocconi.it – www.egeaeditore.it

First edition: June 2025

ISBN Domestic Edition 979-12-80623-66-9
ISBN Digital Domestic Edition 979-12-229-8046-1
ISBN International Edition 979-12-81627-52-9
ISBN Digital International Edition 979-12-81627-53-6
ISBN Epub 979-12-229-8049-2

Content

Foreword
by *Alessandro Terzulli*

Complexity and uncertainty are two of the most used words in economic analyses and comments over the last five years, more so with reference to international trade and the multiple shocks which have affected it.

Internationalization processes have, though, become way more complex before then, due to the acceleration of change caused by the ever more interconnected nature of global markets, the rapid diffusion of technology, and the rise of data-driven decision-making.

Making sense of complexity by harnessing change as a competitive advantage, as the author points out in a very effective way, is therefore very important and – overall - rewarding for companies, also for smaller ones because of the well-known sunk costs of going international in geographically and culturally distant markets.

It is even more challenging to deal with uncertainty. The Trade Policy Uncertainty Index has increased to a record high, considering the impact of the new restrictive measures adopted by the US administration, making global development decisions and the definition of possible scenarios much more difficult. In other words, business planning for international ventures is now highly complicated.

There are anyway high benefits to reap in foreign markets and the new reality requires adaptability as the key not only for a company's survival but - I would add – to be thriving. By a historical excursus of major disruptions in foreign trade, Emiliano Finocchi highlights that firms need therefore to broaden and update their toolbox with: (i) Agile Leadership, to proactively anticipate changes and trends; (ii) Continuous Learning, as a lever to skill-driven and productive organizations; (iii) Digital Transformation, to embrace technological change through automation, including the adoption of AI; and (iv) Sustainable Growth, to ensure long term and enduring performance in both financial and non-financial terms.

Is turning adaptable enough? It is a matter of 3Ws and one H: When, Where, What and How. This is the logical and pragmatic approach, followed in the book, to "Disrupting Internationalization".

As to the "When", the right timing and readiness depend on several internal and external factors. On the former, companies must develop strong internal capabilities, robust supply chains, and a strategic vision before expanding whereas on the latter: financial and operational stability can guarantee capital, both physical and human, technology, and logistics investment capacity; the so-called "one-size fits all" approach to Country Risk analysis and tolerance does not work, doing then the homework on this aspect is time-consuming but essential; last but not least there has to be a clear awareness on the demand preferences for the product and/or service in the target market.

The "Where" part is, in my view, core and paramount for the success of foreign ventures. Classifications help simplify, but oversimplification does not help when dealing with market selection, which cannot be based on a rigid categorization and is instead a "non-linear, multicriteria decision-making challenge". The BRICS example fits well: if this original, appealing and popular acronym, created by Goldman Sachs Chief Economist James O'Neill back in 2001, was effective in identifying global fast-growing emerging markets, it was less so in catching the multidimensionality needed in identifying market opportunities. As a matter of fact, these five countries' growth models are still now structurally very different from each other and have also struggled to be considered as an asset class for financial investors.

A new, more dynamic and human-centered framework is introduced, in an interdisciplinary way, by the author: "Market Pareidolia". Pareidolia originates from psychology and, when applied to markets, this notion proposes that companies should concentrate on identifying emerging patterns that signify real, genuine business prospects, based on their 'age' - a metaphor that correlates economic growth with stages of human development: from rapidly growing, innovative but often unpredictable markets (Adolescent) to highly developed, but potentially saturated and requiring-innovation ones (Senior). Helpful and practical examples of such markets are punctually provided.

It is not a compartmentalized, sequential-only exercise. The timing of international expansion impacts on market selection, which in turn influences the business model of entry, or better the calibration between the company's mode of operation with its aptitudes and market conditions. Before moving then to the third W, it is wisely highlighted that there is a strong interdependence between the When, Where and What here examined, and these dimensions need to be successfully integrated in a strategic framework. Keeping this in mind – many books, guides and specific papers, even the most comprehensive ones, do not well and/or fully address this point of attention - the next question is: What type of internationalization is most suitable?

A thorough review of the different ways businesses engage in international operations is conducted and the number of options can be overwhelming. There is not evidently a magic solution, and it is not surprising that the right entry mode is the one that best fits the company's strategy. It is of paramount importance though to understand there are no free lunches and each mode has trade-offs: licensing is great for low-cost expansion with little financial risk but offers limited control over operations and brand management; foreign direct investment is best for long-term international presence but requires sizeable capital investment and extensive market research. The author introduces a new approach to allow easier decision-making, based on the degree of both risk and involvement.

Finally, internationalization is not just about setting a strategy, a necessary but not sufficient condition. It is equally about How to do it effectively. Even the best-laid plans can fail without a structured process for execution, which often requires local knowledge, regulatory expertise, and an understanding of cultural nuances. To this aim the book suggests six well established international business process models that guide companies in structuring their international development efforts, without ignoring how key are local partnerships - whether with an individual, a business entity, or in a joint venture - in helping a company navigate complexity (e.g. legal compliance, consumer-behavior adaptation) and mitigate country risk (e.g. failing to integrate into foreign business ecosystems).

The reading of "Disrupting Internationalization" has been to me a compelling journey, just like that one of adaptation and growth of going international, which must be a continuous process and can't be taken as a one-time event. Emiliano Finocchi has done a very accurate job, also through a meticulous research and synthesis of the broad academic literature on the topic, in making this clear and in a "user-friendly" way for both practitioners and companies. They can have all the relevant findings they need all at once and with one single refence in this book. I am sure they will enjoy going through it as much as I did.

Dedication

To those who have known darkness, but still chose to reach for the light…
Those who've stumbled, fallen, and wandered far from who they wanted to be.
And yet
found the courage and strength to begin again.
This book is for the fighters, the healers, the rebuilders.
Your story is not one of failure,
but of becoming.

Discover the World of Market Pareidolia

By scanning this QR code, you will be redirected to , the official platform introducing the concept of **Market Pareidolia**. This site offers a unique, human-centric approach to understanding international markets by categorizing 175 countries according to human life stages (**Adolescence**, **Adulthood**, and **Seniority**) based on a comprehensive analysis of socio-economic, political, and developmental indicators.

Through an intuitive framework built on cognitive psychology and advanced market analytics, users will explore detailed profiles of each country, learn how their "market age" influences business strategies, and gain actionable insights for internationalization, investment planning, and risk management. Designed for business leaders, consultants, policymakers, and researchers, the site transforms complex global data into an accessible, empathetic tool for strategic decision-making in today's interconnected world.

Start navigating international markets with greater clarity, empathy, and strategic foresight powered by **Market Pareidolia**.

1 The Acceleration of Change (WHEN)

"It is not the most intellectual of the species that survives; it is not the strongest that survives; but the species that survives is the one that is able best to adapt and adjust to the changing environment in which it finds itself." (Megginson on Charles Darwin's work, 1963, p. 4)

In the dynamic landscape of today's business world, where technological innovations rapidly evolve and market conditions fluctuate unpredictably, the concept of change emerges as a predominant and immutable force. This force propels organizations and individuals toward adaptation, growth, and the realization of new opportunities. Change, in its relentless progression, is inevitable and its pace is accelerating over time. For organizations to thrive, they must embrace change, proactively anticipate it, and drive it forward. The ability to navigate and leverage change has become a critical component of success in the contemporary business environment. The business ecosystem of today is far removed from that of the past, not just in terms of technology but also in how change itself is perceived and managed. Historically, change management was a reactive process, a response to external shifts such as economic downturns, technological advancements, or competitive pressures. Today, however, change is a continuous, integral aspect of an organization's strategy. It demands not just acceptance but a proactive stance from leadership; it requires agile responses, and an organizational culture steeped in continuous learning and innovation. Agile leadership is crucial in this context, as leaders must cultivate an ability to foresee market trends and potential disruptions, making strategic adjustments swiftly and effectively. They must lead by example, fostering a culture where change is viewed as an opportunity rather than a threat. This involves not only strategic foresight but also operational flexibility and the willingness to make difficult decisions that align with long-term goals. Moreover, a culture of continuous learning within an organization is vital for sustaining competitive advantage in a rapidly changing world. This culture encourages ongoing personal and professional development, ensuring that employees not only keep pace with industry changes but also contribute to the organization's innovative capacity. In such environments, learning is not confined to formal training but is part of the everyday workflow, embedded in every project and every challenge encountered. Furthermore, organizations must commit to staying ahead of the curve. This involves investing in new technologies, exploring emerging markets, and continuously improving products and services. It requires a forward-thinking approach where change is integrated into the planning and execution phases of business strategy, not merely reacted to when it becomes unavoidable.

Those who fail to acknowledge the accelerating pace of change risk falling behind. In today's fast-paced business environment, being slow to adapt can lead to missed opportunities and eventual obsolescence (in some cases leads to failure). Companies and individuals who view change as a sporadic disruption rather than a constant aspect of modern business are less likely to succeed in the long term. Today, change is no longer a mere possibility to be managed, it is a perpetual reality that demands a strategic approach and an adaptive mindset. Understanding and harnessing the accelerating pace of change is paramount for businesses and individuals alike to thrive and remain relevant. As markets evolve and new technologies redefine the possible, the ability to adapt swiftly and effectively sets apart successful enterprises from those that falter. To fully appreciate the accelerating pace of change in today's international markets, it is essential to first understand their historical evolution. This understanding not only provides context but also highlights the shifts in strategic thinking required (from reactive to proactive) to navigate this new era of constant, rapid change. As we delve deeper into the mechanisms of change within the global marketplace, it becomes clear that mastery over this dynamic process is foundational to the ongoing success and innovation of any organization.

1.1 The Pretechnological Era

Traditionally, international markets evolved over centuries, shaped by factors such as geographical discoveries, colonial expansions, and trade routes. The Silk Road, for instance, not only facilitated the trade of silk and spices but also acted as a conduit for cultural and technological exchanges between the East and the West. In this era, changes in international markets were predominantly gradual. The slow pace was attributed to limited technological advancements, reliance on manual labor, and rudimentary communication methods. Trade was constrained by long travel times and the risks associated with long-distance sea and land journeys. Information flow was equally slow, with news of market changes taking weeks or months to reach traders and businesses, thereby limiting their ability to respond promptly to market dynamics.

The Silk Road, a term coined in the 19th century, refers to a complex network of trade routes that connected the East to the West and facilitated commerce for over 1,500 years, commencing with the initiation of trade by the Han dynasty of China in 130 B.C. and continuing until 1453 A.D., when trade with the Western world was curtailed by the Ottoman Empire. Yet, the Silk Road's significance transcended the mere trade of goods, as merchants and caravans traversed these routes carrying with them the seeds of cultural exchange such as philosophies, scientific knowledge, and religious beliefs, spilled from their laden baskets and taking root in foreign soils. Technologies that would later define civilizations, such as papermaking and the compass, along with the less tangible but equally vital exchanges in art, literature, and culinary traditions, crossed these boundaries, creating a rich tapestry of shared human heritage. In the context of international markets, the Silk Road exemplified the archetype of gradual change. Bound by the era's technological constraints, with no steam engines to speed their journey or telegraphs to send ahead their news, traders relied on the steady plod of hooves and the rhythmic sway of ships. The unpredictability of travel, compounded by the perils of natural disasters, banditry, and political instability, meant that risk was an inherent companion to trade, reflected in the cost and scarcity of the exotic goods exchanged. The flow of information was equally measured, with news creeping along at the pace of the physical traveler. A merchant in Venice might have waited months to hear of the market prices in Samarkand, and longer still to receive the goods he had commissioned. This sluggish exchange was the norm, not the exception, and set a pace for market movement that was deliberate and restrained. In this manner, the international markets of the time were characterized by their static nature, shaped by the slow but persistent heartbeat of the Silk Road's caravans.

This era's pace of change stands in stark contrast to the rapid, almost instantaneous, market reactions of today. Yet, understanding this epoch is pivotal, as it lays the foundational understanding of how markets can and have evolved. The Silk Road is not merely a relic of the past but a beacon that illuminates the path of commerce from its dawn to the present day. In its story, we see the foreshadowing of globalization and the intricate interplay of supply and demand across continents, a theme that remains ever relevant as we navigate the complexities of modern international markets.

1.2 Emergence of Early Technologies

The landscape of international commerce underwent a profound transformation with the advent of early technological innovations. Central to this transformation was the invention of the printing press in the 15th century by Johannes Gutenberg, a device that radically altered the course of history. The printing press made the mass production of books possible, which in turn made knowledge more accessible. Prior to this, books were handwritten and extremely costly, limiting their availability to a select few. By enabling the widespread distribution of printed material, the printing press democratized information and set the stage for the Enlightenment era and the rise of a more educated and informed middle class.

In terms of international markets, the impact of the printing press was equally revolutionary. For the first time, merchants could disseminate trade information rapidly across vast distances. The publication of tariffs, trade agreements, and mercantile laws became standardized, leading to a more predictable trading environment. Moreover, the proliferation of navigational charts and guides facilitated the expansion of trade routes and the exploration of new territories. The printing press, therefore, was not just a tool for spreading ideas but a catalyst for economic expansion. Yet, the pace of change within market structures and practices was not immediate. While the printing press enabled the faster spread of information, the actual practices of trade and commerce took time to evolve. Traditional methods of trade, reliant on established guilds and familial networks, were entrenched in society and resistant to change. The flow of goods across international borders continued to be a slow and arduous process, dictated by the limitations of contemporary transportation and the vagaries of political alliances. Despite these limitations, the printing press set in motion a series of incremental changes that would eventually culminate in the modernization of market systems. With the greater availability of information, there was a slow but steady push toward standardization and efficiency. Contracts became more complex, and the legal frameworks governing international trade grew more sophisticated. This evolution was gradual, as innovations were assimilated into the existing fabric of trade at a measured pace, reflecting the cautious nature of economic expansion during this period. In essence, the introduction of the printing press and other early technologies provided the kindling for a fire that would, in time, ignite a blaze of change across international markets. These technologies sowed the seeds for future advancements that would accelerate the pace of change, leading to the dynamic and interconnected global economy we experience today.

1.3 Industrial Revolution: A Paradigm Shift

The First Industrial Revolution (1760–1840) was not merely a period of technological advancement; it was a fundamental shift in the very structure of society and the engine of the world's economy. The changes that began in the late 18th century continued into the 19th century, reshaping every aspect of daily life, from how people worked to how they conducted business and interacted with the world.

The invention of the steam engine by James Watt (1763) is often cited as the hallmark of this era. This remarkable innovation provided a source of power that was not dependent on the whims of weather or the strength of flowing water. It revolutionized transportation with the steam locomotive and the steamship, making it possible to move goods and people across distances with a speed and efficiency previously unattainable. The steam engine's impact on industry was profound; factories no longer needed to be situated near rivers or windmills.

They could be located anywhere, and their size and output grew exponentially. Simultaneously, the invention of the telegraph by Samuel Morse in the 1830s laid the foundations for the modern communications era. Information that once took weeks to convey could now be transmitted in minutes. The telegraph not only changed the speed at which business was conducted but also transformed the nature of international diplomacy and news distribution. Markets, once local or regional, became increasingly national and even international, as traders and financiers could learn of price changes and supply disruptions almost instantaneously. With the surge in production capabilities came the establishment of the factory system. The division of labor and the introduction of assembly lines meant that products could be produced on a scale and at a cost that made them accessible to a much broader segment of the population. This mass production fueled a surge in trade volume, as goods that were once the preserve of the affluent became commonplace. The Industrial Revolution also saw the expansion of the financial market. Banks and financial institutions grew in size and number, providing the capital needed for industrial expansion. The rise of the stock market as a barometer of economic health began to take shape during this period. Companies could raise funds by selling shares, and this influx of capital drove further innovation and expansion.

The repercussions of these technological advancements were not confined to the economic realm. Social structures were transformed as people migrated from rural areas to cities, seeking work in the factories. This urbanization brought about significant changes in living conditions and social dynamics. The rise of a new social class, the industrial capitalist, and the burgeoning middle class redefined social hierarchies and power dynamics. The Industrial Revolution marked the beginning of a new age, characterized by rapid change and innovation. It laid the groundwork for the modern international market, introducing changes at a pace previously unimaginable. The era was a crucible of innovation, each invention propelling the next, creating a self-sustaining cycle of growth that would catapult the international markets into a new epoch of progress and complexity.

1.4 From Incremental to Exponential Growth

For centuries, the evolution of international markets has been a slow process. Changes unfolded over a long period of time, as their pace was so gradual that a single human lifespan might witness little more than a ripple in the vast economic continuum. Even as the First Industrial Revolution (1760–1840) and the Second Industrial Revolution (1870–1914) brought about significant technological and social advances, the overall growth trajectory of international markets continued along a largely predictable, linear path through the 19th century and into the early 20th century. However, as the world emerged from the shadows of World War II, it found itself on the cusp of a new era. The geopolitical landscape had been irrevocably altered, with old empires waning and a wave of decolonization sweeping across Asia, Africa, and the Middle East. The formation of new nation-states redrew the global map, and with it, the channels of international trade and commerce were redefined.

The Bretton Woods Conference of 1944 established a new economic order, creating institutions such as the International Monetary Fund (IMF) and the World Bank, which aimed to stabilize global markets and promote international trade. The adoption of the US dollar as the world's primary reserve currency, tied to gold, provided a level of monetary stability that facilitated international business (IB) and investment. In this postwar environment, technological advancements played an increasingly prominent role. The advent of commercial aviation shrank the globe, enabling faster movement of people and goods. The development of the transistor and, subsequently, the microchip, paved the way for the digital revolution that would later explode in the late 20th century. Technologies that had once seemed like the stuff of science fiction have become reality, changing the speed and scope of market interactions.

In the latter decades of the 20th century, the tempo of global market growth shifted gears, entering an era of rapid acceleration fueled by transformative technologies and innovative logistics. This period witnessed a quantitative increase in trade but also a qualitative metamorphosis in the very nature of market expansion and integration. The introduction of container shipping stands as a landmark event in this transformation with Malcolm McLean's innovation (1956) that dramatically cut the costs and time required for sea transport. By standardizing cargo size and streamlining the loading and unloading process, containerization allowed goods to flow across the oceans with unprecedented efficiency. This logistical leap forward was a physical manifestation of what would later be understood through Wright's Law (1936), stating that progress increases with experience, as the more times a task is performed, the lower the cost of doing it. Container shipping was a prime example of this, as the repeated process of global trade became cheaper, faster, and more reliable. In conjunction to this logistical revolution was the proliferation of the television and, subsequently, the internet, which wove a digital fabric across societies and creating the bases for a global consumer culture. Television brought images and desires into living rooms worldwide, while the internet later connected consumers with markets in a direct and immediate way. This burgeoning digital connectivity began to open new markets, driving demand for a diverse array of goods and services, and fostering a culture of immediate gratification and constant innovation. As the century neared its end, the digital revolution began to assert its influence, signaling a shift from linear growth to an exponential one. Moore's Law (1965), which states that the number of transistors on a microchip double approximately every two years, while the cost of computers is halved, predicted this exponential pace of technological improvement, which played out vividly in the international markets. The computing power available to businesses and consumers alike began to increase at a staggering rate, and with it, the capacity for processing, analyzing, and transmitting vast quantities of data.

Ray Kurzweil (2001) extended this concept further, proposing the Law of Accelerating Returns, which suggests that the rate of technological change is exponential because each new generation of technology stands on the shoulders of its predecessors. In terms of market responsiveness, this law was exemplified by the way years of market adjustments were compressed into months, and months into days. Markets began to react in real time to fluctuations and shifts, with algorithms trading stocks in milliseconds and supply chains adjusting dynamically to changes in demand. The deluge of information became the new normal, with market data, news, and trends circulating globally in an instantaneous loop. This ceaseless flow was facilitated by the internet, which broke down the temporal and spatial barriers that once governed international markets. Now, a manufacturer in Shanghai could instantaneously track the inventory of a retailer in New York, adjusting production in near real time. The culmination of these technological and logistical advancements brought about a level of market integration that was previously inconceivable. Moore's Law, Kurzweil's predictions, and Wright's observations provide a framework for understanding the exponential growth of international markets. They underscore the idea that the advancements of the past are not just milestones but also steppingstones to the future, each one setting the stage for the next leap forward in a never-ending dance of progress.

1.5 Embracing Velocity: The Imperative of Adaptability

The seismic shifts in technology and logistics that marked the latter half of the 20th century did more than just accelerate market growth and integration; they fundamentally altered the landscape in which companies operate. In this new era of heightened interconnectivity and rapid technological progression, the ability to adapt has become a core survival trait for any business. For example, for Multinational Corporations (MNCs), the increasing speed of change presents both vast opportunities and significant challenges. On the one hand, these corporations can leverage their global footprint to harness economies of scale, tap into emerging markets more swiftly, and mobilize resources to capitalize on technological advancements. On the other hand, the swift currents of change can disrupt established markets, unseat traditional industry leaders, and create unforeseen compliance complexities as regulations struggle to keep pace with innovation. Small and Medium Enterprises (SMEs), while more agile and often more innovative by necessity, face the daunting task of keeping up with the rapid rate of change without the cushion of vast resources. For these smaller players, adaptability is not just strategic; it is existential. The digital revolution has leveled the playing field in many ways, allowing SMEs to compete on a global stage, but it also requires them to be nimble, to pivot quickly in response to market trends, and to adopt new technologies that can enhance their competitiveness. NGOs and other nonprofit organizations are also impacted by this acceleration. While their missions may not be profit-driven, their effectiveness depends on their ability to leverage technology for coordination, fundraising, and achieving social impact. They too must adapt to the fast-paced digital landscape, employing new technologies to amplify their message and to execute their missions more efficiently in a world where attention is fragmented and the window for action can be brief.

The increasing velocity of change in the international markets necessitates the shift between reacting to a proactive approach to change by applying dynamic management. Companies must cultivate a culture of continuous learning, encourage innovation, and remain vigilant to changes in global markets. They must develop strategies that are flexible and dynamic, able to be reconfigured in response to real-time data and emerging trends. The exponential growth trajectory that businesses face today is not merely a phenomenon to be observed but a clarion call for action. The need for readiness, for an anticipatory rather than a reactive posture, has never been greater. As the past has shown, those who can move with the currents of change, who can embrace and harness its momentum, will survive, and plausibly thrive. The future belongs to the adaptable, to the organizations that view change not as a threat but as the very medium through which they evolve and excel.

1.6 Setting the Stage for the Digital Revolution and Environmental Awareness

The closing decades of the 20th century were marked by a burgeoning awareness of the finite nature of our planet's resources and the boundless potential of digital technology. It was during this period that two pivotal developments began to unfold, each of which would profoundly influence the trajectory of international markets in the years to come. The invention of the computer, which began as a bulky, complex machine used primarily by governments and large corporations, would, over the decades, transform into an indispensable tool for businesses and individuals alike. The rise of personal computing in the late 20th century democratized access to information and computing power, laying the foundation for the digital revolution. This revolution gained further momentum with the advent of the internet, a technology that began to share information between research institutions but quickly expanded to connect the entire globe. The digital revolution reshaped international markets in several fundamental ways. First, it increased the speed at which business could be conducted, from communication to transactions. The internet allowed for instantaneous exchange across continents, facilitating a level of responsiveness that was previously unimaginable. Additionally, the digitization of business processes led to heightened efficiency and cost reductions, from automated supply chains to digital marketing and e-commerce platforms.

Simultaneously, a growing awareness about environmental sustainability began to take root during the mid-20th century, marked by significant cultural and scientific milestones that highlighted the need for ecological preservation. The publication of Rachel Carson's "Silent Spring" in 1962 was a pivotal moment in this awakening. Carson's work, which documented the adverse effects of indiscriminate pesticide use, particularly DDT, on wildlife and human health, sparked widespread public and scientific debate about the relationship between humans and the natural environment. This burgeoning environmental awareness was further amplified by the celebration of the first "Earth Day" on April 22, 1970. Spearheaded by Senator Gaylord Nelson and inspired by the student anti-war movement, Earth Day mobilized millions of Americans across various cities to demonstrate against the deterioration of the environment. This mass mobilization not only raised awareness but also set the stage for the modern environmental movement, leading to significant legislative actions such as the establishment of the United States Environmental Protection Agency (EPA) and the passage of the Clean Air, Clean Water, and Endangered Species Acts. As the scientific understanding of human impacts on the environment expanded, it became increasingly clear that unchecked economic growth could lead to irreversible ecological damage. The realization that economic activities were degrading essential ecosystems, reducing biodiversity, and polluting air and water sources led to a rethinking of traditional economic development models. This shift in thinking was encapsulated in the concept of sustainable development, which emerged prominently in international discourse with the publication of the Brundtland Report, "Our Common Future," in 1987 (Burton, 1987). The report, prepared by the World Commission on Environment and Development, defined sustainable development as development that satisfies current requirements while ensuring that future generations can also fulfill their needs (Burton, 1987). This definition emphasized the need for economic strategies that ensure long-term ecological health, advocating for a balance between economic growth, environmental care, and social well-being. Sustainable development proposed that economies could progress while simultaneously conserving natural resources and enhancing quality of life, ensuring that environmental stewardship became an integral component of global development policies. This evolving understanding of sustainability has continued to influence global policies and practices, leading to initiatives such as the United Nations Sustainable Development Goals (SDGs), adopted in 2015. These goals highlight a global agenda aimed at addressing a range of social, economic, and environmental challenges by the year 2030. As part of this comprehensive framework, sustainable development remains a central theme, reflecting a global consensus on the

necessity of integrating environmental health into the heart of economic planning and decision-making. The convergence of digital transformation and environmental awareness created a synergy that is now integral to modern market
dynamics. On the one hand, digital technologies enable more efficient resource
use and provide platforms for the dissemination of environmental data, thereby
fostering greater transparency and accountability in corporate practices. On the
other hand, the emphasis on sustainability is pushing companies to innovate
and adopt green technologies, which in turn drive further digital advancements.
Today, digital transformation and environmental awareness are not just considerations but imperatives for market success. In an age where consumers are increasingly discerning about the ethical and environmental footprints of their
consumption, businesses must leverage digital tools to meet these demands and
to operate sustainably. Digital technologies offer the data analytics necessary
for understanding and reducing environmental impacts, and they provide the
means to engage with stakeholders who demand corporate responsibility.

As seen, digital transformation and environmental awareness are two paramount forces driving the modern business agenda, and their convergence is
epitomized in the embrace of environmental, social, and governance (ESG) criteria. ESG represents a holistic approach to assessing the impact and sustainability of an organization, blending digital prowess with a commitment to environmental stewardship and social responsibility. In an age where data reigns
supreme, digital transformation provides the tools and methodologies required
to measure and analyze an organization's ESG performance. Advanced analytics, artificial intelligence, and the Internet of Things (IoT) enable the meticulous
tracking of environmental footprints, social impact, and governance practices,
allowing for transparent reporting and accountability. Moreover, digital platforms facilitate stakeholder engagement, enabling companies to communicate
their ESG initiatives and progress directly with consumers, investors, and the
wider community. Sustainability, once a siloed concern, is now a core element
of strategic business models, thanks to the integration of ESG considerations.
It encourages organizations to minimize their environmental impact through
smarter resource management (reducing emissions) and to foster inclusive
workplaces and uphold the highest ethical standards. As businesses undergo
digital transformation, they are also redefining their corporate identity and
value proposition in the market, aligning with the ESG framework to ensure
they meet the growing demands for responsible and sustainable practices in an
increasingly interconnected and digitalized global economy.

As the 21st century progresses, the dual forces of digital transformation
and environmental sustainability will continue to shape the landscape of international markets. They are the twin pillars upon which the future of global trade
rests, challenging businesses to innovate continuously while ensuring that their
operations enhance rather than exploit the natural world. The stage set by the

late 20th century for these movements has led to a new era in IB, one where adaptability and responsibility are key to enduring success.

1.7 ESG and Digital Transformation: A Perfect Match

In recent years, the convergence of digital transformation and ESG criteria has emerged as a pivotal force reshaping the landscape of IB. As companies navigate the complexities of global markets, integrating these two paradigms has become essential for achieving sustainable growth and competitive advantage. This chapter explores the symbiotic relationship between ESG and digital transformation, highlighting how their alignment can drive innovation, enhance corporate responsibility, and foster long-term value creation. Digital transformation refers to the profound integration of digital technologies into all aspects of a business, fundamentally changing how companies operate and deliver value to customers. Technologies such as artificial intelligence (AI), the Internet of Things (IoT), blockchain, and big data analytics are revolutionizing traditional business models, enabling real-time decision-making, automation, and enhanced customer experiences. This transformation is not merely about adopting new technologies but about rethinking organizational processes, culture, and strategies to leverage digital capabilities fully. Simultaneously, ESG criteria have gained prominence as a framework for evaluating a company's commitment to sustainable and ethical practices. The environmental component focuses on a company's impact on the planet, encompassing efforts to reduce carbon emissions, manage waste, and promote resource efficiency. The social aspect examines how a company manages relationships with employees, suppliers, customers, and communities, emphasizing human rights, diversity, and labor practices. Governance pertains to the internal systems, controls, and practices that ensure transparency, accountability, and ethical behavior.

The intersection of ESG and digital transformation is not coincidental but rather a response to evolving market dynamics and stakeholder expectations. Investors, consumers, regulators, and employees increasingly demand that companies not only perform financially but also contribute positively to society and the environment. This shift in expectations necessitates a holistic approach where digital innovation supports and amplifies ESG initiatives. Several factors drive the convergence of ESG and digital transformation. First, the increasing availability of data and advanced analytics enables companies to measure and manage their environmental and social impacts more effectively. For instance, IoT sensors can monitor energy consumption and emissions in real-time, while AI can optimize resource allocation and waste management. Second, digital platforms facilitate greater transparency and accountability, allowing companies to report on ESG metrics and engage with stakeholders more openly. Moreover, the rise of digital natives (consumers and employees who have grown up with technology) has heightened the demand for ethical and sustainable business practices. These stakeholders are more likely to support companies that align with their values and demonstrate a commitment to ESG principles. Furthermore, regulatory frameworks worldwide are evolving to mandate ESG disclosures, with digital tools playing a crucial role in ensuring compliance and facilitating reporting. Integrating ESG and digital transformation is not just a strategic choice but a competitive necessity. Companies that successfully blend these elements can unlock new opportunities for innovation, efficiency, and market differentiation. For instance, by leveraging blockchain for supply chain transparency, businesses can ensure ethical sourcing and enhance consumer trust. Similarly, AI-driven analytics can identify social risks and opportunities, informing strategies that promote diversity, equity, and inclusion.

In conclusion, the convergence of ESG and digital transformation represents a transformative shift in how businesses operate and compete in the global marketplace. By aligning digital capabilities with ESG principles, companies can drive sustainable growth, meet stakeholder expectations, and build resilient, future-ready enterprises. This chapter delves into the practical applications, strategies, and challenges of integrating ESG and digital transformation, providing a roadmap for businesses seeking to thrive in an increasingly interconnected and conscientious world.

2 International Markets Categorization (WHERE)

"International market selection is a non-linear, multi-criteria decision-making problem with overwhelming complexity." (Zhang, Zhuang, Gao, 2007)

Categorization is an essential cognitive and organizational tool, fundamental to both our understanding of the world and the efficiency of our societal structures. At its core, categorization is the process of grouping various elements based on shared characteristics, a practice that is not only instinctive but also critical for simplifying the complexity of our environment. This simplification allows us to process information more efficiently, enabling quicker decision-making and better resource management. The widespread application of categorization in daily life has spurred extensive research in strategic, sociological, and organizational domains, primarily focusing on cognitive and social methodologies (Durand et al., 2017). The cognitive approach to categorization, influenced by Rosch & Mervis (1975), has been further developed in organizational theories by scholars such as Carroll, Hannan, and Hsu (Hannan et al., 2007; Hsu et al., 2009). This approach advocates categorizing a product's value proposition and its producers by evaluating an existing prototype. Durand and Paolella expanded on this concept, proposing that categorization based on prototypes should evolve over time to align with the audience's objectives (Durand & Paolella, 2013; Paolella & Durand, 2016). Alternatively, social constructionists and interactionists, including Rosa and Spanjol (Rosa et al., 1999; Rosa & Spanjol, 2005), have adopted a social lens for categorization. Initially applied to market categorization, this perspective emphasizes the importance of cultural differences and social perceptions in the categorization process, as supported by Durand et al. (2017) and Navis & Glynn (2010).

Categorization's efficacy lies not only in simplifying and ordering the surrounding chaos but also in its dynamic nature, allowing it to evolve with shifting societal values and market trends. Cognitive and social approaches to categorization each play a distinct role in the strategic planning of businesses, especially when they venture into the complex arena of international markets. From the cognitive standpoint, businesses can map out the terrain of global markets by adopting classification systems that recognize universal product attributes and consumer behaviors. As Carroll, Hannan, and Hsu suggest, this involves creating an archetype or prototype within a product category and understanding its appeal to the consumer base. This prototype can be based on factors such as functionality, design, or user experience and serves as a benchmark against which new market entries are evaluated. Over time, these prototypes can evolve or be entirely reimagined to better serve changing consumer needs, as global markets are inherently dynamic entities influenced by technological advancements, economic shifts, and cultural transformations.

On the social front, the market categories are not only shaped by the objective attributes of products or services but are also deeply influenced by the subjective perceptions and culturally constructed meanings. Rosa and Spanjol's research (2005) elucidate how social interactions, and cultural nuances inform the construction of market categories. For instance, the categorization of health-related products varies significantly across different societies, depending on their cultural understanding of health and wellness. These categorizations affect not only the marketing and positioning of products but also the innovation and development within these categories. Moreover, these social perceptions have profound implications for policymakers who are tasked with regulating and promoting healthy market competition. Policies must be adaptive to the fluid nature of market categorizations, which are influenced by cultural shifts, consumer activism, and socioeconomic changes. Recognition of these social constructs allows for a more nuanced approach to market regulation and economic policy, aiming to foster environments that encourage innovation while protecting consumer interests. The convergence of cognitive and social categorization methodologies offers a comprehensive understanding that is critical for IB success. For MNCs and SMEs alike, a blended categorization approach can be instrumental in navigating foreign markets, enabling these entities to recognize both the universal and the particularistic aspects of market dynamics. It allows for the creation of strategies that are globally coherent yet locally resonant, a balance that is increasingly crucial in a world where global integration and local identities often intersect.

In conclusion, the pursuit of a thorough comprehension of market categorization mechanisms is a multifaceted endeavor. It necessitates an appreciation of both the innate human drive to classify and the societal constructs that imbue these categories with deeper meaning. For businesses operating on an international scale, mastering the art of categorization means not only understanding the attributes that define a product but also the cultural narratives that give it value. As companies look to the future, those that can adeptly navigate the interplay between cognitive prototypes and social constructions will be well-positioned to capitalize on the opportunities presented by the ever-evolving tapestry of global markets.

2.1 The Need for a New Categorization of International Markets

In the business world, categorization plays a pivotal role in market analysis, strategy development, and operational efficiency. As Durand et al (2017, p. 4) stated, "categories are groupings of entities that simplify our apprehension of what surrounds us, focusing attention on a limited number of dimensions or features, enabling recognition and action." Companies categorize markets, customers, and products to tailor their strategies effectively. This segmentation enables businesses to address the specific needs of different groups, leading to more targeted and successful marketing strategies, product development, and IB approaches. This organizing principle plays a key role in shaping how organizations interact (Hsu et al., 2009; Rao et al., 2005; Granqvist et al., 2013; Pontikes, 2010; Negro et al., 2010). Managers employ categorization to make sense of the business reality, breaking down complex dimensions and potential futures into digestible and comprehensible data clusters, a concept explored by Durand et al. (2017). Real-life examples include the following:

- Consumer Goods: **Procter & Gamble (P&G)**
  P&G categorizes its vast array of products into segments such as Beauty, Grooming, Health Care, Fabric & Home Care, and Baby, Feminine & Family Care. This segmentation allows P&G to tailor marketing strategies and product innovations to the specific needs and preferences of different demographic groups.
- Automotive Industry: **Toyota**
  Toyota segments its vehicle offerings into categories such as sedans, SUVs, trucks, hybrids, and luxury (under the Lexus brand). By categorizing vehicles according to type and brand prestige, Toyota can effectively target different consumer segments and optimize production.
- Technology Sector: **Apple**
  Apple organizes its product lines into categories such as smartphones (iPhone), tablets (iPad), personal computers (Mac), wearables (Apple Watch), and services (iTunes, iCloud). This helps Apple in crafting specific marketing campaigns and development strategies for each product line, enhancing user engagement and product loyalty.
- Retail Industry: **Walmart**
  Walmart divides its vast product range into categories such as groceries, apparel, electronics, and home goods. Such a categorization allows Walmart to optimize its supply chain management, tailor its in-store layout for better shopping experiences, and develop targeted promotions. This segmentation ensures that marketing efforts resonate with the needs of different consumer groups, enhancing sales and customer satisfaction.

- Financial Services: **JPMorgan Chase**

  JPMorgan segments its services into personal banking, small business banking, commercial banking, and investment banking. This allows the bank to provide tailored financial products and advisory services suitable for each category's unique needs, such as risk management for large enterprises versus personal investment advice for individual clients.

These examples underscore how businesses across various industries leverage categorization to enhance clarity, streamline operations, and achieve strategic goals. By breaking down markets, customer bases, and product lines into manageable segments, companies can more effectively align their resources and strategies to meet the distinct demands of each segment, ultimately driving growth and success.

The categorization process itself involves the separation or grouping of elements based on common physical or material attributes, as noted by Carruthers & Stinchcombe (1999) and Zerubavel (1997). Sometimes, these categories are designed using a custom-made model, as suggested by Casasanto & Lupyan (2015). There are two primary types of category formation: category emergence and category creation (Durand & Kahire; 2017). Category emergence refers to situations where existing classifications are insufficient for the purpose of analysis, necessitating the proposal of new categories that include external data. Category creation, on the other hand, involves the reorganization of existing categories. In the context of IB, both category emergence and category creation are required by companies to effectively manage their international strategy. This is due to existing models failing to meet the company's needs and the overwhelming amount of information that is difficult to evaluate in a structured way, leading to disorientation. Categorization is indispensable for managing the complexity of the world around us. It aids in learning, decision-making, strategic planning, and effective communication, making it a fundamental process in both cognitive function and societal organization. The international market selection process stands as a critical juncture in the journey of a business seeking to expand its business beyond national borders. This decision shapes the future trajectory of a company's expansion, influencing its growth, brand reach, and overall success in the international arena. While the process is underscored by its complexity, as highlighted by Zhang et al. (2007), understanding and navigating through various existing categorizations can significantly streamline this decision-making process.

Durand and Kahire (2017) identified two significant shortcomings in the current approaches to market categorization adopted by researchers, institutions, and governments, which diminish their effectiveness and impact. First, they observed that categories are often established within fixed classification systems without any empirical evidence to substantiate their initial validity. Second, they argue that market categories are both shaped by and contribute to shaping social structures, possessing enough flexibility to be altered, defended, and maintained by organizations active in those markets (Durand & Kahire, 2017, p. 88). These gaps lead to a scenario where categories are formed and adapted based more on subjective goals of the audience rather than objective criteria. Consequently, companies relying on these skewed market categories may develop IB strategies that are inherently biased, potentially leading to sub-par performance outcomes. For example, the Organization for Economic Co-operation and Development's (OECD) country risk classification categorizes nations based on perceived risks, providing guidance on minimum premium rates for credit risk. The classification employs both quantitative and qualitative analyses. The quantitative aspect draws from three groups of risk indicators: member-reported payment experiences, which is inherently subjective, and financial and economic data sourced from the IMF. Despite its widespread acceptance among member states, the OECD's risk categorization methodology reflects concerns raised by Durand and Kahire (2017) regarding the lack of empirical validation. Member-reported payment experiences, integral to the quantitative analysis, may be influenced by political agendas, introducing potential biases. Similarly, the qualitative assessment, conducted by experts from member states, might be swayed by specific national objectives. Furthermore, the primary purpose of this classification is to guide financial institutions in setting minimum premium rates for credit risk, aligning with the prototype-based categorization theory posited by Durand & Paolella (2013) and Paolella & Durand (2016), which suggests that categories evolve over time to meet audience needs.

　　Standard & Poor (S&P)'s country rating methodology offers another illustrative example. Recognized as one of the top three statistical rating organizations alongside Moody's and Fitch (Anders, 2014), S&P approach is detailed in their Guide to Credit Rating Essentials. According to S&P, these "ratings opinions are based on analysis by experienced professionals who evaluate and interpret information received from issuers and other available sources to form a considered opinion. Unlike other types of opinions, such as, for example, those provided by doctors or lawyers, credit ratings opinions are not intended to be a prognosis or recommendation" (S&P Global, 2023, p.4). This highlights that while these ratings are grounded in data, they are ultimately shaped by individual interpretation and do not necessarily predict risk. While both the OECD's country's risk assessment and S&P's country rating are invaluable sources of information, they are merely part of a broader array of tools available to investors. In formulating international strategies, SMEs and MNCs must navigate a complex web of ratings, evaluations, estimates, and statistics. The overwhelming availability of data can lead to information overload, which may confuse managers rather than provide clarity. As a result, the process of developing an international strategy can become prohibitively expensive, and its implementation may carry unrealistic (and unacceptable) risks. This situation often leads to several outcomes:

- *Conservative Market Entry*
  Companies may opt to enter markets that appear similar to their own, potentially overlooking opportunities in markets that, while perceived as risky, offer substantial growth potential. This can limit a company's ability to diversify and tap into new consumer bases.
- *Missed Opportunities*
  In regions such as Africa, South America, and Far East Asia, perceived risks might deter entry, despite the high potential for returns. Companies may miss out on first-mover advantages in these emerging markets.
- *Low Rate of Success*
  Despite the numerous factors influencing success in international strategies, such as the company's country of origin, size, and industry, the success rate remains low, with few companies achieving their internationalization goals (Stadler et al., 2015)
- *Complexity in Strategy Implementation*
  The complexity of internationalization may discourage managers from pursuing this ambition. Companies might find themselves overwhelmed by the demands of adapting to multiple, poorly understood markets, leading some to retract from international endeavors altogether.
- *Evaluation Challenges*
  The intricate process of evaluating and entering international markets can become convoluted. This often results in lost opportunities as companies struggle to navigate through the fog of overwhelming data.

To address these challenges, there is a pressing need for the development of more robust, empirically validated categorization frameworks that can adapt to the evolving dynamics of global markets. Such frameworks should not only reflect the current economic, social, and political landscapes of these markets but also be recognized by the interested party. By improving the accuracy and relevance of market categorization, companies can enhance their strategic decision-making processes, tailor their approaches to meet the specific needs of diverse markets, and ultimately, improve their overall success rates in internationalization. The goal is to move beyond the existing paradigms and innovate new categorization methods that truly reflect the complex realities of global markets. Such advancements in categorization will equip companies with the necessary tools to strategically navigate the challenges of IB, ensuring that they can capitalize on opportunities while minimizing risks.

2.2 Existing International Market Categories

Many categories group international markets based on a few common variables which do not represent the single market but rather a set of markets grouped by a few common characteristics. While such groupings offer a rudimentary framework for market analysis, as previously said, they may obscure the nuanced realities of each country's unique market dynamics. This oversimplification can lead to a misleading homogenization that fails to capture the complex fabric of individual markets, rendering these categories less useful for strategic decision-making processes. Take, for instance, the designation of countries as "developed" markets. This grouping might place Japan and Portugal within the same category, suggesting a degree of similarity that overlooks significant differences. Japan, with its advanced technology sector and sizable economy, exhibits market characteristics such as high consumer purchasing power, sophisticated infrastructure, and a competitive high-tech industry. Portugal, while sharing the developed market tag, presents a vastly different profile with its smaller economy, distinct cultural factors, and varied industry strengths. The economic scales, consumer behaviors, regulatory environments, and market maturity levels diverge substantially between the two nations. This categorization conundrum extends beyond developed markets. Emerging and frontier markets, often seen as monoliths, are anything but uniform. Grouping rapidly industrializing countries with diverse economic structures and varying stages of regulatory, financial, and infrastructural development dilutes the strategic insight that firms need. A business looking to expand must consider a plethora of factors, including local consumer preferences, legal frameworks, competitive landscapes, and political risks, which are often unique and cannot be homogenized without losing critical detail. Today, international markets are categorized in different ways, next is a description of the most common ones.

2.2.1 Categorization by Market Development

Categorizing international markets by market development provides a framework for understanding and analyzing the economic conditions, growth potential, and investment risks associated with different countries. This categorization typically divides markets into three primary groups: Developed, Emerging, and Frontier.

a. Developed Markets

Developed markets are characterized by high levels of income, well-developed infrastructure, and mature industrial sectors. These countries have stable political and economic ecosystems, low levels of corruption, and robust legal frameworks that protect investor interests. The economies in developed markets are usually diversified, with significant contributions from advanced manufacturing, services, and technology sectors. The populations in these countries tend to have high standards of

living, with well-established social safety nets and high consumer purchasing power. Examples of developed markets include the United
States, Eurozone countries, Japan, and Australia, among others.

b. Emerging Markets

Emerging markets are nations in the midst of rapid industrialization and
economic growth. These countries typically exhibit growth rates above
the global average and are characterized by rising middle classes, increasing urbanization, and significant improvements in infrastructure
and technology. Emerging markets are transitioning from low-income
to middle-income status, driven by industrialization, increased foreign
direct investment (FDI), and economic reforms. Examples of emerging
markets include Brazil, Russia, India, and Mexico, among others.

c. Frontier Markets

Frontier markets represent a subcategory of emerging markets, distin-
guished by their smaller and less developed capital markets and economies. Once called underdeveloped countries, these markets are often in
the early stages of economic development, with limited financial infrastructure and lower levels of industrialization compared to their emerging counterparts. Examples of frontier markets include Bangladesh,
Cameroon, Mozambique, and Mali, among others.

Example of the positive and negative effects of this category are shown in Table
2.1.

Advantages:

- *Strategic Market Entry and Resource Planning:* Enables businesses to
  assess a country's economic environment, craft tailored market entry
  strategies and allocate resources efficiently to maximize returns.
  - Example: Starbucks assessed China's economic environment
    and tailored its entry strategy by focusing on urban centers with
    high disposable incomes. By gradually expanding from Tier-1
    cities such as Shanghai to smaller Tier-2 and Tier-3 cities, Star-
    bucks efficiently allocated resources to maximize returns.
- *Risk and Political Stability Assessment*: Helps businesses evaluate both
  political and economic risks, allowing them to mitigate potential dangers when entering new regions. More developed countries are generally
  politically stable, while emerging or frontier markets may pose higher
  risks but may offer greater rewards.
  - Example: Tesla prioritized expanding into Norway due to its po-
    litical stability and incentives for electric vehicles (EVs). Con-

versely, Tesla cautiously approached markets such as Venezuela, where political and economic instability posed significant risks despite potential opportunities.

- *Growth Potential Assessment:* Enables companies to gauge the potential for future growth, with emerging and frontier markets often offering lower competition, albeit with increased risks.
  - Example: In the 2000s, Unilever identified India as a high-growth market due to its expanding middle class and increasing demand for consumer goods. Despite the challenges of operating in a developing market, Unilever capitalized on the lower level of competition and invested heavily in local operations.
- *Investor Alignment:* Assists companies in aligning their internationalization efforts with investor expectations, as certain investors may prefer exposure to developed, stable markets while others may seek the high returns associated with emerging or frontier markets.
  - Example: A private equity fund (name is undisclosed) seeking stable returns invested in Germany's renewable energy sector, citing its mature regulatory environment. Meanwhile, a venture capital firm (name is undisclosed) targeted fintech startups in Kenya, an emerging market, aiming for high returns despite higher risks.
- *Benchmarking and Comparison:* Provides a benchmark for comparing countries within the same development category, allowing businesses to identify competitive advantages and challenges in similar markets.
  - Example: McDonald's benchmarked its performance in developed markets such as the US and Canada, comparing key metrics such as average customer spending and store profitability. This allowed them to identify areas for improvement and adopt the best practices across similarly developed markets.
- *Long-Term Strategic Planning:* Offers a structured approach to plan long-term international expansion by targeting specific types of markets as the business grows and its risk appetite evolves.
  - Example: BMW first focused on developed markets such as the US and Western Europe before gradually entering emerging markets such as China and India as the company's risk tolerance and global infrastructure expanded over decades.
- *Simplification:* Helps businesses quickly identify the characteristics and risks associated with each market type, simplifying the formulation of entry and expansion strategies, though it may not always be entirely accurate.
  - Example: IKEA categorized Brazil as an emerging market with high potential but simplified its initial entry strategy by focusing

on São Paulo, assuming it represented the country's overall urban consumer base. While this approach streamlined planning, it initially underestimated the challenges posed by regional disparities in Brazil.

Table 2.1 Positive and negative effects of categorization by Market Development

Example of positive effect	Example of negative effect
Portugal and Spain are categorized as developed countries. In fact, they share most of their market and cultural traits, favoring benchmarks and integration of products. A company operating in Portugal may successfully implement a similar market approach for market penetration in Spain as implemented in Portugal (and vice versa). In this context, probabilities of similar market reaction to the company's internationalization process are highly predictable.	Portugal and Japan are categorized as developed countries. However, their cultural and economic traits are far from being similar. Portugal has a service-based economy with a relaxed work culture, valuing family and community, while Japan is a highly industrialized economy with a demanding work culture, emphasizing collective responsibility and harmony. Culturally, Portugal is more individualistic with direct communication, whereas Japan is group-oriented with indirect communication and a strong focus on etiquette and tradition. Thinking about benchmarking or seeking similar market reactions to a possible internationalization process may lead to oversimplification bias and consequently to an increase in risk and a potential failure.

2.2.2 Categorization by Geography

Categorizing international markets by geography provides a framework for understanding and analyzing regions based on their location, plausible cultural similarities, and economic ties. This method divides the world into major geographic regions, each with distinct characteristics and opportunities for businesses. The most common categories include EMEA (Europe, the Middle East, and Africa), NA (North America), LATAM (Latin America), and APAC (Asia and Pacific).

a. EMEA

The EMEA region is a diverse and expansive market encompassing a wide range of economies, cultures, and political environments. Europe is characterized by highly developed economies with well-established infrastructure and regulatory frameworks. The Middle East, while rich in oil and natural gas, presents both opportunities and challenges due to political instability and varying levels of economic development. Africa is a continent of contrasts, with some rapidly growing economies alongside others that are still developing.

b. **NA**

   North America, primarily encompassing the United States, Canada, and Mexico, is a region known for its economic stability, advanced infrastructure, and significant consumer purchasing power. The region is highly integrated, with strong trade agreements such as the United States–Mexico–Canada Agreement (USMCA) facilitating cross-border business activities.

c. **LATAM**

   Latin America is a region with significant economic potential, characterized by a mix of emerging markets and developing economies. The region is known for its rich cultural heritage, natural resources, and youthful demographics. However, it also faces challenges such as political instability, economic volatility, and infrastructure deficits.

d. **APAC**

   The Asia and Pacific region is one of the most dynamic and diverse markets globally, ranging from highly developed economies such as Japan and Australia to rapidly growing emerging markets such as China, India, and Southeast Asian nations. APAC is a hub for global manufacturing, technology innovation, and economic growth.

Example of the positive and negative effects of this category are shown in Table 2.2.

Advantages:

- *Simplified Regional Analysis:* Provides a clear framework for understanding and analyzing regional markets.
    - Example: A multinational company such as Coca-Cola divides its global operations into regions such as EMEA, NA, and APAC. This regional segmentation helps Coca-Cola streamline market analysis by focusing on shared economic and cultural characteristics within each region.
- *Tailored Strategies:* Allows companies to tailor strategies based on regional characteristics.
    - Example: Netflix adapts its content strategy based on regional preferences. For instance, in the APAC region, Netflix invests in local-language productions like South Korean dramas, whereas in North America, it emphasizes blockbuster shows and movies.
- *Regional Synergies:* Leverages commonalities in economic ties, trade agreements, and consumer behavior within regions.
    - Example: The automotive industry leverages regional synergies in Europe through the European Union's trade agreements and common standards. For instance, Volkswagen benefits from free trade

and unified regulatory requirements across EU member states, simplifying its operations and market entry within the region.

- *Operational Efficiency:* Facilitates more efficient allocation of resources and operations across regions.
    - Example: P&G optimizes its supply chain by establishing regional distribution hubs in areas such as Latin America and APAC. This regional approach reduces transportation costs and ensures faster delivery to local markets, boosting operational efficiency.

Table 2.2 Positive and negative effects of categorization by Geography

Example of positive effect	Example of negative effect
Morocco and Egypt, both part of the EMEA region, share numerous market and cultural characteristics, which creates favorable conditions for benchmarking and integrating products across these two countries. Given the similarities in consumer behavior, preferences, and economic environments, a company operating in Morocco can effectively replicate its market entry strategies in Egypt with a high likelihood of success, and vice versa. The cultural and market commonalities between the two nations suggest that the response to a company's internationalization efforts will likely be consistent, making market reactions in these regions more predictable and easier to manage.	Morocco and Italy are both part of the EMEA region, yet their cultural and economic traits differ significantly. Morocco has an emerging economy characterized by agriculture, mining, and a growing tourism sector, with a market that is still developing and adapting to global trends. On the other hand, Italy boasts a highly industrialized economy, known for its strong manufacturing base, particularly in fashion, automotive, and luxury goods, as well as a well-established services sector. Culturally, Morocco is more traditional, with strong ties to Arab and Berber heritage, emphasizing community and family values. In contrast, Italy has a rich cultural history rooted in the Renaissance, with a focus on art, fashion, and a Western lifestyle. Attempting to benchmark or predict similar market reactions to a company's internationalization strategy in these two distinct markets can lead to oversimplification, increasing the risk of misalignment and potential failure.

2.2.3 Categorization by Political/Economical Groups

Categorizing international markets by political or economic groups provides a framework for understanding and analyzing countries based on their membership in specific agreements, coalitions, or organizations. This method helps businesses assess market potential, trade advantages, and economic stability based on the collective characteristics and goals of these groups. Key categories include USMCA, MINT (Mexico, Indonesia, Nigeria, and Turkey), BRICS (Brazil, Russia, India, China, and South Africa), GCC (Gulf Cooperation Council), and other regional or global economic organizations.

a. USMCA

The USMCA is a regional trade agreement that replaced NAFTA in July 2020, involving the United States, Mexico, and Canada. It aims to facilitate trade, reduce tariffs, and create a more integrated North American economy. The agreement supports streamlined cross-border trade, enhanced intellectual property (IP) protections, and fair labor practices across the member states.

b. MINT

The MINT countries are characterized by large populations, strategic geographic locations, and significant economic potential. These countries are seen as emerging markets with strong growth prospects, each playing a crucial role in their respective regions. Members were selected for their strategic geographical locations, which are used as commercial hubs within their regions. Mexico covers the American continent, Indonesia covers the Pacific region, Nigeria covers Africa, and Turkey covers Europe and the Middle East.

c. BRICS

BRICS represents a coalition of major emerging economies that are recognized for their large populations, significant natural resources, and growing influence in global economic and political affairs. These countries are seen as key drivers of global economic growth and development, empowered by the access of huge natural resources.

d. GCC

The GCC consists of Bahrain, Kuwait, Oman, Qatar, Saudi Arabia, and the United Arab Emirates (UAE). These countries are known for their significant oil and gas reserves, high-income levels, strong liquidity, and efforts to diversify their economies beyond hydrocarbons. The concept behind the creation of GCC is to promote economic growth within the Arabic peninsula.

Various other regional and global organizations play a significant role in international markets, including, but not limited to, Southern Africa Development Community (SADC), Common Market for Eastern and Southern Africa (COMESA), OECD, World Trade Organization (WTO), Asia-Pacific Economic Cooperation (APEC), and Association of Southeast Asian Nations (ASEAN). These groups facilitate trade, economic cooperation, and regional integration among member states, providing businesses with opportunities to expand into new markets under favorable conditions.

Example of the positive and negative effects of this category are shown in Table 2.3.

Advantages:

- *Enhanced Trade Opportunities:* Access to favorable trade agreements, reduced tariffs, and integrated markets.
    - Example: Companies operating within the European Union benefit from tariff-free trade and simplified regulations across member countries, enabling smoother cross-border operations and reducing costs. For instance, BMW easily exports vehicles from Germany to France without additional tariffs, enhancing competitiveness.
- *Strategic Market Insights:* Provides insights into collective economic and political characteristics of member countries.
    - Example: The USMCA provides insights into the shared economic characteristics of North American markets, such as strong manufacturing sectors and cross-border trade dependencies. Ford uses these insights to optimize its supply chain across the three countries.
- *Market Integration and Synergies*: Facilitates easier cross-border operations and integrated supply chains.
    - Example: Coca-Cola leverages the integrated supply chains within ASEAN to streamline production and distribution across member states, reducing costs and improving efficiency in serving regional markets.
- *Economic Diversification*: Groups often include diverse economies, providing opportunities across various sectors.
    - Example: GE (General Electric) capitalized on the MINT countries by investing in Mexico's advanced manufacturing sector, Indonesia's energy market, Nigeria's infrastructure projects, and Turkey's healthcare systems. This diversification allowed GE to balance risk while tapping into varied high-growth opportunities across multiple sectors.
- *Influence in Global Affairs*: Groups such as BRICS or OECD have significant economic influence, offering strategic advantages in global trade.
    - Example: Huawei expanded into BRICS nations, leveraging the group's collective influence in advocating for alternative global trade practices. These nations' collective economic power facilitated Huawei's market access and countered trade restrictions in other regions, enhancing the company's global footprint.

Table 2.3 Positive and negative effects of categorization by Political/Economical Groups

Example of positive effect	Example of negative effect
Both the United States and Canada are members of the USMCA, which facilitates trade and economic integration between the two countries. The agreement ensures reduced tariffs, streamlined regulations, and enhanced market access, creating a stable and predictable business environment. Companies operating within the USMCA framework benefit from strong legal protections, robust infrastructure, and high consumer purchasing power in both markets. This alignment under the same political/economic group allows businesses to implement similar strategies across both countries, leveraging the integrated supply chains and harmonized standards.	While the United States and Mexico are both members of the USMCA, offering trade benefits and economic integration, they are also categorized differently within broader political/economic groupings, such as MINT. The US represents a stable and advanced economy with high consumer purchasing power and a strong regulatory framework, whereas Mexico, while benefiting from USMCA, is also part of MINT, reflecting its status as an emerging market with higher economic volatility, different regulatory challenges, and a less developed infrastructure. This dual categorization shows the limitations of grouping countries solely by political/economic agreements, as it overlooks significant differences in economic maturity, market dynamics, and operational risks.

2.2.4 Categorization by Market Maturity

Categorizing international markets by their level of maturity provides a framework for understanding and analyzing markets based on their growth stage, competitive dynamics, and consumer behavior. This method helps businesses identify opportunities and challenges specific to each stage of market development, guiding strategic decisions for market entry, product development, and competitive positioning. The key categories include Mature Markets and Growing Markets.

a. Mature Markets
    Mature markets are characterized by a state of equilibrium and stability, with slower growth rates and relatively predictable market dynamics. These markets have well-established competition, with numerous players vying for market share. Consumers in mature markets are generally well-informed, with clear preferences and significant purchasing power. Most consumer needs and desires are already met by existing products and services, leading to high market saturation. Innovation in mature markets tends to be incremental rather than disruptive, focusing on product enhancements and efficiency improvements. Examples of mature markets include Eurozone countries, South Korea, the United States of America, and Australia, among others.

b. Growing Markets

Growing markets are those experiencing rapid expansion, often representing emerging economies or sectors influenced by technological, demographic, or socioeconomic trends. These markets are characterized
by high growth rates, evolving consumer behavior, and increasing competition as new players enter to capitalize on emerging opportunities.
Consumer needs in growing markets are still developing, with significant
demand for new products and services that address unmet needs. Growing markets offer ample room for expansion and innovation, making
them attractive for businesses seeking high-growth opportunities. Examples of growing markets include Indonesia, India, Brazil, and Nigeria, among others.

Example of the positive and negative effects of this category are shown in Table
2.4.

Advantages:

- *Resource Allocation Efficiency*: Helps companies allocate resources effectively by identifying which markets require more aggressive investment (growing markets) versus those that require maintenance or niche
focus (mature markets).
    - Example: Starbucks invests aggressively in the Middle East, a
    growing market with expanding consumer demand for premium
    coffee, while adopting a more maintenance-focused approach in
    mature markets like Western Europe, where coffee culture is
    well-established, and competition is intense.
- *Competitive Positioning Insight:* Offers insights into competitive dynamics, with mature markets often requiring differentiation strategies
and growing markets offering opportunities for market entry and expansion.
    - Example: Apple employs differentiation strategies in mature
    markets such as Japan, emphasizing premium features and
    brand loyalty, while in growing markets such as Vietnam, it fo-
    cuses on affordability and accessibility to gain market share.
- *Facilitates Long-Term Planning:* Helps in long-term strategic planning
by providing a general understanding of market life cycles and where
markets are headed.
    - Example: Tesla leverages market maturity categorization by
    identifying China as a growing market for EVs and planning
    long-term investments in manufacturing and infrastructure to
    dominate this rapidly evolving sector.

- *Consumer Behavior Understanding:* Enables companies to better understand consumer behavior patterns in different market stages, aiding in product development and marketing strategies.
  - Example: Nestlé develops smaller, affordable packaging for products like instant coffee in growing markets such as Nigeria, where affordability is key, while in mature markets such as Switzerland, it focuses on premium and niche offerings like organic and fair-trade coffee to cater to more sophisticated consumer preferences.

Table 2.4 Positive and negative effects of categorization by Market Maturity

Example of positive effect	Example of negative effect
United States and Germany are categorized as mature markets characterized by stable economies, advanced infrastructure, high consumer purchasing power, and intense competition. Companies can adopt similar strategic approaches in both markets, such as focusing on quality, innovation, and premium offerings, due to the alignment in market dynamics and consumer behavior. This categorization effectively supports the development of comparable strategies across these two countries.	Although both the United States and Italy are classified as mature markets, they exhibit significant differences in economic and market dynamics. The US market emphasizes innovation with a competitive environment driven by consumer demand for new products. In contrast, Italy's market, while mature, is more traditional and conservative, with a complex regulatory environment and a high taxation system. This discrepancy highlights the limitations of categorizing markets solely by maturity, as it overlooks important economic, cultural, and regulatory differences between countries within the same category.

2.2.5 Categorization by Degree of Freedom

Categorizing international markets by their degree of freedom provides a framework for understanding and analyzing the accessibility, regulatory environment, and business conditions in different countries. This method helps businesses assess the ease of market entry, the level of government intervention, and the associated risks. The key categories include Opened Markets, Restricted or Closed Markets, and High-Risk Markets.

a. Opened Markets
   Open markets are highly accessible to foreign businesses, characterized by minimal regulatory restrictions, favorable policies, and ease of doing business (EDB). These markets often have free trade agreements in place, strong legal protections for investors, and a transparent regulatory environment that facilitates smooth market entry and operations.

Examples of opened markets include Eurozone countries, Singapore, the United States of America, and the United Kingdom.
b. Restricted or Closed Markets
Restricted or closed markets are characterized by significant barriers for foreign entities, often aimed at protecting national interests and industries or for political reasons. These markets feature strict regulations, state monopolies, limited access to certain sectors, ownership restrictions, and usually require partnerships with local firms. Examples include North Korea, Cuba, Venezuela, and Iran.
c. High-Risk Markets
High-risk markets are defined by political instability, economic volatility, or significant business challenges. These markets are characterized by unpredictable conditions due to government changes, economic crises, ongoing conflicts, or other disruptive factors. Examples of high-risk markets include Afghanistan, Yemen, Libya, Sudan, Mali, and Somalia.

Example of the positive and negative effects of this category are shown in Table 2.5.

Advantages:

- *Risk Assessment and Mitigation*: Helps businesses assess and plan for the risks associated with entering different markets based on their accessibility and stability.
    - Example: Uber's expansion into Germany required navigating stringent labor laws and regulatory hurdles, helping the company assess high-entry barriers and plan for legal challenges compared to its smoother entry into markets with less stringent regulations, such as Mexico.
- *Resource Allocation:* Facilitates efficient allocation of resources by identifying markets with low entry barriers versus those that require significant investment to overcome restrictions.
    - Example: Amazon invested heavily in Brazil, where logistical challenges, regulatory complexities, and infrastructure gaps required substantial resources, compared to its expansion into Canada, a market with minimal trade barriers and well-developed infrastructure, allowing for a more straightforward entry.
- *Operational Planning:* Assists in developing operational plans that are aligned with the regulatory environment and risk profile of each market.
    - Example: Pfizer adjusted its operational plans for entering China, focusing on compliance with strict pharmaceutical regulations and local partnerships, while using a more standardized

approach in the UK, where regulatory frameworks align closely with its existing operations.

Table 2.5 Positive and negative effects of categorization by Degree of Freedom

Example of positive effect	Example of negative effect
United Kingdom and Singapore are categorized as opened markets, characterized by minimal barriers to entry, strong legal protections, and stable business environments. Companies can implement similar strategies in both markets, such as focusing on high-value sectors, leveraging advanced infrastructure, and taking advantage of favorable regulatory conditions. This alignment allows businesses to confidently expand and operate in these markets, benefiting from the predictability and supportiveness of the business environment.	United Kingdom and Greece are categorized as opened markets, with minimal regulatory barriers and policies that generally support foreign business operations. However, the economic and business environments in these two countries differ significantly. The UK is characterized by a stable economy, strong legal protections, and a predictable regulatory framework, making it highly attractive for IBs. In contrast, Greece, while also categorized as an opened market, has faced economic challenges, including a prolonged debt crisis, high levels of bureaucracy, and less stable economic conditions. These differences highlight the limitations of relying solely on the degree of freedom categorization, as it may obscure critical economic and operational risks specific to each market, leading to potentially flawed strategic decisions.

2.2.6 Categorization by Political Risk

Categorizing international markets by political risk involves assessing countries based on their capacity to maintain political stability, continuity of governance, and the level of geopolitical threats. This categorization considers various factors such as the quality of governance, the likelihood of expropriation, and the presence of internal or external conflicts. Organizations like export credit agencies (ECAs), such as SACE in Italy, Export-Import Bank of the United States (Ex-Im Bank), and Euler Hermes in Germany, use these assessments to evaluate the political risks associated with different countries, providing insights for businesses seeking to enter or operate in these markets.

a. *High-Risk Markets*

High-risk markets are characterized by volatile political environments, weak governance, and significant geopolitical threats. These countries may face frequent government changes, civil unrest, or conflict, which can disrupt business operations and pose a threat to investments. The risk of expropriation, where governments seize foreign assets without adequate compensation, is also higher in these markets.

b. *Moderate-Risk Markets*

Moderate-risk markets have a more stable political environment than high-risk markets but still face some degree of political uncertainty. These countries typically have better governance structures and less frequent political upheaval, though they may still experience occasional instability or regional conflicts. The risk of expropriation is lower than in high-risk markets but still present.

c. *Low-Risk Markets*

Low-risk markets are characterized by strong governance, political stability, and minimal geopolitical threats. These countries typically have well-established legal frameworks, transparent regulatory environments, and a low risk of expropriation. Businesses operating in low-risk markets benefit from a high degree of predictability and security, making these markets attractive for long-term investments.

Example of the positive and negative effects of this category are shown in Table 2.6.

Advantages:

- *Risk Mitigation:* Helps businesses avoid or prepare for risks associated with political instability.
  - Example: Coca-Cola avoided expanding into Venezuela during periods of political unrest, mitigating the risk of disrupted operations and economic losses.
- *Informed Decision-Making:* Provides a clear framework for assessing the potential risks associated with different markets.
  - Example: Siemens used political risk assessments to decide on entering Vietnam, recognizing manageable risks tied to its political stability and high potential for industrial growth.
- *Insurance and Protection:* Supports access to insurance and risk protection from ECAs.
  - Example: Boeing secured coverage from the US Export-Import Bank to protect its investments in politically unstable markets such as Pakistan, ensuring compensation in case of unforeseen disruptions.
- *Strategic Allocation of Resources:* Allows companies to allocate resources more effectively, focusing on markets with manageable risks.
  - Example: Nestlé allocated greater resources to the UAE, a politically stable environment, while limiting exposure in Sudan, where high political risks made significant investment less feasible.

- *Long-Term Planning*: Facilitates long-term strategic planning by identifying stable environments for investment.
  - Example: ExxonMobil prioritized long-term investments in politically stable markets such as Canada for energy exploration, while delaying projects in Libya due to its unpredictable political climate.

Table 2.6 Positive and negative effects of categorization by Political Risk

Example of positive effect	Example of negative effect
Mexico and Uruguay are categorized as politically moderate-risk markets by SACE Country Risk Assessment (Italy's ECA), reflecting their relatively stable political environments, improving governance, and growing economies. This categorization allows businesses to identify these countries as viable opportunities for investment and expansion, with a balanced approach to risk and reward. Companies can capitalize on Mexico's large consumer market and strategic location within North America, while Uruguay offers a stable legal framework and strong democratic institutions, making it an attractive gateway to the Southern Cone of Latin America.	While both Mexico and Botswana are categorized as politically moderate-risk markets by SACE, this categorization can obscure important differences in their political and economic landscapes. For example, Mexico faces challenges such as ongoing issues with organized crime and corruption, which can significantly impact business operations and investor confidence. In contrast, Botswana, despite being categorized similarly, is known for its strong governance, low levels of corruption, and political stability. The oversimplification in categorization could lead businesses to overlook these critical distinctions, potentially resulting in misaligned strategies and unforeseen risks when entering these markets.

2.2.7 Categorization by Financial Risk

Categorizing international markets by financial risk involves evaluating countries based on their creditworthiness, considering factors such as economic conditions, fiscal stability, and debt levels. This method is crucial for investors and businesses as it helps them assess the likelihood of a country defaulting on its sovereign or commercial debts, thereby informing investment decisions. Renowned credit rating agencies such as Moody's, Fitch, and S&P provide ratings that categorize countries based on their financial risk, ranging from low-risk "AAA" ratings to high-risk "C" or "D" ratings.

a. High-Rated Markets ("AAA," "AA")
   Countries with "AAA" or "AA" ratings are considered to have the highest level of creditworthiness. These markets are typically characterized by strong economic fundamentals, political stability, robust legal systems, and low levels of debt. They are viewed as safe havens for investment, offering low risk of default.
b. Medium-Rated Markets ("A," "BBB")

Markets with "A" or "BBB" ratings are considered medium risk. These countries generally have stable economic conditions but may face challenges such as higher debt levels, less diversified economies, or moderate political risks. These markets are still attractive for investment but require careful risk management.

c. Low-Rated Markets ("BB," "B")
Low-rated markets, with ratings such as "BB" or "B," are considered high risk. These countries often face significant economic challenges, such as high debt levels, political instability, and less developed financial systems. While they offer potential for high returns, investments in these markets come with a substantial risk of default.

d. Very Low-Rated Markets, or Junks ("CCC," "CC," "C," "D")
Markets with very low ratings, such as "CCC," "CC," "C," or "D," are at the highest risk of default. These countries typically face severe economic difficulties, political turmoil, and high levels of debt. Investments in these markets are highly speculative and carry the greatest risk of loss.

Example of the positive and negative effects of this category are shown in Table 2.7.

Advantages:

- *Informed Investment Decisions*: Provides a clear understanding of the creditworthiness and financial risk of countries.
    - Example: Apple's decision to invest in Ireland was influenced by the country's high credit rating, signaling strong financial stability and low investment risk.
- *Risk Management*: Helps investors and businesses manage risk by avoiding high-risk markets or preparing for potential risks.
    - Example: Shell avoided expanding operations in Zimbabwe due to its low credit rating and high financial risk, mitigating potential economic losses.
- *Strategic Portfolio Diversification*: Allows investors to diversify their portfolios by balancing investments across high-, medium-, and low-risk markets.
    - Example: A global investment fund (name is undisclosed) balanced its portfolio by investing in low-risk markets such as Germany for stable returns and medium-risk markets such as Brazil for higher growth potential.
- *Transparency and Predictability*: Credit ratings offer a transparent and predictable method for assessing market risk.

- Example: BlackRock relied on Moody's credit ratings to evaluate market risk when expanding into Chile, using the transparent methodology to guide financial decision-making.
- *Guidance for Interest Rates and Bond Yields*: Credit ratings help set
  benchmarks for interest rates and bond yields, aiding in financial planning.
  - Example: The Indian government's sovereign credit rating in-
    fluenced bond yields, helping foreign investors such as JPMor-
    gan determine acceptable interest rates for lending and invest-
    ments in India.
- *Ease of Comparison*: Facilitates easy comparison of financial risks
  across different countries and regions.
  - Example: HSBC compared financial risks between Mexico and
    Argentina using credit ratings, enabling a straightforward anal-
    ysis that informed decisions on regional market expansion.

Table 2.7 Positive and negative effects of categorization by Financial Risk

Example of positive effect	Example of negative effect
Japan and Sweden, both holding an "A+" S&P rating, are considered relatively stable markets with moderate financial risk. Japan, known for its advanced technology sector and large economy, and Sweden, recognized for its strong welfare system and innovation-driven economy, both offer attractive investment opportunities. The shared rating indicates a balanced risk environment, making them appealing to investors looking for stable returns in developed markets.	Japan and South Korea, despite both having an "A+" S&P rating, present different levels of underlying risk. Japan, while economically stable, faces challenges such as an aging population and high public debt, which could impact long-term growth. South Korea, although sharing the same credit rating, is subject to geopolitical tensions with North Korea and has a more export-dependent economy, making it vulnerable to global market fluctuations. This example highlights how identical ratings can conceal country-specific risks, which investors need to consider when making decisions.

2.2.8 Potential Biases of Using Categories for an International Strategy Expansion

Whren using a methodology to develop a strategy, advantages and disadvantages of the methodology shall be compared and balanced. The selection of
a specific categorization methodology to draft an IB strategy shall be based on
the company's need for reliability of that method, confronting and balancing
both advantages and biases, as this can influence the accuracy and effectiveness

of the analysis. Unforeseen biases can lead to misinterpretation of data and result in flawed decision-making. Here are some of the key potential biases for
any categorization method:

- *Economic Bias:* This bias occurs when a categorization places too much
  weight on economic metrics such as GDP, income levels, and industrial
  output, potentially ignoring other crucial factors such as social stability,
  governance, and environmental sustainability laws. This can lead to an
  incomplete understanding of a market's true development level and potential.
    - Example: Despite high GDP from oil revenues, businesses in Ve-
      nezuela in the early 2000s overlooked political instability, gover-
      nance issues, and social unrest. Companies misclassified Vene-
      zuela as an emerging market, focusing too heavily on economic
      metrics, which led to financial losses and failed market entries.
- *Cultural Bias:* Often, developed markets are defined by standards and
  metrics that are rooted in Western economic and cultural norms. This
  can lead to an underestimation of the potential in non-Western markets
  or a mischaracterization of how business is conducted in those regions,
  which may have different cultural, social, and economic dynamics.
    - Example: When Walmart decided to enter South Korea, applied
      Western business models, disregarding local consumer preferen-
      ces and cultural shopping habits. This led to poor performance,
      and in 2006, Walmart exited the market after failing to adapt to
      the unique dynamics of South Korean retail culture. Another
      example is Chevrolet's "Nova" car, which faced challenges in
      Spanish-speaking markets, as "No Va" translates to "it doesn't
      go," which was similarly problematic in Italian ("Non Va").
- *Recency Bias:* When placing too much emphasis on recent economic or
  political events in a country, the long-term view of a market's development and potential may be distorted. A temporary economic downturn
  in an emerging market might lead to its incorrect categorization as
  higher risk or lower potential.
    - Example: In Brazil's 2015–2016 recession, due to the temporary
      economic downturn, many companies and investors prematu-
      rely categorized Brazil as a high-risk, low-potential market.
      However, this short-term focus ignored Brazil's long-term eco-
      nomic potential, and the market rebounded significantly in sub-
      sequent years.
- *Survivorship Bias:* This occurs when only the most successful markets or
  companies within a certain category are considered, while those that

failed or underperformed are ignored. This can lead to an overly optimistic view of a market category, underestimating the risks and challenges.

- – Example: A prime example of this bias is seen in the early 2000s tech boom in India. Investors and companies focused on the success of major IT firms such as Infosys and Wipro, while ignoring numerous smaller tech ventures that failed. This led to an overly optimistic view of India's tech sector, underestimating the risks for new entrants.

- **Selection Bias:** If the data used to categorize markets is not representative of the entire market or is skewed toward certain regions or industries, the resulting categorization may be biased. For example, using data from only urban centers in an emerging market might overlook the challenges faced in rural areas, leading to a skewed perception of market potential.
  - – Example: In the 1990s, China's market potential was misleading as many companies used data primarily from urban centers such as Beijing and Shanghai, overlooking the challenges in rural areas. This led to an overly optimistic view of China's overall market readiness for expansion, neglecting significant rural barriers.

- **Anchoring Bias:** Decision-makers might become anchored to the first piece of information they receive about a market (such as an initial categorization) and fail to adjust their perceptions based on new data or insights. This can result in outdated or overly rigid views of a market's development stage.
  - – Example: Anchoring bias can be seen in the initial categorization of Eastern European countries in the early 1990s after the fall of the Soviet Union. Many decision-makers remained anchored to the perception of these markets as risky post-communist economies, even as reforms and economic growth transformed some of them into promising markets for investment.

- **Political Bias:** The process of categorization might be influenced by political considerations, where certain countries are categorized in a way that aligns with the interests or perspectives of powerful stakeholders. This can lead to biased categorizations that do not accurately reflect the market's true characteristics.
  - – Example: During the 2008 financial crisis, Greece's credit rating was downgraded significantly, in part reflecting political pressures from the EU. The categorization of Greece as a high-risk country was influenced by broader political dynamics, which did not fully capture the market's recovery potential (as it did).

- *Regional Stereotyping:* Overgeneralizing regions based on common stereotypes can lead to misinterpretations of market potential or risks.
  - Example: Africa being stereotyped as a uniformly high-risk, underdeveloped region. This bias led many companies to overlook high-potential markets such as Rwanda, which has consistently ranked as one of the easiest places to do business in Africa due to its stable governance and investor-friendly policies.
- *Anchoring on Historical Data:* Relying too heavily on historical data to define geographic regions can result in outdated perceptions, missing the dynamic changes within regions such as APAC, where rapid economic transformations are common.
  - Example: The perception of Vietnam in the 1990s as a war-torn, underdeveloped country, lead businesses that clung to this outdated view to overlook Vietnam's rapid economic transformation in the 2000s, missing opportunities as it became a manufacturing hub and one of Asia's fastest-growing economies.
- *Herd Mentality:* Strategies relying on simple categorization methods might select markets based on industry trends or their competitors' actions, rather than conducting independent, in-depth analysis. This approach assumes that markets within the same category behave similarly, leading to a bandwagon effect where multiple companies adopt the same strategy without recognizing unique market dynamics. Such an approach can result in missed opportunities or unforeseen challenges and can lead to failure.
  - Example: Domino's Pizza's failed attempt to penetrate the Italian market. Believing they could replicate their US strategy and capture market share from small local pizzerias, Domino's overlooked the distinct culinary and cultural preferences of Italy. In 2022, Domino's Italy declared bankruptcy, highlighting the risks of herd mentality.
- *Group Homogenization:* There is a tendency to treat all member countries within a group as similar, which can lead to oversimplified strategies that do not account for significant internal differences.
  - Example: Many companies entering the EU treat all member countries as having similar consumer behavior and market dynamics. However, strategies that work in Germany, with its efficiency-driven culture, often fail in markets such as Greece, where consumer preferences and economic conditions differ significantly.
- *Confirmation Bias:* Companies might focus on the benefits highlighted by the group's promotional materials or historical successes, while downplaying potential risks or challenges within the member countries.

- Example: Within BRICS, Brazil has a strong international promotional policy incentivizing agriculture supply chain and tourism, whereas China pushes on being the world's industrial system.

- *Overreliance on Group Characteristics:* Businesses may rely too heavily on the collective characteristics of the group, overlooking specific market risks or opportunities unique to individual member states.
  - Example: Within the SADC region, South Africa is the major producer and exporter of services and consumer goods, form where Mozambique (and many of the SADC members) imports most of the country's needs, making them two different and distinctive market targets.

- *Geopolitical Bias:* The geopolitical relationships and tensions within or between these groups can lead to biased perceptions of market stability, especially if one country's instability is projected onto the entire group.
  - Example: The Qatar diplomatic crisis (2017–2021) involved the Saudi-led coalition accusing Qatar of supporting terrorism and violating a 2014 GCC agreement, leading to a significant deterioration of ties between Qatar and the Arab League, and leading to a potential misperception of an imminent crisis to the Qatari economy.

- *Overgeneralization Bias:* There is a tendency to generalize market characteristics based on their maturity, potentially overlooking unique dynamics within individual markets.
  - Example: While the Eurozone is categorized as mature, there are significant differences between its member countries such as France and Romania, which might not be captured in a broad categorization.

- *Static Perception Bias:* Categorizing markets with non-evolving traits can result in a static and overly simplistic view, where businesses fail to account for the dynamic nature of market conditions over time. Rapidly evolving markets may be misclassified, leading to missed opportunities or the adoption of inappropriate strategies.
  - Example: A prime example of this was China in the 1980s, where many Western companies underestimated the country's potential, resulting in lost opportunities for those unable to adapt. Today, a similar situation is unfolding in India; however, many companies, having learned from past experiences, are now proactively positioning themselves to penetrate this vibrant and rapidly growing market.

- **Risk Aversion Bias:** Categorizations might encourage businesses to avoid high risk or restricted markets altogether, potentially missing out on niche opportunities or markets that are beginning to open up.
    - Example: Companies avoided Myanmar for decades due to its high political and economic risks. However, when reforms began in 2011, early movers such as Coca-Cola capitalized on niche opportunities as the market opened, gaining a first-mover advantage.
- **Overreliance on Credit Ratings:** There is a risk of overemphasizing credit ratings as the sole measure of financial risk, which can lead to overlooking other critical factors such as political stability, social unrest, or sector-specific risks that might affect investments.
    - Example: In the lead-up to the 2008 financial crisis, Lehman Brothers held an investment-grade credit rating from major agencies shortly before its collapse. Investors who relied solely on these ratings overlooked underlying risks in the company's asset portfolio, leading to massive financial losses.
- **Rating Agency Bias:** Credit rating agencies may have inherent biases based on their methodologies, geographical focus, or historical performance. These biases can influence the ratings assigned to different countries, potentially leading to misclassification.
    - Example: During the 1997 Asian financial crisis, credit rating agencies were criticized for downgrading countries such as South Korea and Indonesia too rapidly, exacerbating investor panic. This bias stemmed from methodologies that overly penalized short-term volatility, despite the countries' long-term potential for recovery.

2.2.9 The Need for a New Categorization for International Markets

As seen, in the realm of IB, a critical examination of current market categorization reveals a significant issue: Many existing categories are inadvertently skewed or fail to provide the depth of information necessary for managers to craft a comprehensive and effective IB strategy. This inadequacy in market categorization can lead to strategic missteps and missed opportunities in the global marketplace. Recognizing this gap urges a pressing need for the development of a new, more informative category, which will be established through a category emergency approach.

The creation of such a category is not just about adding more data; it's about providing clarity and actionable insights that empower managers to make informed decisions. This new category should serve as a navigational tool, guiding managers in developing strategies that are not only aligned with their company's goals but also responsive to the nuances of the international market landscape. To address this need, the upcoming chapter introduces a groundbreaking concept: "Market Pareidolia." Drawing inspiration from the psychological phenomenon of pareidolia, where the mind perceives familiar patterns in random or ambiguous stimuli, this concept applies a similar principle to the categorization of international markets. Market Pareidolia is about seeing beyond the apparent chaos and complexity of global markets to discern patterns and opportunities that are not immediately obvious. This innovative approach to market categorization promises to provide managers with a more nuanced and insightful framework for developing their short-to-long-term IB strategies. It represents a significant step forward in the way companies approach global market analysis and strategy formulation, offering a fresh perspective that is both practical and strategically sound.

2.3 Market Pareidolia

Market Pareidolia transcends traditional market analysis, providing a holistic, humanized approach to international business strategy. It aligns business practices with the psychological and developmental profiles of markets, thereby fostering a deeper, more intuitive connection between companies and the global markets they serve.

Pareidolia is a type of sensory illusion where external stimuli evoke perceptions of entities that don't actually exist, resulting from incorrect correlations between internal representations and sensory inputs (Liu et al., 2014). "Individuals often report seeing a face in the clouds, Jesus in toasts, or the Virgin Mary in a tortilla" (Liu et al., 2014, p. 61). This phenomenon is an evolutionary adaptation in humans, developed as a defense mechanism for detecting the presence of other humans or predators, along with their intentions or emotional states, in their surroundings (Adams et al., 2011). This widely observed defense mechanism (Adams et al., 2011; Liu et al., 2014; Palmer & Clifford, 2020) assists the human brain in interpreting otherwise ambiguous data.

In the complex arena of IB, entities such as MNCs and SMEs grapple with the daunting task of understanding and penetrating diverse global markets. With the seen plethora of market categories, ratings, and evaluations at their disposal, these businesses often encounter a perplexing array of data that complicates the formulation of effective international strategies. Applying pareidolia mechanisms within the interpretation of market behaviors has created a new market category system defined as Market Pareidolia. Its objective is to establish a novel categorization framework for international markets, one that leverages the sensory illusion of pareidolia to transform complex and often perplexing market variables into familiar, human-like patterns. This approach aims to enhance managers' understanding of foreign markets by stimulating their perception through the recognition of patterns that resemble human characteristics. By doing so, it seeks to simplify the complexity of international market analysis, making it more intuitive and relatable for those formulating global business strategies.

This approach offers a novel framework for navigating the global business landscape, providing profound implications for MNCs and SMEs. By utilizing human developmental analogies, firms gain an empathetic understanding of market idiosyncrasies, which enhances their strategic decision-making. For example, an "adolescent" market, characterized as vibrant and risk-embracing, guides companies to introduce innovative products that resonate with a daring consumer psychology. Moreover, Market Pareidolia serves as an invaluable tool for policymakers, enabling them to formulate trade and investment strategies that align with a market's developmental "age." For instance, "adult" markets, indicative of stability and maturity, might benefit from policies fostering long-term investments, while "adolescent" markets may require policies with greater adaptability. This approach also streamlines the strategic planning process by humanizing market categories, thus allowing businesses to develop strategies aligned with anthropomorphized market traits. It informs risk management by providing insights into the inherent challenges of markets at various developmental stages, facilitating the creation of resilient operational models.

Market Pareidolia draws inspiration from the human age classification framework developed by Nithyashri and Kulanthaivel (2012), identifying four main stages of human life: childhood, adolescence, adulthood, and seniority. Enriched by further scholarly insights, this new categorization deepens the understanding of each life stage, translating eighteen distinct human age markers into comparable/compatible market development indicators. This cross-disciplinary methodology aims to enrich traditional market categorization by drawing parallels between the progression of human age and market evolution. For practical application in the realm of IB, Market Pareidolia selectively focuses on the stages of adolescence, adulthood, and seniority. These phases embody economic agency and activity, making them relevant to market indicator analyses. Unlike childhood, characterized by economic dependency and absent decision-making autonomy, these later stages mirror the active engagement in market dynamics. This approach advocates for a holistic view of markets as entities progressing through life-like stages, each with distinct traits and behaviors. It situates markets within a lifecycle context, providing deeper insights into their current state and potential trajectory. This innovative strategy not only simplifies the intricate task of market categorization but also aligns IB practices with the more intuitive and familiar patterns of human development, promising enhanced empathy, and effectiveness in global market engagement.

2.3.1 Adolescent Markets

Fitton et al. (2013, p. 207) identified six primary characteristics of adolescence (Table 2.8): "desire for independence and autonomy, aspiration to develop/maintain individual identity, preference for association with peers, high susceptibility to peer influence, willingness to take risks, and increasing detachment from parents/guardians." In the context of Market Pareidolia, the goal is to identify market indicators that logically correspond to these adolescent traits, providing a nuanced understanding of markets in this life stage.

1. *Desire for Independence and Autonomy*

   The concept of democracy, rooted in the Greek words "demos" (people) and "kratos" (power), signifies the idea of authority residing with the people. This makes the Democracy Index a fitting analogy for a market's pursuit of independence and autonomy. The Democracy Index, compiled by the Economist Intelligence Unit (EIU), evaluates the state of democracy across various countries and serves as a proxy for this particular aspect of adolescent markets. Countries in the adolescent stage typically score low on this index, reflecting a limited level of democratic governance.

   For companies considering entry into these markets, it is crucial to understand that operating in such environments requires a willingness to adhere to the country's rules, both formal regulations and the often unwritten, implied norms. This necessitates a flexible compliance process and an open-minded corporate culture that can adapt to the unique challenges of these markets. However, these environments also present potential risks, particularly when companies find themselves navigating legally gray areas without fully comprehending the associated dangers. In today's complex landscape of global compliance requirements, adolescent markets may offer opportunities that are entangled with unclear or ambiguous processes, tempting companies to venture into precarious zones. For businesses already facing economic difficulties, this can be especially perilous. Therefore, it is essential that companies entering these markets are financially stable and prepared to manage the inherent risks. A solid economic foundation is critical, as it provides the resilience needed to navigate the uncertainties of markets with lower democratic standards, where the rules of engagement may be fluid and unpredictable.

2. *Aspiration to Develop/Maintain Individual Identity*

   Adolescence is a pivotal stage in the formation of individual identity, a process that significantly influences both personal and professional decisions (Tatum, 2000). In the economic realm, the Index of Economic

Freedom, as defined by the Heritage Foundation (Kim et al., 2023), mirrors this quest for autonomy, reflecting the extent to which individuals can control their labor and property. Markets in this adolescent phase are often in the midst of developing (or only partially developing) their economic identity.

This stage of economic evolution is marked by instability, with political dynamics playing a crucial role in determining the future trajectory of the country. Such markets possess a high degree of unexpressed potential, offering both opportunities and risks. The latent potential within these markets could either be harnessed effectively, leading to significant growth, or it may remain unrealized, resulting in stagnation. For companies with substantial experience, entering such markets can be highly advantageous; these companies can serve as role models, helping to shape the market's development and encouraging the realization of its potential. However, for companies with limited experience, these markets can present significant challenges. Without the necessary expertise and strategic approach, they risk falling into a cycle of investment with minimal returns, unable to effectively capitalize on the market's latent opportunities.

3. *Preference for Association with Peers*

In today's digital era, many adolescents view social media as a crucial tool for strengthening friendships and building networks (Anderson et al., 2023), seeking association with peers. This observation translates into the business world, where the percentage of internet users within a market can serve as a proxy for this adolescent trait. The Internet Access and Usage Index, provided by Statista, quantifies the proportion of a population with internet access, offering valuable insight into how connected and peer-oriented a market is.

In adolescent markets, networking plays a pivotal role in gaining access to opportunities. While networking is important in any market, its significance is magnified in adolescent markets, where rules (especially the unwritten ones) are often unclear, and where making a strong network is essential for securing a favorable position in the competitive landscape. A robust network enables companies to stay abreast of the market's constantly evolving rules and conditions, which are often fluid and unpredictable. Without a strong network, companies face a high likelihood of failure, as they may struggle to navigate the complexities and nuances of the market. Therefore, it is imperative for companies entering these markets to allocate sufficient resources to build and maintain a strong network. This involves not just traditional business activities but also investing in relationship-building efforts such as dinners, events, subsidies, sponsorships, and other initiatives that enhance their image and strengthen their connections. By doing so, companies can establish a solid foothold in the market, ensuring they remain agile and responsive to their ever-changing dynamics.

4. *High Susceptibility to Peer Influence*

Adolescents are often highly influenced by their peers, a trait that is reflected on the global stage by the Global Soft Power Index, developed by Brand Finance. This index assesses the influence of nations and the perceptions they hold of one another, effectively measuring a market's susceptibility to external influences. In adolescent markets, this susceptibility is manifested as a heightened vulnerability to international geopolitical dynamics. Understanding this trait is crucial when approaching such markets, as they represent the most fragile links in the global economic chain.

Adolescent markets tend to align themselves with the political blocs that offer the most immediate benefits, which can lead to various challenges, ranging from international compliance issues to disruptions in supply chains that could adversely affect a company's local operations. For example, following the conflict in Ukraine, Russia faced numerous UN sanctions that extended not only to Russia itself but also to countries conducting certain types of business with it. African nations maintaining favorable relations with Russia were compelled to navigate this new geopolitical landscape, leading to potential compliance challenges for companies operating within these countries. In essence, adolescent markets are more susceptible to the influences of international geopolitics than their more mature counterparts. Companies entering these markets must remain acutely aware of the broader geopolitical context and be prepared to adapt to the shifting alliances and tensions that can impact their business activities. Failing to account for these external pressures can lead to significant operational and strategic risks, underscoring the importance of a well-informed and flexible approach when engaging with these volatile markets.

5. *Willingness to Take Risks*

The natural inclination toward risk-taking in adolescence can be observed in markets by examining the Central Government Debt (CGD) as a percentage of GDP, an economic indicator provided by the IMF. This metric reflects a nation's willingness to engage in financial risks, with higher debt levels relative to GDP indicating riskier economic behaviors, paralleling the adventurous and often impulsive nature of adolescence. Across cultures, adolescence is commonly associated with a heightened propensity for risk-taking. Young people, with their limited perception of danger, are more likely to take risks, often finding in these risks a sense of excitement and a way to "feel alive." This psychological drive is the root of many adrenaline-driven pursuits that begin in youth, as individuals develop a dependency on the thrill of risk.

Similarly, adolescent markets exhibit a comparable approach to risk. These markets are characterized by high levels of uncertainty and volatility, where the potential for significant gains is matched by equally substantial risks. Just as adolescents are drawn to the excitement and challenge of risky behaviors, companies entering adolescent markets may be attracted by the prospect of high returns. However, these markets are often speculative in nature, where fortunes can be made or lost quickly, depending on how well companies navigate the inherent risks. For businesses considering entry into these markets, it is crucial to approach them with caution. Companies should only allocate resources that they can afford to lose, given the volatile and unpredictable environment that defines these markets. While the potential rewards can be substantial, the risks are equally pronounced, making it essential for companies to carefully weigh their risk tolerance against the possible outcomes. Entering these markets requires not just a strategic approach but also a clear understanding of the risks involved and a readiness to adapt to rapidly changing conditions.

6. *Increasing Dissociation from Parents/Guardians*
    As adolescents strive for independence, they often begin to distance themselves from parental guidance. In the global economic landscape, this detachment is mirrored by the level of foreign aid a country receives. Lower levels of foreign aid (LFA) indicate a market's increasing independence and a reduced reliance on external support, much like an adolescent stepping away from parental oversight. This indicator, sourced from World Bank data, is used in Market Pareidolia, where the variable is inverted (higher LFA correspond to a lower "age" of the market).

    Economically, this suggests that adolescent markets tend to deviate from adhering strictly to international norms and standards (the guidance). In these markets, unspoken local customs and practices often hold greater sway than internationally recognized rules and requirements. Companies considering entry into such markets must carefully assess their willingness to navigate these local dynamics, which may challenge their ethical and operational standards. For instance, many adolescent markets have minimal environmental protection policies, leading to frequent environmental degradation by both companies and local communities. While certain practices may be legally permissible in these markets, companies must critically evaluate whether they align with broader ethical and moral standards. The question companies need to address before entering these markets is not just about legality but also about ethics: Are they prepared to operate in an environment where local practices may conflict with global ethical norms? Before venturing into these markets, companies must establish clear ethical and moral boundaries that they are not willing to cross. This involves not only understanding the legal landscape but also considering the long-term implications of their actions on their reputation and on the communities in which they operate. Setting these boundaries is essential for maintaining corporate integrity and ensuring that business practices are aligned with the company's core values, even in challenging environments.

Table 2.8 Adolescent markets' corresponding indexes

Human age marker	Corresponding Market Index	Market trait
Desire for independence and autonomy	Democracy Index	Flexible compliance and open-minded corporate culture
Desire to develop/maintain individual identity	Economic freedom	Unexpressed potential
Desire for association with peers	Internet access usage	Network predominance
High susceptibility to peer influence	Global Soft Power Index	High influence from international geopolitics
Willingness to take risks	Central government debt in percentage	High levels of risk
Increasing dissociation with parents/guardians	Net official aid received divided by their GDP	Challenging ethical and moral boundaries

2.3.2 Adult Markets

Benson and Furstenberg (2006) presented a new interpretation of adulthood markers, shifting the focus from traditional indicators like parenthood to contemporary markers that emphasize responsibility and independence. Building on previous research, they identified six key markers of adulthood (Table 2.9) that include emotional, educational, financial, and social maturity, as well as legal and economic independence.

1. *Emotional Maturity*
   Emotional maturity in adults is often marked by a progression from dependence to autonomy, a reduction in feelings of inferiority, diminished egotism, and a decrease in competitiveness. This concept aligns with what Saul (1947) described as the "genital level" of development, a stage theoretically preparing individuals for parenthood. However, the choice to have children is not necessarily an indicator of emotional maturity. Paradoxically, a strong desire for many offspring can sometimes reflect a lack of emotional maturity, particularly if it stems from motives that conflict with self-reliance and autonomy. To quantify emotional ma-

59

turity at a societal level, the Population Growth Rate (PGR), as monitored by the United Nations Department of Economic and Social Affairs, provides a useful indicator. A balanced growth rate may suggest societal emotional maturity, while a high PGR could indicate collective immaturity, signaling that the market is still navigating the challenges of maturation. In Market Pareidolia, the PGR is inversely proportional, meaning that higher population growth corresponds to lower levels of emotional maturity.

From an economic perspective, companies considering entry into these markets can typically expect a more stable economic environment compared to adolescent markets, though they must be mindful of the potential for a "mid-life crisis" that could disrupt their investments. Adult markets, characterized by greater emotional stability, are generally well-positioned to accommodate significant opportunities. These markets are more likely to adhere to international laws and compliance standards, and they prioritize long-term gains over short-term, speculative ventures. Companies entering adult markets can therefore anticipate a more predictable and secure business environment, making these markets ideal for strategies focused on sustainable growth and mid- to long-term investment.

2. *Educational Maturity*

Educational maturity within a country is best reflected by its average years of schooling (AYS), with longer durations indicating a more advanced stage of societal progress in educational development. This metric serves as a marker of national educational maturity, akin to the concept of adult educational maturity. AYS is a key indicator sourced from the UNDP Human Development Index Report, offering insights into the overall educational attainment of the population.

From an economic standpoint, this metric directly correlates with the local availability of skilled human resources, which is a critical consideration for companies, particularly those looking to invest in production lines. In adult markets, the workforce typically boasts a mid-to-high level of education, reducing the need for costly expatriate employees since local talent can perform the required tasks. This is a significant advantage, as it allows companies to tap into a well-educated labor pool that can effectively support their operations at lower costs. In some adult markets, the local workforce is so sufficiently skilled that companies may find no need to bring in foreign workers to manage their investments. Instead, they can rely entirely on the local population to handle most operational tasks, requiring only periodic monitoring and training from the parent company. This not only lowers operational costs but also facilitates smoother integration into the local business environment, fostering sustainable growth and long-term success.

3. *Financial Maturity*

   Financial maturity in individuals is reflected in their ability to achieve financial independence, accumulate savings, and meet financial needs through their professional endeavors. On a national level, this maturity is mirrored in a market's capacity to attract financing, as measured by international benchmarks such as Moody's country's ratings. The ability to attract finance serves as an indicator of a market's financial maturity, with ratings ranging from C to AAA, as provided by Moody's.

   Financial maturity is crucial for companies looking to enter a market, as it signifies the presence of a reliable and robust financial system. Adult markets typically have strong connections to major financial institutions, including well-established corresponding banks and international banks with a solid local presence. This financial infrastructure provides companies with the assurance that they can access the necessary capital to support their operations and growth strategies. Additionally, these markets generally offer a relatively stable currency environment, which helps to mitigate currency risks associated with long-term projects. However, it is important to note that despite their financial maturity, adult markets remain vulnerable to international economic crises. When a global economic downturn occurs, these markets often bear the brunt of the impact, leading to significant disruptions in their financial systems and posing challenges for foreign investments. Companies operating in adult markets must be aware of this vulnerability and should prepare for potential economic volatility by implementing robust risk management strategies. While the financial infrastructure in these markets is generally strong, the interconnected nature of the global economy means that even the most mature markets can experience instability during times of international crisis.

4. *Social Maturity*

   Social maturity, as defined by Goleman (2006), encompasses the ability to navigate and comprehend interpersonal relationships, effectively manage social situations, and interact harmoniously with others. This maturity is grounded in an understanding of societal dynamics and a deep sense of mutual respect. The Social Progress Index (SPI), developed by the Social Progress Imperative, serves as a robust measure of social advancement, integrating 53 indicators that cover a wide range of social and environmental outcomes. The SPI offers a comprehensive assessment of social maturity at the national level, reflecting the overall social well-being and development of a society.

   In adult markets, a high level of social maturity is typically observed. These markets are characterized by the presence of a significant middle class, which plays a crucial role in driving economic growth. A thriving and effective middle class contributes to a more stable society, where basic needs have been met and the focus shifts toward improving quality of life. In such societies, the workforce is often composed of motivated and ambitious individuals who are eager to improve their economic standing by improving the company's returns. These workers, typically earning lower wages compared to those in more mature markets, present a competitive advantage for companies looking to maximize their return and lower their operational costs. This dynamic, if managed effectively, can yield substantial benefits for businesses operating in these markets. The combination of a stable social environment, a motivated workforce, and competitive labor costs creates an attractive landscape for investment. Companies that recognize and leverage the social maturity of these markets can tap into a productive and driven labor force, ultimately enhancing their operational efficiency and profitability. Understanding the social fabric of adult markets is therefore essential for businesses seeking to capitalize on the unique opportunities these markets offer.

5. *Legal Emancipation*

Legal emancipation, as described by H. Clark (1968), signifies the critical transition where a minor is released from parental authority and assumes full legal responsibility for their actions. This legal milestone typically occurs at age 18 or 21 in some jurisdictions, marking the individual's entry into adulthood, where adherence to the law becomes a fundamental aspect of societal participation. In the context of international markets, the Rule of Law Index (RLI), developed by the World Justice Project, serves as a valuable metric that reflects this concept of legal maturity. The RLI evaluates countries based on several key aspects, including constraints on governmental power, the absence of corruption, government transparency, the protection of fundamental rights, societal order and security, regulatory enforcement, and the effectiveness of civil and criminal justice systems.

In adult markets that score highly on the RLI, businesses can typically rely on a relatively independent legal system that upholds the principles of law and order. In these markets, the rule of law and the separation of powers are established and are often a source of national pride. Corruption tends to be lower, and basic rights are generally guaranteed, creating a more stable and predictable environment for companies and their investments. This legal stability reduces the risks associated with doing business, as companies can operate with greater confidence that their rights will be upheld and that they will be treated fairly under the law. For businesses, entering markets with a strong rule of law offers significant advantages. The reduced prevalence of corruption, coupled with the assurance that legal disputes will be handled transparently and justly, provides a solid foundation for long-term investment and growth. Companies can focus on expanding their operations and pursuing opportunities without the constant concern of legal uncertainties or unfair practices. In this way, high RLI scores in adult markets signal a favorable environment for businesses, where legal protections and regulatory frameworks support both economic activities and the broader social order.

6. *Economic Independence*

Economic independence, a hallmark of adulthood, is reflected on the national level by a country's reserves of foreign exchange (Forex). Significant reserves signal a nation's economic self-sufficiency and stability within the global economic framework. The Forex reserves serve as a crucial indicator of economic independence, demonstrating a country's ability to engage confidently and autonomously on the international stage.

From an economic perspective, substantial Forex reserves suggest that the country has achieved higher purchasing power. This economic strength often correlates with the rise of the middle class that prioritizes quality over price in its consumption habits. In such markets, there is a noticeable shift toward consumerism, with a growing appetite for new products and innovations. These markets are characterized by an eager consumer base, increasingly oriented toward acquiring goods and services that mirror the lifestyles of more mature economies. In these economies, people are not only willing but also enthusiastic about spending to obtain products that are popular in more developed countries. This consumer behavior reflects a broader societal trend toward emulating the material and lifestyle standards seen in wealthier nations. For companies, this represents a significant opportunity: Entering these markets can be highly lucrative, as there is a strong demand for new and innovative products that meet the rising expectations of the burgeoning middle class. The drive for consumption in these markets makes them aggressive and dynamic environments, ripe for businesses that can cater to the desires of consumers eager to experience the quality and variety of products available in more mature economies. However, first come first served, and latecomers may find the market saturated faster than expected.

Table 2.9 Adult markets' corresponding indexes

Human age marker	Corresponding Market Index	Market trait
Emotional maturity	Population Growth Index	Prioritization of long-term gains over short-term speculative ventures
Educational maturity	Average years of schooling	Well-educated labor pool
Financial maturity	Moody's country rating	Strong connections to major financial institutions
Social maturity	Social Progress Index	Productive and driven labor force
Legal emancipation	Rule of Law Index	Relatively independent legal system
Economic independence	Foreign exchange reserves	Higher purchasing power

2.3.3 Senior Markets

After identifying the markers for adolescence and adulthood, Freud and Smith (1999) explored how senior adults perceive their own identities, emphasizing the importance of self-definition in shaping how individuals view themselves. The authors highlight that "self-definition is not about an objective portrayal of an individual, but centers on those self-conceptions that individuals deem fundamental to their personal identity" (Freud and Smith, 1999, p. 55). Their research revealed that, compared to other age groups, seniors place greater significance on specific aspects of their lives (Table 2.10), which can be mirrored in market analysis.

1. *Integrity*

   Integrity, a key characteristic of senior adulthood, embodies moral uprightness and honesty. In the context of international markets, this trait is mirrored by the Corruption Perception Index, developed by Transparency International. Just as integrity reflects the ethical standards of an individual, the Corruption Perception Index measures the perceived integrity and transparency of a country's institutions and public sector. A higher score on this index corresponds to a lower level of perceived corruption, aligning closely with the senior value of integrity. Economically speaking, countries that score highly on this index are typically those where the separation of powers in government is well-established, and the justice system operates independently and fairly. These nations provide an environment where businesses can operate securely, guided by clear, well-defined laws with no reliance on unwritten rules or practices. In such markets, there are no ambiguous or gray areas; the legal framework is transparent, and companies can proceed with confidence, knowing they are protected from power abuse or any criminal acts against their investments. In senior markets there is a strong sense for the rule of law.

2. *Coping with Physical Decline*

   As individuals age, they often experience a decline in physical abilities, which can significantly impact their overall well-being and ability to reenter the workforce after retirement (Sibbritt et al., 2007). This decline is mirrored in the economic context by the Unemployment Rate Index, which serves as a relevant market metric to capture the challenges associated with an aging population. In Market Pareidolia, the Unemployment Rate Index, sourced from The World Bank, is inverted, meaning that a higher unemployment rate corresponds to a lower ability of a market to cope with its "physical decline." This metric reflects the difficulties a market faces in sustaining its workforce as its population ages.

In senior markets this phenomenon is indirectly related to a slower economic pace. Senior markets typically experience slow growth, rarely exceeding 3% annually, with the average growth rate often falling below 1%. Despite this matter, senior markets offer low and stable inflation levels, coupled with a reliable monetary system, providing a degree of economic stability (slow but stable growth). The high GDP per capita characteristic of these markets means that achieving significant growth is more challenging. For example, increasing GDP per capita by 1% in a senior market, where the per capita GDP may already be around $40,000, is considerably more difficult than a 10% increase in a younger market where the GDP per capita might be only $1,000. In younger markets, moving from $1,000 to $1,500 GDP per capita per year is less daunting than the incremental growth required in senior markets to shift from $40,000 to $42,000 GDP per capita per year. The relative effort required for such growth is significantly greater in senior markets due to their already high economic baseline. However, this also means that younger markets are rapidly catching up, which is an encouraging sign for global economic development.

3. *Confirmation/Loss of Professional Status*
In senior adulthood, the affirmation or loss of professional status becomes a significant concern, reflecting how individuals relate to their past career achievements and current economic roles. This concept finds its parallel in a country's EDB ranking, which indicates its economic standing and its ability to maintain or improve its business environment. A higher rank on this scale suggests that a country, much like an individual, is successfully managing its professional and economic identity on the global stage.

From an economic standpoint, maintaining and improving the EDB requires a robust and well-functioning bureaucratic system that ensures stability and fairness within the business context. However, the complexity of such systems can have a dual effect. On the one hand, a strong bureaucratic framework can provide the necessary structure to safeguard business operations, ensuring that regulations are followed and that the market remains orderly and predictable. On the other hand, an overly complex or burdensome bureaucracy can deter investment, as it often requires significant resources to navigate, potentially discouraging smaller international investors from entering the market. The challenge lies in creating a balanced bureaucratic system that supports economic stability and fairness while remaining accessible and efficient. This balance is reflected in a country's EDB Index, where senior markets typically exhibit more complex, and sometimes costly, bureaucratic systems. While these systems contribute to a stable and reliable business environment, they can also act as a barrier to entry for smaller investors who may be deterred by the additional costs and complexities involved. For companies looking to invest in senior markets, it is crucial to be prepared for the intricate bureaucratic processes that come with the territory. Successfully navigating these processes is often essential for establishing a foothold in these markets, where the rewards of a stable and mature business environment can be significant, but the path to entry may require careful planning and substantial compliance efforts.

4. *Commitment Levels to Life's Roles and Obligations*

As individuals age, their commitment to life's roles and obligations, particularly those involving family responsibilities, becomes increasingly significant. This often includes ensuring financial stability to meet the needs and expectations of family members, such as providing support for adult children. On a national scale, a market proxy for this sense of commitment is the Gross Domestic Saving (% of GDP), which measures a country's ability to save and effectively manage its financial obligations. This indicator underscores the importance of savings strategies in maintaining economic stability and fulfilling long-term commitments.

This deepened sense of responsibility and accountability is mirrored in senior markets, where both companies are held to high standards of conduct. In these markets, accountability is not just a corporate buzzword; it is a fundamental expectation. Consumers in senior markets are typically well-informed, highly educated, and possess strong purchasing power, and these attributes translate into a consumer base that is exceptionally demanding and discerning, with a clear preference for companies that uphold ethical standards and demonstrate responsible behavior. In senior markets, a company's reputation is inextricably linked to its financial success. Consumers, empowered by their ability to choose from a wide range of products, are more likely to support companies that have established a solid ethical reputation. In this environment, any misconduct or unethical practices can have immediate and significant repercussions, directly impacting revenues and long-term business viability. Governments and societies in these markets place a high value on accountability, expecting companies to take responsibility for their actions across the entire supply chain. For companies looking to expand into senior markets, it is crucial to embody strong and transparent values throughout their operations. This means not only adhering to high ethical standards but also ensuring that these values are consistently applied at every stage of the supply chain. In doing so, companies can build and maintain the trust of consumers, securing their position in these mature and demanding markets.

5. *High Quality of Life*

As individuals reach senior adulthood, the emphasis on quality of life becomes increasingly pronounced. In this stage of life, priorities shift toward economic stability, access to healthcare, and security within a stable political and economic framework. The World Health Organization defines Quality of Life as "an individual's perception of their position in life in the context of the culture and value systems in which they live and in relation to their goals, expectations, standards, and concerns." The Quality-of-Life Index, developed by World Data, serves as a relevant market variable, capturing the overall well-being and satisfaction of a population. A higher score on this index indicates that a market provides the conditions necessary for a high quality of life, closely aligning with the values and priorities of senior adults.

However, maintaining a high quality of life in these markets comes with its own set of challenges, particularly in the form of elevated living costs. To sustain a society that enjoys a high quality of life, senior markets must bear significant operational costs. These include costly human resources, high taxes, expensive raw materials, and substantial marketing expenditures. The economic environment in these markets is characterized by higher costs across the board, which can pose challenges for companies looking to establish or expand their presence. On the positive side, consumers in senior markets typically possess strong purchasing power, enabling them to support these higher costs. This purchasing power creates opportunities for companies that can successfully navigate the financial demands of operating in such environments. However, businesses must be aware that entering these markets will require significant investments. The initial outlay for establishing operations, coupled with ongoing costs, can be substantial, but the potential returns from a consumer base that values quality and is willing to pay for it can make these investments worthwhile. For companies eager to enter senior markets, understanding the balance between high operational costs and the purchasing power of the local population is crucial. Success in these markets depends on the ability to offer products and services that meet the high expectations of consumers while managing the costs associated with delivering a high standard of living. With careful planning and substantial investment, companies can thrive in these environments, benefiting from the stability and prosperity that characterize senior markets.

6. *Life's Achievements*

In senior adulthood, individuals often engage in reflection on their life's achievements and overall satisfaction. This period of introspection can be analogized to a country's ranking in the World Happiness Report, which offers insights into the collective well-being and fulfillment of its citizens. A higher ranking in the World Happiness Report suggests that a nation's population is generally content with their lives and accomplishments, mirroring the personal reflections of senior adults on their life's work and successes. This metric acts as a proxy for a market's overall sense of contentment and success, akin to an individual's sense of life fulfillment.

A society that ranks highly in happiness typically exhibits a well-balanced approach to life, maintaining harmony between work, family, and leisure. Achieving this balance is largely possible through the implementation of processes and tools that simplify daily life and offer individuals greater freedom of choice. How did (and does) humanity create these tools? The answer lies in technological development. Technology is the cornerstone of modern-day choices, enabling people to work from home through the internet, cultivate vast areas of land with advanced machinery, and stay informed via news channels. Technology has endowed humanity with the ability to choose a higher standard of living. In senior markets, technology plays a pivotal role in maintaining and enhancing this quality of life. Companies seeking to enter these markets will encounter high technological standards across every industry. Businesses that are technologically averse or lagging in innovation may struggle to compete effectively in these environments. To thrive in senior markets, companies must prioritize technological competitiveness, ensuring that their products, services, and operations meet or exceed the advanced expectations of these markets. Embracing and leveraging technology is not just an advantage but a necessity for companies aiming to succeed in markets where the integration of cutting-edge innovations is integral to both business and daily life.

Table 2.10 Senior markets' corresponding indexes

Human age marker	Corresponding Market Index	Market trait
Integrity	Corruption Index	Clear separation of powers and strong rule of law
Coping with physical decline	Unemployment rate	Slow and stable growth
Confirmation/loss of professional status	Ease of doing business rank	Complex bureaucratic systems
Confirmation/decrease in professional and family roles and obligations	Gross domestic savings divided by GDP	High levels of accountability
High quality of life	Quality of life	High investment costs
Life's achievements	World Happiness Report by country	technologically advanced

2.3.4 From Human Age to Market Age

As seen in the previous chapter, 18 human markers were identified, each corresponding to specific stages of human development (adolescence, adulthood, and seniority) and were matched with 18 economic indexes representing similar traits in global markets. The aim was to create a comprehensive model that could effectively categorize countries by their "market age," providing businesses with a clearer understanding of which markets align with their strategic goals. However, some of these 18 variables may represent similar data, adding little contribution to the whole context, and working with 18 separate variables can be complex and unwieldy, particularly when trying to apply this model in a practical, real-world context. Therefore, a factor analysis was conducted to simplify and refine the model, making it more accessible and accurate. Factor analysis is a statistical method used to identify underlying relationships between a large set of variables, grouping them into factors that can explain the observed variances with fewer dimensions. In the context of the Market Pareidolia model, the factor analysis aimed to condense the 18 identified economic indexes into a smaller number of factors, each representing a broader but cohesive aspect of a market's characteristics. The goal was to reduce redundancy, highlight the most significant variables, and simplify the decision-making process to calculate the "humanized" age of a market.

The factor analysis was successful in consolidating 16 of the 18 variables into four distinct factors, each encapsulating a different aspect of a country's market characteristics. Two variables did not load into any of the factors, which indicates that they capture unique aspects of the market that are not closely related to the other variables. As a result, these two variables were retained as standalone indicators, contributing independently to the overall market age calculation. This refinement meant that the initial set of 18 variables could now be represented more efficiently by four factors and two independent variables, streamlining the model while preserving its analytical power. Each of the four factors derived from the analysis encapsulates a specific dimension of a market's overall profile:

- *Factor 1* – Socio-Political and Economic (SPE) Stability
  Variables
  1. Levels of Democracy (LOD)
  2. Economic Freedom Index (EFI)
  3. Rule of Law Index (RLI)
  4. Easiness to Attract Finance (EAF)
  5. Corruption Perceptions Index (CPI)
  6. Quality of Life (QOL)
  7. World Happiness Report (WHR)

Context
This factor was interpreted as representing the SPE Stability Index. It aggregates multiple indicators that collectively reflect the quality of governance, the strength of democratic institutions, the level of economic freedom, and the overall well-being of the population. Countries scoring high on this factor typically have robust legal systems, low corruption, strong democratic processes, and a high quality of life. These elements together contribute to a stable and predictable environment, which is crucial for long-term economic growth and investment security.

Significance
The SPE Stability Index is particularly important for companies looking to invest in markets where long-term stability and predictability are critical. A high score in this factor suggests that the country offers a secure and conducive environment for business operations, minimizing the risks associated with political and economic instability.

- *Factor 2* – Global Influence and Financial (GIF) Stability
  Variables
  1. Global Soft Power Index (GSP)
  2. Foreign Exchange Reserves (RFE)

Context
This factor measures a country's global influence and financial stability. The Global Soft Power Index reflects the country's cultural, diplomatic, and political influence on the world stage, while Foreign Exchange Reserves indicate the country's financial resilience and ability to manage economic shocks. High scores in this factor suggest that the country is not only influential on a global scale but also has the financial stability necessary to support sustained economic growth.

Significance
The Global Influence and Financial Stability factor is crucial for companies aiming to enter markets that serve as regional or global hubs. Countries that score highly here can provide businesses with strategic advantages, such as access to influential networks, stable financial systems, and the ability to leverage the country's global reputation for business expansion.

- *Factor 3* – Economic Development and Human Capital (EDH)
  Variables

1. Internet Access Usage (IAU)
2. Levels of Foreign Aid (LFA)
3. Population Growth Rate (PGR)
4. Average Years of Schooling (AYS)
5. Social Progress Index (SPI)
6. Ease of Doing Business (EDB).

Context
This factor captures the level of economic development and human capital within a country. High internet access and educational attainment levels, combined with low population growth, are indicators of a well-developed economy with a strong human capital base. The inclusion of the SPI and EDB further reflects the country's commitment to social development and the ease with which businesses can operate.

Significance
The Economic Development and Human Capital factor is particularly relevant for companies that rely on skilled labor and advanced infrastructure. Markets that score highly in this factor are likely to provide the necessary resources and environment for companies to thrive, particularly in knowledge-intensive industries or sectors requiring a high level of technical expertise.

- *Factor 4* – Central Government Debt (CGD)
  Variables
  1. CGD.

Context
This factor is represented by a single variable – CGD. This index reflects the financial burden on the government and its capacity to support economic growth through public investment. High levels of government debt can constrain a country's ability to invest in infrastructure, education, and other areas critical to long-term economic development.

Significance
The CGD factor is a critical indicator of a country's fiscal health. For companies, a high government debt level may signal potential risks, such as austerity measures, higher taxes, or reduced government spending, all of which can negatively impact the business environment. Conversely, low government debt suggests greater fiscal flexibility and a more supportive environment for business expansion.

- The Two Standalone Variables
  1. Unemployment Rate Index (URI)

     Context
     The unemployment rate reflects the health of the labor market and the availability of human resources. High unemployment can indicate economic distress, while low unemployment suggests a robust economy with strong labor demand.

  2. Gross Domestic Savings (GDS) as a Percentage of GDP

     Context
     This variable measures the level of savings within an economy relative to its GDP. High savings rates indicate a population that is financially prudent and a country that has the capital necessary for investment in growth opportunities.

After identifying the four factors and the two standalone variables, the next step was to assign a "partial age" to each factor and variable, ranging from 13 to 100 years. This was accomplished by mapping the lowest z-score to 0 years and the highest z-score to 100 years, with intermediate z-scores proportionally translated within this range. Each factor and non-loaded variable were then assigned equal weight, contributing one-sixth to the total calculated age (comprising four factors and two variables). This method ensured a balanced and comprehensive approach to calculating a country's "human age," which was derived by summing these weighted partial ages. The transition from 18 variables to 4 factors and 2 standalone variables represents a significant refinement of the Market Pareidolia model. This streamlined approach not only simplifies the model but also enhances its practical utility, making it easier for companies to assess and compare markets based on a comprehensible framework. By focusing on the most critical aspects of a market's characteristics, this refined model offers a robust tool for guiding strategic decisions in internationalization efforts.

2.3.5 Evolutionary Characteristic of Market Pareidolia

The concept of Market Pareidolia is fundamentally evolutionary in nature, offering a nuanced approach to understanding and categorizing markets. It is crucial to emphasize that Market Pareidolia does not rigidly classify markets into the three distinct stages of adolescence, adulthood, and seniority. Instead, much like the progression of human development, it provides a corresponding age that reflects the market's characteristics at a given time. Just as adolescence can extend beyond the age of 18, and adulthood can begin before the age of 21, markets, too, can exhibit traits from different stages simultaneously. By assigning a human age to markets, Market Pareidolia equips companies with the tools to analyze these markets in their full complexity. A market's age not only defines its current state but also signals its growth potential. For example, a country scoring over 70 on the Market Pareidolia scale will display certain well-defined characteristics typical of that stage. However, countries that fall within the transitional ages (between adolescence, adulthood, and seniority) may exhibit traits from more than one age category. This overlapping of characteristics is what makes Market Pareidolia an evolutionary tool, capable of capturing the dynamic nature of markets as they develop and mature.

This evolutionary perspective is particularly valuable for companies' considering entry into new markets. Understanding that a market may possess a blend of traits from different developmental stages allows businesses to approach market entry with greater flexibility and insight. Markets in transition can present both opportunities and challenges, as they may combine the productive and driven labor force of adulthood with an excessively rigid and complex bureaucratic system of seniority. Therefore, Market Pareidolia encourages companies to ask the right questions about a market's age and developmental stage before making strategic decisions. Market Pareidolia provides a powerful framework for analyzing markets, recognizing that markets, like humans, are not static but are constantly evolving. By understanding the evolutionary nature of Market Pareidolia, companies can better navigate the complexities of international markets, making informed decisions that align with the unique characteristics and potential of each market. This approach not only helps in identifying the current state of the market but also in anticipating its future trajectory, enabling businesses to strategically position themselves for long-term success. A full list by country's age can be consulted in Table 2.11 and Table 2.12.

Table 2.11 List of countries by Market Pareidolia age

Markets	Age	Country
senior	86.27	Japan
	85.53	Singapore
	79.00	USA
	73.39	United Kingdom
	73.04	Germany
	71.76	Switzerland
	71.05	South Korea

	70.3	France
	69.85	Italy
	68.37	Netherlands
	68.17	Ireland
	67.59	China
	67.46	United Arab Emirates
	66.46	Qatar
	66.2	Canada
	65.97	Belgium
	65.88	Norway
	65.19	Finland
	65.04	Australia
	65.03	New Zealand
	64.94	Denmark
	64.41	Austria
	63.96	Bahrain
	63.93	Portugal
	63.53	Sweden
	63.06	Czechia
	62.97	Israel
	62.96	Luxembourg
	61.87	Russia
	60.9	Cyprus
	60.83	Spain
	60.81	Iceland
	59.53	Poland
adult	59.41	Hungary
	59.25	Slovenia
	58.79	Thailand
	58.07	Malaysia
	57.08	Malta
	56.48	Maldives
	56.44	Estonia
	56.26	Greece
	55.68	Saudi Arabia
	55.68	Lithuania

55.51	Slovakia
55.11	Bhutan
54.63	Croatia
54.39	Latvia
53.12	India
52.28	Romania
52.18	Sri Lanka
51.87	Uruguay
51.86	Barbados
51.77	Oman
51.39	Indonesia
51.16	Bulgaria
50.78	Dominica
50.73	Chile
50.47	Argentina
50.21	Vietnam
50.08	Mexico
49.99	Jamaica
49.64	Suriname
49.39	Brazil
49.02	Fiji
48.59	Kazakhstan
48.58	Belarus
48.04	Ukraine
47.95	Mauritius
47.8	Zambia
47.74	Mongolia
47.59	Trinidad and Tobago
47.2	Ghana
47.11	Kuwait
47.05	Panama
47.04	Cuba
47.03	Bahamas
47.02	Laos
46.74	Brunei
46.59	Cabo Verde
46.11	Peru

45.87	Serbia
45.84	Philippines
45.5	Seychelles
45.13	Azerbaijan
44.93	Myanmar
44.72	Costa Rica
44.49	Ecuador
44.39	Moldova
44.23	Uzbekistan
44.19	Turkey
44.17	Morocco
44.11	Vanuatu
43.54	Georgia
42.93	Dominican Republic
42.72	Senegal
42.59	Belize
42.25	Cambodia
42.19	Gambia
42.08	Paraguay
41.99	Albania
41.98	Armenia
41.67	Tanzania
41.67	North Macedonia
41.55	Bolivia
41.19	Saint Lucia
41.11	Papua New Guinea
40.99	Benin
40.98	Timor-Leste
40.9	Eritrea
40.78	Côte d'Ivoire
40.23	El Salvador
40.22	Kyrgyzstan
40.03	Malawi
39.98	Iran
39.86	Algeria
39.67	Montenegro
39.48	St. Vincent & the Grenadines

	39.03	Kenya
	38.82	Colombia
	38.61	Togo
	38.54	South Africa
	37.89	Bangladesh
	37.84	Mozambique
	37.83	Angola
	37.69	Liberia
	37.54	Samoa
	37.43	Venezuela
	37.26	Egypt
	36.95	Nigeria
	36.8	Guinea-Bissau
	36.52	Burkina Faso
	36.23	Guatemala
	36.18	Solomon Islands
	36.14	Nicaragua
	35.92	Tunisia
	35.85	Guyana
	35.75	Mauritania
	35.43	Pakistan
	35.38	Bosnia and Herzegovina
	35.26	Gabon
	35.19	Jordan
	35.12	Niger
	34.91	Madagascar
	34.79	Mali
	34.76	Libya
adolescents	34.45	Tajikistan
	34.39	Turkmenistan
	34.3	Sao Tome and Principe
	34.24	Zimbabwe
	34.16	Sierra Leone
	34.01	Uganda
	33.93	Honduras
	33.29	Ethiopia
	33.25	Rwanda

	32.72	Chad
	32.69	Cameroon
	32.18	CAR
	31.86	Burundi
	31.37	DRC
	31.28	Guinea
	31.04	Iraq
	30.75	Nepal
	30.42	Afghanistan
	30.3	Equatorial Guinea
	30.28	Botswana
	30.25	Congo
	29.99	Namibia
	27.37	Lebanon
	26.77	Syria
	26.6	Eswatini
	25.58	Sudan
	25.07	Comoros
	24.42	Djibouti
	23.95	Lesotho
	21.67	Hait

Figure 2.1: Countries by Market Pareidolia age

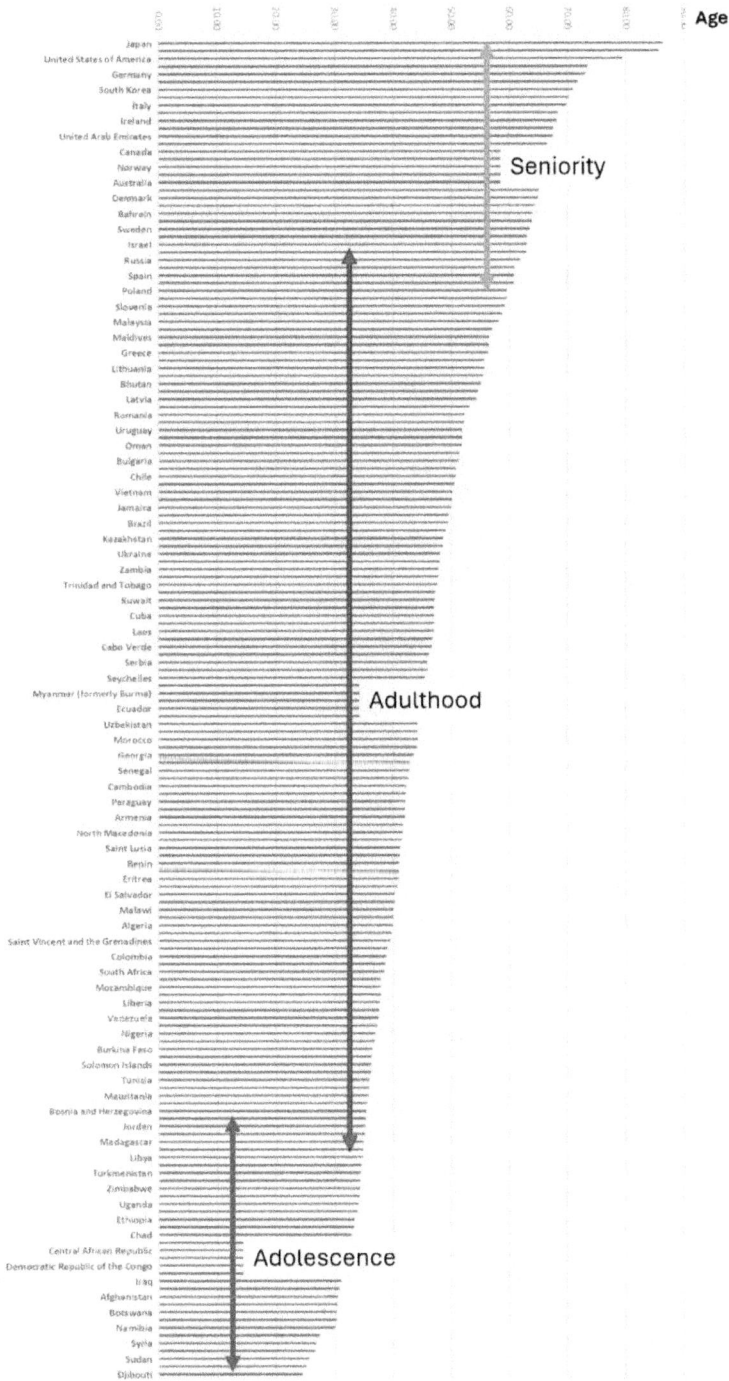

2.4 Empirical Evidence of Market Pareidolia – by Luca Gatto

How effective could Market Pareidolia be? As seen in the previous chapter, Market Pareidolia categorization model is a new tool for companies and managers to evaluate their entry into new markets by leveraging on the human sensory illusion of human behavior given by their age within international markets. A first evaluation of the effectiveness of Market Pareidolia was provided by sharing and comparing the model with potential users in Italy to assure effectiveness and user friendliness. The decision was made to engage directly with those managers active in foreign markets (Export Managers). These professionals play a key role in the internationalization process, not only developing foreign markets but also advising top management or business owners on which target markets to pursue. Replying to a questionnaire, the international senior consultant specialized in African countries, Umberto Trulli, stated:

> "Too often this function is confusing with that of foreign sales, which in micro and small enterprises obviously overlap. The Export Manager must be able to select appropriate sources of information, validate them, and direct strategic decision-making processes for internationalization toward value creation. Therefore, if in large organizations these analyses are carried out using the variety of skills available internally (MAKE), in SMEs or micros they must be acquired (BUY). For the above reasons, the Export Manager must possess managerial skills and attitudes".

Trying to record empirical evidence on the applicability and usefulness of Market Pareidolia's model in real-world scenarios, Italy was selected as a test ground for being within the ten largest exporters in the world. Based on LinkedIn database and network, it was revealed that there are approximately 43,000 Export Managers in the country, with over 20% connected to the author's network. Leveraging the educational activities conducted in recent years and reference publications, the decision was made to engage this community in evaluating the model's relevance and effectiveness. The engagement process followed a structured approach with multiple activities. Initially, the Market Pareidolia model, a collaboration between Prof. Emiliano Finocchi and Dr. Luca Gatto, was presented to the community. The goal was to gauge the level of knowledge and interest through a LinkedIn poll. The feedback received was insightful and has been integrated into the model's development.

The concept of Market Pareidolia was introduced using the familiar example of the "face on Mars," but this phenomenon can also be observed in the recognition of familiar shapes in clouds, shades, and rocks or in any other object or natural event. As seen previously, pareidolia is a psychological phenomenon where the brain attempts to create order and familiarity out of chaotic images. In the business context, the search for order is critical when approaching new international markets, a process that demands significant investments in both human and financial resources, thus, essential to categorize and understand the external market context. However, existing market categorization methodologies have two main limitations: They are often static and not based on robust empirical evidence, and they are influenced by social structures, leading to expectations-driven outcomes. Therefore, the development of a more realistic and expectation-immune market categorization model, such as Market Pareidolia, can provide substantial support to companies in their internationalization efforts.

"A great deal of work is being done in the field of neuro-management on managerial decision-making processes and the mechanisms underlying them. As seen, a large body of scientific literature sees the interplay between noise, bias, heuristics, cognitive loadings, emotions, interoception, perception, memory and more. The case studied for categorizing markets, in terms of decision-making, also responds to these logics. One method used is to analyze the same element from different perspectives of interest, hence the need to create appropriately governed and result-oriented multidisciplinary teams" (Umberto Trulli).

For Mariella Di Pinto, Senior Export Manager for IC&Partner, a consulting firm that supports Italian companies to develop international projects, her extensive professional experience has led her to understand that the ability to "read" markets is a skill that develops over time. She stated:

"Market Pareidolia, the tendency to attribute human characteristics to markets, is a phenomenon I have repeatedly observed. Every time I negotiate with a foreign partner, analyze trends in an emerging market, or decide to invest in a new sector, I am actually attributing almost all human characteristics to that market, product, or interlocutor. It's as if I'm trying to anticipate their developments, dynamics, and perspectives. This ability to create narratives, though subjective, is a valuable starting point. However, it must be complemented by a scientific, data-driven approach. The balance between intuition and analysis, when well-managed, becomes a powerful tool for navigating market complexity and making effective strategic decisions".

As previously seen, the Market Pareidolia approach begins with the idea that a country's age can be compared to that of an individual, where, throughout life, everyone experiences adolescence, adulthood, and seniority phases of life. These life stages possess distinctive traits that transcend culture, habits, and language as they are tied to the universal experience of human development. By applying pareidolia to global markets, the concept of assigning a human age to a market can help, in this specific case, entrepreneurs and Export Managers make more intuitive and strategic decisions. Next, the chapter delves into the process and results derived from LinkedIn community engagement with Market Pareidolia.

"In my opinion, this model will express its potentiality and usefulness for our Export Managers at the utmost, when it will be applied not only to a country's economy tout court but to a specific good or service market within a country." (Riccardo Fichera, Senior Export Manager for Società Cooperativa Fattorie Garofalo, an Italian leading buffalo mozzarella production company, with 55% exports in 45 countries)

2.4.1 Different Age Groups

1. Adolescence

A first LinkedIn post was released introducing the Market Pareidolia concept and its initial six parameters, which identified the traits of adolescence in human development and their corresponding economic indexes, reflecting the analogous traits in markets (as discussed in the previous chapter):

- *Desire for Independence*: Democracy Index (Economist).
- *Individual Identity*: Economic Freedom Index (The Heritage Foundation)
- Associations with Peers: IAU (World Bank)
- *Peer Influence*: Global Soft Power Index (Brand Finance)
- *Risk Appetite*: Debt Percentage of GDP (IMF)
- *Parental Detachment*: Net Official Aid Received/GDP (World Bank)

The LinkedIn community was then asked to provide feedback on the model. The results were insightful:

- *General Interest:*
  All respondents showed interest in the survey, indicating a strong desire to understand better how to categorize markets and interest in the proposed model. The consensus was that current categorizations are insufficient for comprehending the important dynamics that guide market selection.
- *Degree of Agreement:*
  10% were interested but did not fully understand the variables, likely because some variables are less familiar or not directly related to business contexts. 50% partially agreed with the model, recognizing its usefulness but expressing reservations about the indicators used (this could be due to a lack of familiarity with the indices or a belief that other indices might be more appropriate. 40% agreed with the reasoning and variables related to adolescence, indicating significant interest in this innovative, holistic model).

Overall, 90% of respondents agreed, in whole or in part, with the choice of market indicators explaining adolescence, signaling strong interest in the model and its potential application.

2. Adulthood
In the second LinkedIn post, adulthood stage was presented to the community, as well as their six correspondent adulthood market traits:

- Emotional Maturity: Average Population Growth (The UN Department of Economic and Social Affairs, Population Division)
- *Educational Maturity*: AYS (Human Development Index Report)
- *Financial Maturity*: Moody's Rating Scale
- *Social Maturity*: Social Progress Index (Social Progress Imperative)
- *Legal Emancipation*: Rule of Law Index (World Justice Project)
- *Economic Independence*: Reserves of Foreign Exchange (CIA Fact Book)

The LinkedIn community was again consulted, with the following results:

- *General Interest:*
  Only 8% of respondents were not interested in the survey, suggesting that most see value in understanding market categorization during adulthood. 42% showed interest but lacked full familiarity with the variables, indicating a latent need that has not yet been fully articulated. The Moody's scale was the only widely recognized indicator.
- *Degree of Agreement:*
  17% partially agreed, likely due to unfamiliarity with some indices. 33% agreed with the model and its adulthood indicators, showing substantial interest in and alignment with the proposed model.

Overall, 50% of respondents agreed, in whole or in part, with the choice of variables explaining adulthood, with 42% showing interest in the proposed model, indicating that it meets a real and latent community need.

3. Seniority
The third and last stage of life, seniority, was then submitted as the third LinkedIn post, always defining and explaining the six-correspondent Market Index for seniority:

- *Integrity*: Corruption Perception Index (Transparency International)
- *Managing Physical Decline*: The Unemployment Rate Index (The World Bank)

- Professional Status: EDB (World Bank)
- *Commitment to Responsibilities*: Gross Domestic Savings (World Bank)
- *Quality of Life*: Quality of Life Index (World Data)
- *Life's Achievements*: World Happiness Report

Once again, the LinkedIn community was asked for feedback:

- *General Interest:*
  22% of respondents were not interested in the survey, possibly be-cause the community is predominantly under 60 years old and may not directly relate to this age group. None of the respondents lacked knowledge of the variables, indicating interest in the model and an adequate understanding of the indicators.
- *Degree of Agreement:*
  52% partially agreed, recognizing the model's usefulness but ques-tioning the chosen indicators, possibly due to unfamiliarity with some indices or belief in alternative indicators. 22% agreed with the model and its senior age indicators, showing moderate but signifi-cant interest.

Overall, 74% of respondents agreed, in whole or in part, with the choice of variables explaining senior age, indicating that the model can meet a signifi-cant community need.

"Evaluating markets using the Market Pareidolia method was very accurate both regarding senior established markets (e.g. UK), as well as for mature but still relatively developing markets development such as Poland. When comparing my knowledge of the latter market with the Market Pareidolia method, there is a perfect match with what the method itself suggests: a market that is making its own transition from Adult to Senior" (Nicola Petronio, Senior Export Manager at Basaltina srl, an Italian leader company in the production and processing of basalt stone, having 60% of export in 70 countries).

Next, the model was evaluated as a whole, and the aggregated responses re-vealed significant interest:

- *Disinterest*: 10% of respondents were not interested in the Pareidolia Market Model, a small but expected percentage given the diversity of the community.

- *Interest with Knowledge Gaps*: 18% showed interest but lacked full understanding of the model, highlighting a need for further clarification and training.
- *Partial Agreement*: 40% partially agreed with the model, recognizing its potential but suggesting the need for fine-tuning, which will be addressed through further testing.
- *Strong Agreement*: 32% fully agreed with the model, indicating that it meets a clear need for better market categorization to guide target market selection.

Overall, 72% of respondents agreed, in whole or in part, with the proposed model, showing that current models do not fully address these needs, while the Pareidolia Market model is a good candidate.

2.4.2 Market Age

Lastly, the process for which Market age was calculated using a factor analysis was presented to the LinkedIn community, providing a corresponding human age to 175 countries. Japan came to be the oldest market in the world, being slightly over 86 years. The first 33 countries are considered "senior," with ages of at least 60 years (including Poland, rounded by excess). Markets ranging from 35 to 59 years fell into the "adult" category, as some adolescent traits are seen in older countries, reaching the approximate age of 35 years (which could be identified as "late adolescents"). Adult markets are the most numerous, with a total of 112 countries in this category. "Adolescent" markets, aged up to 35 years, represent the category with the lowest members, containing only 30 countries. The final empirical test with the LinkedIn community was to share the ages of various countries to assess whether there was a positive match and potential use in the market identification process. The survey revealed that Export Managers showed strong interest in the Market Pareidolia model, with 90% of respondents considering it a useful tool for target market selection. Breaking down the positive responses:

- *Full Agreement*: 10% fully agreed with the model, likely representing managers with cross-disciplinary skills who understand the different variables within the model.
- *Partial Agreement*: 30% partially agreed, using the model in conjunction with other information. This is reasonable given that the model is new and offers a more cross-sectional approach.
- *Interest in Further Exploration*: 50% were interested in delving deeper into the model, indicating that it meets a need but requires further exploration of both variables and practical application. This percentage

aligns with the average response across the age group pools, making the overall responses more coherent.

"In general, the method was also accurate for other markets of my knowledge such as Lebanon, Malaysia, Singapore, and Brazil (as well as the UK and Poland). However, I believe that in the modern world "network predominance" and "high influence from international geopolitics" can still favor, perhaps, success in a certain market" (Nicola Petronio).

Rita Aricò, senior Export Manager at Wide Range stated that

"Using pareidolia in sales, as in marketing or advertising, is an interesting approach, as focusing on what can arouse interest is a very strategic move. In today's society, which is somehow evolved, but also fragile, it is very apt to exploit psychology as a study of markets, as I don't believe it is effective to categorize the various target audiences into fixed segments, as there are too many variables to consider: what was logical and sensible only a few years ago is no longer applicable in today's world. However, it is important to consider the experience of each reality. I agree with the authors that every company has a unique path. Very often there are outdated managers that are not open to studying the market from a different and innovative point of view. What is often overlooked is that every single country, in which one wants to expand one's market, has religious, political and ethical customs that can incisively influence the outcome of a negotiation if not known or underestimated. Finally, it is important to use pareidolia in an ethical and responsible manner, avoiding misleading or manipulating consumers, the risk being that an interesting model may not be used correctly".

Moreover, Marcella Uttaro, senior manager for International Trade at Andersen, with a presence in over 170 countries and over 425 offices worldwide, stated that international markets are

"Hard to categorize, and that each company has a unique path. Behind a deal are people who decide to establish a relationship of trust that entices them to share their experiences toward a common end. There are so many factors that come into play, not just statistical but intuitional, also often driven by emotions and personal ambitions. They are worth exploring further."

To conclude, Paolo Rovelli (Chief of Export Sales Officer at Ultramar Caffè SpA) said:

"I believe Market Pareidolia's model is innovative for guiding a company's choices in foreign trading, but its true potential lies in predicting how a country/market will evolve with respect to a commodity category".

Following these suggestions, the Market Pareidolia model could potentially become the right model to support companies in better selecting international markets. However, it has been noted that the model must be:

- Further refined
- Empirically validated and potentially integrated with additional data
- Simplified (were possible) and automated
- Widely disseminated to become an operational and practical tool for businesses

3 International Business Modes (WHAT)

"IB is a business that crosses national borders, that is, it includes the comparative study of business as an organizational form in different countries, cross-border activities of businesses, and interactions of business with the international environment." (Eden, Dai, Li, 2010, p. 58)

International Business (IB) has evolved into a complex and dynamic field, encompassing a wide array of activities that span across national borders. The essence of IB lies in its ability to navigate the intricate web of interactions between businesses and the diverse international environments in which they operate. As Eden, Dai, and Li (2010) aptly describe, IB involves not only the comparative study of business as an organizational form in different countries but also the cross-border activities of businesses and their interactions with the global environment. In today's globalized economy, companies are increasingly seeking to expand beyond their domestic markets, driven by the pursuit of new opportunities, the need for diversification, and the desire to gain a competitive edge. The way through which businesses engage in international operations (modes) are varied and multifaceted, reflecting the diverse strategies and objectives of firms as they adapt to different cultural, economic, and regulatory environments.

This chapter explores existing modes in which companies enter and operate in international markets and proposes a new perspective by grouping these modes into a more comprehensible manner. It delves into the different actions that businesses employ to manage their cross-border activities effectively, from the simple import–export operations to more complex arrangements like joint ventures (JVs), franchising, and wholly owned subsidiaries. Each mode of IB presents unique challenges and opportunities.

3.1 Existing International Business Modes

Eden et al. (2010) definition for IB is exhaustive per se; however, it gives no indication on the complexity and countless execution modes involving IB. Business practices offer companies an extensive choice on the type of modes by which to develop their IB strategy. However, selecting the appropriate IB mode can be challenging. Much like market categorization, the sheer number of available modes can be overwhelming and potentially misleading. Therefore, it is essential to simplify the selection process by organizing these modes into more comprehensible categories. To begin, let us explore the major IB modes that are prevalent today.

3.1.1 International Trade

International trade is the oldest and most fundamental mode of IB, forming the bedrock of global commerce. It involves the exchange of goods and services across national borders, enabling countries and companies to access a broader array of products, services, and resources than what is available domestically. Through international trade, businesses can reach new markets, increase their customer base, and optimize production by exploiting global efficiencies. At its core, international trade is driven by the principle of comparative advantage, where countries specialize in producing goods and services that they can produce most efficiently while trading for those that other countries produce more efficiently. This specialization and exchange benefit all parties involved, leading to a more efficient allocation of global resources, lower prices for consumers, and enhanced economic growth. For businesses, international trade offers the opportunity to expand beyond the limitations of their domestic markets. Companies can sell products to a larger, more diverse customer base, leading to increased revenues and economies of scale. Additionally, international trade allows companies to diversify their markets, reducing dependence on any single economy and mitigating the risks associated with domestic economic downturns.

Challenges to International Trade

Despite its advantages, international trade is not without challenges. Companies must navigate various barriers, including tariffs, import quotas, and nontariff barriers such as strict regulatory standards. These barriers can increase the cost and complexity of trading across borders. Additionally, fluctuations in exchange rates can impact on the profitability of international transactions, making financial planning more difficult. Moreover, companies engaged in international trade must be aware of political and economic risks. Trade policies can change with shifts in government, and economic crises in key markets can disrupt trade flows. For example, the US–China trade war, which began in 2018, led to the imposition of tariffs on hundreds of billions of dollars' worth of goods, disrupting supply chains and increasing costs for businesses on both sides.

Case Snapshot: Apple Inc. and Its Global Supply Chain

One of the most prominent examples of international trade in action is Apple Inc. Apple's products, such as the iPhone, are designed in the United States but rely on a complex global supply chain. Key components are sourced from various countries: semiconductors from South Korea, memory chips from Japan, and displays from China. These components are then assembled in China, taking advantage of the country's manufacturing expertise and cost efficiencies. The finished products are subsequently exported worldwide. This international trade model allows Apple to maintain high-quality standards while keeping production costs competitive. It also enables the company to respond quickly to global demand, ensuring that its products are available in markets around the world shortly after launch. Apple's success illustrates how international trade facilitates innovation and growth by leveraging the strengths of different economies.

Case Snapshot: Toyota and the Export of Vehicles

Toyota Motor Corporation is another example of a company that has mastered international trade. Toyota, a Japanese automaker, exports vehicles to over 170 countries, making it one of the largest car manufacturers globally. Toyota's production system, renowned for its efficiency and quality, allows the company to produce vehicles in Japan that are highly competitive in international markets. Toyota's international trade strategy includes not only exporting vehicles but also establishing regional production hubs to serve specific markets better. For instance, Toyota has manufacturing plants in North America, Europe, and Asia, which produce vehicles tailored to the preferences and regulatory requirements of those regions. These plants also export vehicles to neighboring countries, maximizing Toyota's global reach. Toyota's success in international trade highlights the importance of understanding and adapting to different market needs. By carefully selecting which models to produce domestically and which to manufacture abroad, Toyota optimizes its supply chain, reduces shipping costs, and ensures that its vehicles meet the diverse demands of its global customer base.

3.1.2 Foreign Direct Investment (FDI)

FDI is one of the most strategic and impactful modes of IB, allowing companies to establish a significant presence in foreign markets by directly investing in business operations. Unlike international trade, which primarily involves the exchange of goods and services across borders, FDI requires a company to commit substantial resources, such as capital, technology, and management expertise, to establish or acquire business operations in another country. This mode of entry offers companies the ability to exert greater control over their international operations, enhance their global competitiveness, and gain direct access to new markets and resources. FDI can take various forms, including the establishment of new facilities (commonly known as Greenfield investments), acquisitions of existing businesses (Brownfield investments), and the creation of wholly owned subsidiaries. Companies engage in FDI to achieve multiple objectives, such as securing a stable supply chain, reducing production costs, accessing new consumer markets, and benefiting from favorable regulatory environments. FDI is often driven by the desire to be closer to key markets, reduce transportation costs, and adapt products and services to local preferences and standards. One of the key advantages of FDI is the level of control it provides. By owning and operating facilities in a foreign country, a company can directly manage its business operations, ensuring that its global standards and practices are maintained. This control also enables companies to respond more effectively to local market conditions and regulatory requirements, thereby reducing risks and improving operational efficiency.

Challenges in Foreign Direct Investment

While FDI offers numerous advantages, it also presents significant challenges. Companies must navigate complex regulatory environments, which can vary widely between countries. Compliance with local laws, labor regulations, and environmental standards can increase operational costs and require significant legal and managerial resources. Additionally, political risk is a major concern in FDI. Changes in government policies, nationalization of industries, or political instability can threaten the security of foreign investments. Cultural differences also pose challenges for companies engaging in FDI. Understanding and adapting to local business practices, consumer behavior, and cultural norms is critical for success. Failure to do so can lead to miscommunication, operational inefficiencies, and even reputational damage. Moreover, FDI requires substantial capital investment, which carries financial risks. The cost of establishing new facilities, acquiring companies, or setting up subsidiaries can be high, and the returns on investment may take years to materialize. Economic downturns in the host country can also impact on the profitability of foreign operations, potentially leading to losses.

Case Snapshot: BMW's Spartanburg Plant

A prime example of successful FDI is BMW's investment in a manufacturing plant in Spartanburg, South Carolina. Established in 1994, the Spartanburg plant represents a significant Greenfield investment by the German automaker. BMW chose this location to produce its popular line of Sports Activity Vehicles (SAVs), primarily for the North American market but also for export to other regions. The plant has since become the largest BMW production facility in the world, producing over 400,000 vehicles annually. BMW's decision to invest in the United States was influenced by several factors, including the country's stable economic environment, skilled labor force, and access to key markets in North America. By manufacturing vehicles in the United States, BMW significantly reduced transportation costs and tariffs associated with exporting vehicles from Germany. Additionally, the Spartanburg plant allowed BMW to tailor its products to meet the specific preferences of American consumers, enhancing its competitiveness in the US market. The success of BMW's Spartanburg plant illustrates the strategic benefits of FDI. By establishing a direct manufacturing presence in the United States, BMW not only strengthened its position in the North American market but also created a robust export base, contributing to its global growth and profitability.

Case Snapshot: Unilever's Acquisition of Dollar Shave Club

Another compelling example of FDI is Unilever's acquisition of Dollar Shave Club in 2016 for $1 billion. Dollar Shave Club, an American subscription-based razor delivery service, was a rapidly growing company with a strong brand presence in the United States. Unilever, a British-Dutch multinational company, saw the acquisition as an opportunity to expand its footprint in the male grooming market and enhance its digital and direct-to-consumer capabilities. This Brownfield investment allowed Unilever to immediately gain a strong position in the US market without the time and resources required to build a similar business from scratch. By acquiring Dollar Shave Club, Unilever also gained valuable insights into consumer behavior and preferences in the rapidly growing e-commerce segment, which it could leverage across its global operations. The acquisition demonstrates how FDI through mergers and acquisitions (M&A) can be an effective strategy for quickly entering and scaling foreign markets. Unilever's investment in Dollar Shave Club enabled the company to diversify its product portfolio, tap into a new customer base, and strengthen its competitive position in the global personal care industry.

3.1.3 Licensing and Franchising

Licensing and franchising are two widely used modes of IB that allow companies to expand globally by leveraging their IP, brand reputation, and business models without the need for significant capital investment or direct operational control. These modes are particularly appealing for companies seeking to enter new markets quickly and with reduced risk. While both licensing and franchising involve granting rights to a foreign entity, they differ in the scope of those rights and the level of control retained by the original company. Licensing is a business arrangement in which a company (the licensor) grants permission to a foreign company (the licensee) to use its IP, such as patents, trademarks, or technology, to manufacture, market, or sell products. This agreement typically involves the payment of royalties or fees by the licensee to the licensor. Licensing allows companies to monetize their IP and enter foreign markets without the need for significant investment or the establishment of physical operations. One of the primary advantages of licensing is that it provides a relatively low-risk way to enter new markets. The licensor can expand its brand and product reach globally while the licensee benefits from using an established brand or technology to attract customers in their local market. Licensing is especially effective in industries where IP, such as technology, entertainment, and consumer goods, plays a significant role.

Franchising is a more comprehensive business arrangement where a company (the franchisor) grants a foreign entity (the franchisee) the right to operate a business under the franchisor's brand, using its established business model, products, and services. In return, the franchisee typically pays an initial franchise fee and ongoing royalties based on revenue. Franchising goes beyond licensing by providing the franchisee with access to the franchisor's entire business system, including training, marketing support, and operational guidelines. Franchising is particularly effective in industries such as fast food, retail, and hospitality, where brand consistency and customer experience are critical to success. It allows companies to expand rapidly across multiple markets while maintaining control over how their brand is represented and ensuring that customers receive a consistent experience, regardless of location.

Challenges in Licensing and Franchising

While licensing and franchising offer significant advantages, they also present challenges, as both licensing and franchising require robust legal agreements to protect the interests of both parties. These agreements must clearly define the rights and obligations of each party, including the scope of the license or franchise, quality control measures, and dispute resolution mechanisms. Navigating the legal and regulatory complexities of different countries can be challenging and require careful planning and expert guidance. One of the main risks associated with licensing is the potential loss of control over how the IP is used. If the licensee does not adhere to the quality standards or brand guidelines set by the licensor, it can damage the brand's reputation and erode consumer trust. Franchising, while offering more control than licensing, still requires a delicate balance between maintaining brand consistency and allowing franchisees flexibility to adapt to local market conditions. The success of a franchise largely depends on the franchisee's ability to execute the franchisor's business model effectively. Poor management or failure to adhere to the franchisor's standards can lead to operational issues and reputational damage.

Case Snapshot: Disney's Licensing Agreements

The Walt Disney Company is a prime example of how licensing can be used effectively in IB. Disney licenses its popular characters, such as Mickey Mouse, and its franchises, such as Star Wars and Marvel, to manufacturers and retailers around the world. These licensees produce and sell a wide range of products, from toys and apparel to home goods and stationery, all bearing Disney's iconic characters. This licensing strategy has allowed Disney to extend its brand reach globally without directly managing the production or distribution of these products. For example, in Japan, Disney has licensed its characters to companies such as UNIQLO, which designs and sells clothing featuring Disney characters, catering to local consumer preferences. This approach not only generates significant revenue for Disney but also strengthens its brand presence in international markets.

Case Snapshot: McDonald's Global Franchising Model

We can't talk about franchising without talking about McDonald. McDonald's is one of the most successful examples of international franchising. The fast-food giant operates in over 100 countries, with more than 90% of its restaurants owned and operated by local franchisees. McDonald's franchising model is built on providing franchisees with a well-established business framework, including access to proprietary recipes, supply chain networks, marketing campaigns, and operational support. In India, for example, McDonald's has adapted its menu to cater to local tastes and cultural preferences, offering vegetarian options and avoiding beef and pork products. This adaptation is made possible through close collaboration between McDonald's and its Indian franchisees, ensuring that the brand remains relevant to local consumers while maintaining the quality and consistency that McDonald's is known for globally. The franchising model allows McDonald's to scale quickly and efficiently, leveraging local entrepreneurs' knowledge and expertise while retaining control over key aspects of the brand. This approach has been instrumental in McDonald's ability to dominate the global fast-food industry.

3.1.4 International Joint Ventures (JVs)

JVs represent a strategic mode of IB in which companies from different countries come together to create a new, jointly owned entity. This collaborative approach allows businesses to pool resources, share risks, and capitalize on each partner's strengths while entering or expanding within foreign markets. International JVs are particularly advantageous in complex or highly regulated markets where local knowledge and expertise are crucial for success. A JV is formed when two or more companies agree to establish a new business entity, with each partner contributing assets such as capital, technology, IP, or market access. In an international context, JVs often involve companies from different countries, with the venture operating in one or more of the partners' home markets or in a third-country market. International JVs are used across a wide range of industries, from manufacturing and energy to technology and finance. They are particularly effective in markets where local regulations require foreign companies to partner with a domestic firm or where market entry is too risky or costly for a single company to undertake alone. JVs enable companies to gain access to new markets, leverage local expertise, and distribute risks while benefiting from the synergies created by the collaboration.

Challenges in International Joint Ventures

While international JVs offer numerous benefits, they also come with significant challenges. One of the primary challenges is managing the relationship between the partners. Differences in corporate culture, management styles, and strategic priorities can lead to conflicts, which, if not managed effectively, can undermine the success of the JV. Clear communication, mutual trust, and a shared vision are essential for overcoming these challenges. Another challenge is the complexity of navigating different legal and regulatory environments. International JVs often operate in countries with different laws governing business practices, taxation, labor, and environmental standards. Ensuring compliance with all relevant regulations requires careful planning and coordination between the partners. The financial structure of a JV can also be a source of complexity. Partners must agree on how to share profits, losses, and liabilities, and how to finance the venture. Disagreements over financial matters can strain the partnership and threaten the viability of the JV. Additionally, JVs may face challenges related to IP protection. When partners share technology and know-how, there is a risk that IP could be misused or leaked, potentially harming the interests of one or more partners. Therefore, it is crucial to establish clear agreements on IP rights and protections from the outset.

Case Snapshot: Sony Ericsson

One of the most successful examples of an international JV is Sony Ericsson, a JV formed in 2001 between Sony Corporation of Japan and Ericsson of Sweden. The venture combined Sony's consumer electronics expertise with Ericsson's telecommunications technology to create a company focused on mobile phones. At the time, both companies faced challenges in the highly competitive mobile phone market, and the JV provided a way to combine their strengths and compete more effectively. Sony Ericsson quickly became a leading player in the global mobile phone market, known for its innovative designs and advanced features. The collaboration allowed the partners to share the costs and risks associated with research and development (R&D), marketing, and global distribution. The JV was particularly successful in Europe and Asia, where it captured a significant market share. While the JV eventually dissolved in 2012, with Sony buying out Ericsson's stake, Sony Ericsson remains a prime example of how two companies can collaborate through a JV to achieve greater market success than either could have achieved alone.

Case Snapshot: BP and Reliance Industries Limited

Another notable example of an international JV is the partnership between BP (British Petroleum) and Reliance Industries Limited (RIL), one of India's largest conglomerates. In 2011, BP and RIL entered into a JV to explore and produce oil and natural gas in India. The venture was driven by BP's desire to expand its presence in India's rapidly growing energy market and RIL's need for the technological expertise and financial resources that BP could provide. The JV allowed BP to gain a foothold in the Indian market, which has significant potential for energy production and consumption. For RIL, the partnership with BP brought in advanced technology and global best practices in exploration and production, enhancing its capabilities in the sector. The JV has been instrumental in developing India's energy resources, contributing to the country's energy security and economic growth. The success of the BP-RIL JV highlights the importance of choosing the right partner with complementary strengths. By combining BP's global expertise with RIL's local knowledge and market presence, the JV was able to achieve its strategic objectives and create value for both companies.

3.1.5 Strategic Alliances

Strategic alliances are a flexible and increasingly popular mode of IB that allows companies to collaborate on specific projects or achieve common objectives while maintaining their independence. Unlike JVs, where a new, jointly owned entity is created, strategic alliances involve a less formal partnership in which each company continues to operate independently but cooperates closely with one or more partners to achieve mutual benefits. This mode of business is particularly advantageous in dynamic and fast-evolving industries where speed, innovation, and resource sharing are critical to success. A strategic alliance is a partnership between companies from different countries (or within the same country) that agree to work together on specific initiatives while remaining independent entities. These alliances can take many forms, including technology sharing, co-development of products, joint marketing efforts, or shared distribution networks. The key to a successful strategic alliance is that it leverages the unique strengths of each partner, allowing them to achieve goals that would be more difficult or costly to accomplish individually. Strategic alliances are commonly used in industries such as technology, pharmaceuticals, automotive, and telecommunications, where rapid innovation, large-scale investments, and access to new markets or technologies are crucial. These alliances enable companies to pool their resources, share risks, and access new capabilities, markets, or customer bases without the need for significant capital investment or loss of control over their core operations.

Challenges in Strategic Alliances

While strategic alliances offer significant benefits, they also come with challenges that must be carefully managed. One of the main challenges is aligning the goals and expectations of the partners. Each company may have different objectives for the alliance, such as entering a new market, gaining access to new technology, or enhancing its product portfolio. Ensuring that both partners are committed to the same goals and have a clear understanding of each other's expectations is critical to the success of the alliance. Another challenge is managing the relationship between the partners. Differences in corporate culture, management styles, and decision-making processes can lead to misunderstandings or conflicts. Regular communication, transparency, and a strong foundation of trust are essential for overcoming these challenges and maintaining a productive partnership. IP protection is also a significant concern in strategic alliances, particularly when the partnership involves technology sharing or co-development. Companies must establish clear agreements on IP ownership, usage rights, and confidentiality to protect their interests and prevent potential disputes. Furthermore, the success of a strategic alliance depends on the ability to adapt to changing market conditions. As markets evolve, the original objectives of the alliance may need to be reassessed, and the partnership may require adjustments to remain relevant and effective. Flexibility and a willingness to renegotiate terms are important for sustaining a long-term strategic alliance.

Case Snapshot: The Renault–Nissan–Mitsubishi Alliance

One of the most successful examples of a strategic alliance is the Renault–Nissan–Mitsubishi Alliance. Formed in 1999 initially as a partnership between Renault (France) and Nissan (Japan), and later joined by Mitsubishi (Japan) in 2016, this alliance has become one of the largest and most successful automotive partnerships in the world. The alliance allows the three companies to collaborate on various aspects of their businesses while maintaining their distinct brands and operations. They share R&D costs, jointly develop platforms and technologies, and integrate their supply chains to achieve economies of scale. For example, the alliance has developed common platforms for EVs and autonomous driving technologies, enabling them to compete more effectively in these rapidly growing segments. The strategic alliance has enabled Renault, Nissan, and Mitsubishi to remain competitive in a highly globalized and capital-intensive industry. By sharing resources and capabilities, the alliance partners have been able to reduce costs, accelerate innovation, and expand their global market reach. Despite the challenges of coordinating between three different companies with distinct cultures and management structures, the alliance has continued to thrive, demonstrating the effectiveness of strategic alliances in the automotive industry.

Case Snapshot: Starbucks and PepsiCo

Another notable example of a strategic alliance is the partnership between Starbucks and PepsiCo. In 1994, Starbucks and PepsiCo formed an alliance to jointly develop and distribute ready-to-drink (RTD) coffee beverages under the Starbucks brand. At the time, Starbucks was focused on its core coffee shop business and lacked the distribution capabilities to enter the RTD beverage market. PepsiCo, on the other hand, had extensive experience and a vast distribution network in the beverage industry. The strategic alliance allowed Starbucks to leverage PepsiCo's distribution expertise to quickly and efficiently bring its RTD coffee products to market. The collaboration resulted in the successful launch of the Starbucks Frappuccino® bottled beverages, which became a market leader in the RTD coffee segment. The partnership has since expanded to include other products, such as Starbucks Doubleshot® and Starbucks Refreshers®. This strategic alliance benefited both companies: Starbucks was able to extend its brand into a new product category and reach a broader consumer base, while PepsiCo gained access to a premium brand and a growing market segment. The success of the Starbucks–PepsiCo alliance highlights the value of combining complementary strengths in a strategic partnership to achieve mutual growth.

3.1.6 Consortiums

Consortiums represent a unique and specialized mode of IB where multiple companies come together to collaborate on a specific project, typically of a large scale or complex nature. Unlike JVs and strategic alliances, which may involve long-term cooperation and the formation of new entities or ongoing partnerships, consortiums are often formed for a single, well-defined objective, and the partnership is typically more temporary and less formal. This mode of business is particularly common in industries such as construction, engineering, and technology, where projects require significant capital investment, diverse expertise, and shared resources. A consortium is a partnership of several companies, often from different countries, that join forces to work on a particular project. Each member of the consortium contributes specific expertise, resources, or technology, and they typically share the costs, risks, and rewards associated with the project. Unlike a JV, where a new, jointly owned entity is created, a consortium is a collaborative agreement where the participating companies maintain their independence and work together for the duration of the project. Once the project is completed, the consortium is typically dissolved.

Difference between a Consortium, JV, and Strategic Alliance

JVs involve the creation of a new, jointly owned entity by two or more companies. The partners share ownership, management, and profits or losses of the new entity. JVs are generally more structured and of long term, often involving significant integration of operations between the partnering companies. Strategic alliances are partnerships where companies collaborate on specific goals or projects while maintaining their independence. Unlike JVs, strategic alliances do not involve the creation of a new entity, and the relationship can be more flexible and less formal, often centered around shared technology, marketing efforts, or co-development. Consortiums, on the other hand, are typically incorporated for a single, large-scale project. The partnership in a consortium is usually more temporary and project-specific, without the creation of a new entity or the deep integration seen in JVs. Each member of the consortium retains its independence and contributes to the project according to its expertise.

Challenges in Consortiums

While consortiums offer significant advantages for managing large-scale and complex projects, they also come with challenges that need careful management. One of the primary challenges is coordinating between multiple independent companies, each with its own management structure, corporate culture, and strategic objectives. Effective communication and collaboration are critical to ensure that the consortium operates smoothly and that all members are aligned with the project's goals. Another challenge is the allocation of responsibilities, costs, and risks among the consortium members. Disagreements over these aspects can lead to delays or disruptions in the project. It is essential to establish clear agreements and governance structures at the outset to manage these issues effectively. Additionally, consortiums often operate in highly regulated environments, particularly in sectors such as energy, infrastructure, and defense. Navigating the legal and regulatory frameworks of multiple countries requires careful planning and compliance to avoid legal pitfalls and ensure the project's success. Finally, the temporary and project-specific nature of consortiums can also be a challenge. Once the project is completed, the consortium is typically dissolved, which means that collaborative relationships and shared resources may not be available for future projects. Companies need to plan for the transition and manage the winding down of the consortium to avoid operational disruptions.

Case Snapshot: Airbus Consortium

One of the most well-known examples of a successful consortium is the Airbus Consortium. Founded in 1970, Airbus began as a consortium of European aerospace manufacturers, including companies from France, Germany, Spain, and the United Kingdom. The goal was to compete with American aerospace giants such as Boeing and McDonnell Douglas by pooling resources, expertise, and technology to develop a new line of commercial aircraft. Each member of the Airbus Consortium contributed specific expertise and components: for example, France focused on the cockpit, Germany on the fuselage, and the UK on the wings. By sharing the costs and risks of developing new aircraft, the consortium was able to produce innovative and competitive products such as the Airbus A320 and the A380, which have become iconic in global aviation. The Airbus Consortium eventually evolved into Airbus SE, a fully integrated company, but its origins as a consortium demonstrate how this mode of collaboration can be highly effective in achieving complex, large-scale goals. The consortium structure allowed the participating companies to leverage their collective strengths and mitigate individual risks, leading to the successful establishment of Airbus as a major player in the global aerospace industry.

Case Snapshot: TAPI Pipeline Consortium

Another example of a consortium in action is the TAPI (Turkmenistan–Afghanistan–Pakistan–India) Pipeline project. This ambitious project aims to construct a natural gas pipeline running through Turkmenistan, Afghanistan, Pakistan, and India, supplying natural gas from Central Asia to South Asia. Given the project's complexity and the political and security challenges in the region, it was necessary to form a consortium of companies from the countries involved to manage the project. The consortium includes state-owned gas companies from Turkmenistan (Turkmengas), Afghanistan (Afghan Gas Enterprise), Pakistan (Inter State Gas Systems), and India (GAIL). Each company is responsible for the construction and management of the pipeline within its national borders, and they collectively share the financial, technical, and logistical challenges of the project. The TAPI Pipeline Consortium illustrates the utility of consortiums in managing large-scale infrastructure projects that require cooperation across multiple borders and stakeholders. By working together, the consortium members aim to enhance energy security and foster regional cooperation, demonstrating the strategic importance of consortiums in IB.

3.1.7 Turnkey Projects

Turnkey projects represent a unique mode of IB, wherein a company is contracted to design, construct, and fully equip a facility, infrastructure, or system, and then hand it over to the client in a ready-to-operate state. The term "turn-key" implies that the client only needs to "turn the key" to start operations, with everything already in place. This approach is particularly common in large-scale industrial projects, such as power plants, oil refineries, airports, and manufacturing facilities, where the complexities and technical expertise required are beyond the capabilities of the client. Turnkey projects are comprehensive, all-encompassing solutions provided by a contractor or a consortium of companies, who take responsibility for the entire life cycle of the project – from design and engineering to construction, commissioning, and final delivery. The contractor manages all aspects of the project, including sourcing materials, hiring labor, installing equipment, and ensuring that the facility meets the required operational standards. Once completed, the facility is handed over to the client, who can immediately begin operations. This mode of business is particularly advantageous for clients in emerging markets or industries where the necessary expertise and resources to manage such complex projects are lacking. Turnkey projects allow clients to focus on their core business activities while relying on the expertise of the contractor to deliver a fully functional facility on time and within budget.

Challenges in Turnkey Projects

While turnkey projects offer substantial benefits, they also come with significant challenges. One of the primary challenges is the complexity of managing such large-scale projects, which often involve multiple stakeholders, extensive coordination, and a high degree of technical expertise. Contractors must carefully plan and execute every phase of the project to ensure that it meets the client's requirements and is completed on time and within budget. Another challenge is the financial risk associated with turnkey projects. Contractors typically bear full responsibility for the project's success, including any cost overruns, delays, or technical issues that may arise. This means that any unforeseen problems can have a significant financial impact on the contractor. As a result, contractors must conduct thorough risk assessments and implement robust project management practices to mitigate these risks. Additionally, turnkey projects often require contractors to work in foreign countries with different legal, regulatory, and cultural environments. Navigating these complexities requires a deep understanding of the local context and close collaboration with local partners and authorities. Contractors must ensure compliance with local laws and regulations while also adapting to cultural differences that may affect the project's execution.

Case Snapshot: Bechtel's Role in the Jubail Industrial City

One of the most significant examples of a turnkey project is Bechtel Corporation's involvement in the development of Jubail Industrial City in Saudi Arabia.

Jubail is one of the largest industrial complexes in the world, covering over 1,000 square kilometers and housing a wide range of industrial facilities, including petrochemical plants, refineries, and manufacturing units. The project was initiated by the Saudi government to diversify its economy and reduce dependence on oil exports by developing a robust industrial base. Bechtel was contracted to provide a turnkey solution for the development of the city's infrastructure, including roads, utilities, port facilities, and residential areas. The company was responsible for designing and constructing the entire city, from initial planning and engineering to the final delivery of fully operational facilities. Bechtel managed all aspects of the project, including procurement, construction, and commissioning, ensuring that the city was ready for industrial operations upon completion. The success of Jubail Industrial City is a testament to the effectiveness of turnkey projects in delivering large-scale, complex infrastructure solutions. By entrusting the project to Bechtel, the Saudi government was able to leverage the company's global expertise and experience in industrial construction, ensuring that the project was completed on time and met the highest standards of quality and safety.

Case Snapshot: Siemens' Turnkey Power Plants

Siemens AG, a global leader in engineering and technology, is another company that frequently engages in turnkey projects, particularly in the energy sector. Siemens has been contracted to design, construct, and commission power plants in various countries around the world, providing turnkey solutions that include everything from engineering and procurement to installation and testing. For instance, Siemens was awarded a contract to deliver a turnkey solution for the Beni Suef combined-cycle power plant in Egypt, one of the largest gas-fired power plants in the world. The project was part of Egypt's plan to increase its electricity generation capacity to meet growing demand. Siemens was responsible for the complete execution of the project, including the design, supply, and installation of turbines, generators, and other key components, as well as the construction of the plant's infrastructure. Upon completion, the Beni Suef power plant added 4.8 gigawatts of electricity to Egypt's national grid, significantly boosting the country's energy supply. Siemens' turnkey approach allowed the Egyptian government to quickly and efficiently expand its power generation capacity, demonstrating the value of turnkey projects in meeting critical infrastructure needs.

3.1.8 Management Contracts

Management contracts are a distinctive mode of IB that enable companies to extend their global reach by managing the operations of a business in another country without owning the business itself. In this arrangement, a company (the contractor) is hired by a foreign entity (the client) to manage its operations in exchange for a fee. The contractor provides managerial expertise, operational know-how, and sometimes even the personnel needed to run the business, while the ownership and financial risks remain with the client. Management contracts are particularly useful in industries such as hospitality, real estate, and public utilities, where operational excellence and expertise are critical to success. Management contracts are typically used when the owner of a business lacks the necessary expertise or experience to manage the operations effectively, particularly in sectors that require specialized skills. By hiring a company with the relevant expertise, the business can improve its performance and profitability while the owner retains control over the strategic direction and financial aspects. This mode of IB allows companies to expand their influence and generate revenue from foreign markets without the need for capital investment or ownership stakes. The contractor provides services such as strategic planning, operational management, marketing, and staff training, ensuring that the business operates efficiently and meets its objectives. Management contracts can be short-term or long-term, depending on the needs of the client and the nature of the business.

Challenges in Management Contracts

While management contracts offer substantial benefits, they also present several challenges. One of the primary challenges is the potential for conflicts of interest between the contractor and the client. The contractor is responsible for managing the operations, but the client retains ownership and ultimate control. Misalignment of goals, expectations, or operational strategies can lead to tensions, making it essential for both parties to establish clear terms and maintain open communication. Another challenge is to ensure that the contractor meets the performance standards agreed upon in the contract. The client must carefully monitor the contractor's performance to ensure that the business is being managed effectively and that the desired outcomes are achieved. Performance-based incentives or penalties are often included in management contracts to align the contractor's interests with those of the client and to ensure accountability. Cultural differences can also pose challenges in international management contracts. When the contractor and the client are from different countries, differences in business practices, management styles, and cultural norms can affect the relationship and the success of the contract. Contractors must be culturally sensitive and adaptable, ensuring that they can effectively manage the business while respecting local customs and expectations. Additionally, management contracts may involve transferring knowledge and skills to the client's employees, particularly in cases where the contract is temporary. This transfer of knowledge is crucial for ensuring that the client can continue to operate the business successfully after the contract ends. However, it requires a commitment to training and capacity-building, which can be resource-intensive and time-consuming.

Case Snapshot: Marriott International

Marriott International is one of the most well-known examples of a company that extensively uses management contracts in its global operations. Marriott, a leading global hotel chain, operates a significant number of its hotels worldwide through management contracts. In this arrangement, Marriott manages the day-to-day operations of the hotel, including staffing, marketing, and customer service, while the hotel's ownership remains with the property owner, which could be an individual, a corporation, or a real estate investment trust (REIT). For example, the Marriott Marquis Hotel in New York City, one of the brand's flagship properties, is operated under a management contract. Marriott is responsible for all aspects of the hotel's operations, from guest services to food and beverage management, while the property is owned by Host Hotels & Resorts, a REIT. This arrangement allows Host Hotels to benefit from Marriott's global brand recognition, operational expertise, and loyalty programs, while Marriott earns management fees and strengthens its brand presence in a key market. This model has enabled Marriott to rapidly expand its global footprint with minimal capital investment. By managing hotels on behalf of property owners, Marriott can focus on its core competencies, hospitality management and brand development, while providing property owners with the operational excellence needed to achieve high occupancy rates and customer satisfaction.

Case Snapshot: Veolia and the Johannesburg Water Management Contract

Another notable example of a management contract is Veolia's contract with the City of Johannesburg, South Africa, to manage the city's water supply and sanitation services. Veolia, a global leader in environmental services, was brought in to manage Johannesburg's water infrastructure, which had been facing significant challenges, including aging infrastructure, inefficiencies, and service delivery issues. Under the management contract, Veolia was responsible for overseeing the operations of Johannesburg Water, including maintenance, customer service, billing, and the implementation of water conservation measures. The contract also involved transferring skills and knowledge to the local workforce, ensuring that the city would have the capacity to manage the water services independently in the future. Veolia's involvement led to significant improvements in the efficiency and reliability of Johannesburg's water services. The management contract allowed the city to benefit from Veolia's global expertise in water management, while Veolia gained valuable experience and a foothold in the South African market. This example highlights how management contracts can be used to improve public services in developing countries by leveraging the expertise of international companies.

3.1.9 E-commerce

E-commerce has revolutionized the way businesses operate and connect with customers, becoming a powerful mode of IB that transcends geographical boundaries. Through online platforms, companies can sell products and services to consumers and businesses worldwide, bypassing traditional barriers to market entry such as physical presence, distribution networks, and local regulations. E-commerce not only enables companies to reach a global audience but also provides consumers with unprecedented access to a wide range of products and services from around the world. E-commerce, or electronic commerce, refers to the buying and selling of goods and services over the internet. It encompasses a variety of business models, including business-to-consumer (B2C), business-to-business (B2B), and consumer-to-consumer (C2C) transactions. The rise in e-commerce has been driven by the proliferation of internet access, the growth of mobile technology, and the increasing preference for online shopping among consumers. One of the key advantages of e-commerce is its ability to operate 24/7, allowing businesses to engage with customers at any time, regardless of time zones. Additionally, e-commerce platforms provide businesses with valuable data on consumer behavior, preferences, and purchasing patterns, enabling them to tailor their offerings and marketing strategies to better meet the needs of their target audience. For businesses, e-commerce offers a cost-effective way to enter international markets without the need for significant capital investment in physical infrastructure. Companies can establish an online presence, reach customers globally, and conduct transactions in multiple currencies, all while maintaining centralized operations. This flexibility makes e-commerce an attractive option for both large MNCs and small to medium-sized enterprises (SMEs) seeking to expand their global footprint.

Challenges in E-commerce

While e-commerce offers significant opportunities for IB, it also presents several challenges that companies must navigate. One of the primary challenges is managing cross-border logistics, including shipping, customs clearance, and delivery. Ensuring that products reach customers in a timely and cost-effective manner requires a well-coordinated logistics strategy and partnerships with reliable service providers. Another challenge is dealing with the regulatory complexities of different countries. E-commerce businesses must comply with various legal requirements, including consumer protection laws, data privacy regulations, and tax policies, which can vary significantly across markets. Failure to comply with these regulations can result in fines, legal disputes, and damage to the company's reputation. Cultural differences also play a crucial role in the success of e-commerce in international markets. Companies must understand and adapt to local consumer behavior, preferences, and shopping habits. This may involve customizing product offerings, payment methods, and marketing strategies to resonate with the target audience in each market. Cybersecurity is another critical concern for e-commerce businesses. As online transactions involve the exchange of sensitive information, such as credit card details and personal data, companies must invest in robust security measures to protect their customers from fraud and data breaches. Maintaining customer trust is essential for the long-term success of any e-commerce business.

Case Snapshot: Amazon's Global Marketplace

Amazon, the e-commerce by definition, the world's largest online retailer, is a prime example of how e-commerce can be used to build a global business. Founded in the United States, Amazon has expanded its operations to over 190 countries, offering millions of products through its global marketplace. Amazon's e-commerce platform allows third-party sellers from around the world to list their products, reaching customers in virtually every corner of the globe. One of Amazon's key strategies for global expansion has been the localization of its e-commerce platforms. In countries such as the United Kingdom, Germany, Japan, and India, Amazon has developed country-specific websites that cater to local languages, currencies, and consumer preferences. This localization strategy has enabled Amazon to build a strong presence in these markets, where it is now a dominant player in the e-commerce sector. Amazon's global fulfillment network, which includes warehouses, distribution centers, and logistics services, is another critical component of its e-commerce strategy. This network allows Amazon to offer fast and reliable delivery to customers worldwide, further enhancing its competitive advantage. By leveraging e-commerce, Amazon has transformed itself from a small online bookstore into a global retail powerhouse, demonstrating the vast potential of e-commerce as a mode of IB.

Case Snapshot: Alibaba and Cross-Border E-commerce

Alibaba Group, China's largest e-commerce company, has also harnessed the power of e-commerce to expand its global reach. Alibaba operates several e-commerce platforms, including Alibaba.com (B2B), Taobao (C2C), and Tmall (B2C), which connect buyers and sellers across the globe. One of Alibaba's most successful ventures in international e-commerce is AliExpress, a platform that allows Chinese manufacturers and retailers to sell directly to consumers in over 200 countries. AliExpress has become a popular platform for international shoppers seeking affordable products, particularly in categories such as electronics, fashion, and home goods. The platform's global reach is supported by Alibaba's sophisticated logistics network, which includes partnerships with shipping companies and the use of advanced technology to streamline cross-border transactions. Alibaba has also introduced payment solutions such as Alipay, which facilitates secure international transactions in multiple currencies, further reducing barriers to cross-border e-commerce. By providing a seamless shopping experience for consumers and offering businesses a platform to reach global markets, Alibaba has solidified its position as a leader in the global e-commerce industry.

3.1.10 Piggybacking

Piggybacking is an innovative and resource-efficient mode of IB that allows companies, especially SMEs, to enter foreign markets by leveraging the established distribution channels, sales teams, or logistical capabilities of a more prominent, established company. This approach provides a cost-effective way to gain access to international markets without the need for significant capital investment or the complexities of setting up independent operations abroad. In a piggybacking arrangement, a smaller company (the "rider") partners with a larger, well-established company (the "carrier") that already has a presence in the target international market. The carrier allows the rider to use its distribution networks, sales force, and logistical infrastructure to sell the rider's products in the foreign market. This arrangement is mutually beneficial: The rider gains access to new markets with reduced risk and lower costs, while the carrier can enhance its product offering, strengthen its market position, and potentially earn additional revenue from the partnership. Piggybacking is particularly advantageous for SMEs that have innovative or niche products but lack the resources or market knowledge to enter foreign markets independently. By partnering with a larger company that has already established its brand and operations in the target market, the smaller company can overcome many of the barriers associated with international expansion, such as high entry costs, complex regulations, and cultural differences.

Challenges in Piggybacking

While piggybacking offers numerous advantages, it also comes with challenges that companies must carefully manage. One of the main challenges is maintaining control over brand identity and customer experience. Since the rider relies on the carrier's distribution network and sales force, there is a risk that the rider's products may not be marketed or presented in a way that aligns with its brand values and positioning. To mitigate this risk, it is crucial for the rider to establish clear guidelines and maintain close communication with the carrier. Another challenge is the potential for conflicts of interest. The carrier may prioritize its own products or other partnerships, potentially leading to less attention or support for the rider's products. To avoid this, companies must carefully select partners whose goals and interests align with their own and establish mutually beneficial terms that incentivize the carrier to actively promote the rider's products. Additionally, cultural and market differences can pose challenges in a piggybacking arrangement. The rider must ensure that its products are adapted to meet the preferences and expectations of customers in the target market. This may involve modifying product features, packaging, or marketing strategies to resonate with local consumers. The rider must also be aware of the regulatory environment in the target market, as the carrier's compliance efforts may not fully cover the specific requirements related to the rider's products.

Case Snapshot: Nestlé and Coca-Cola's Partnership for Nescafé

A classic example of piggybacking is the partnership between Nestlé and Coca-Cola to distribute Nescafé RTD coffee products in various international markets. Nestlé, a global leader in food and beverages, wanted to expand its Nescafé brand into the RTD coffee segment but faced challenges in setting up the necessary distribution channels in new markets. Coca-Cola, on the other hand, already had an extensive global distribution network and expertise in the beverage industry. In 2001, Nestlé and Coca-Cola formed a JV called Beverage Partners Worldwide (BPW) to capitalize on each other's strengths. Nestlé provided product and brand expertise, while Coca-Cola leveraged its global distribution network to market and distributed Nescafé RTD coffee products in various regions, including North America, Europe, and Asia. This piggybacking arrangement allowed Nescafé to quickly penetrate new markets and compete in the growing RTD coffee segment without the need to build its own distribution infrastructure from scratch. Coca-Cola benefited from adding a new product category to its portfolio, enhancing its market presence and driving additional sales through its established channels. The partnership was a win–win situation for both companies, demonstrating the effectiveness of piggybacking as a strategy for international market entry.

Case Snapshot: Leveraging Local Expertise with MNCs

Another example of piggybacking can be seen in the relationship between MNCs and local distributors in emerging markets. Many MNCs, such as P&G, utilize local distributors in regions such as Africa, Southeast Asia, and Latin America to market and sell their products. These local distributors have deep market knowledge, established customer relationships, and existing distribution networks, making them ideal partners for MNCs looking to expand their reach in these markets. For instance, P&G, a global consumer goods giant, often partners with local distributors in smaller or less developed markets where it does not have a direct presence. By piggybacking on the local distributor's network, P&G can quickly and cost-effectively enter these markets, offering its products to a broader audience without the need for a significant upfront investment. The local distributor benefits from having a renowned global brand in its portfolio, which can attract more customers and boost sales. At the same time, P&G gains access to the market knowledge and distribution capabilities of the local partner, helping to navigate the complexities of the local market and achieve faster growth. This approach is particularly valuable in markets where setting up independent operations would be too costly or where the market size does not justify such an investment.

3.1.11 Countertrade

Countertrade is a unique and often necessary mode of IB that involves the exchange of goods and services between countries or companies without using money as a medium of exchange. Instead of a typical cash transaction, countertrade agreements are based on barter, where goods and services are traded directly for other goods and services. This mode of trade is particularly prevalent in situations where currency exchange is restricted, where countries face a shortage of hard currency, or where specific political or economic circumstances make conventional trade challenging. Countertrade encompasses a variety of trade practices, including barter, counter-purchase, buyback, and offset agreements. Each of these methods allows companies and countries to engage in international trade by circumventing the challenges posed by currency limitations, trade deficits, or unstable financial systems. Countertrade is often used in transactions involving developing or emerging markets, where currency issues are more common, but it can also be employed between developed nations in certain situations.

1. *Barter:*
This is the simplest form of countertrade, where two parties agree to exchange goods or services directly without the use of money. Each party provides a set quantity of goods or services that are deemed to be of equal value.
2. *Counter-purchase:*
In this arrangement, one party agrees to purchase goods from another, with the understanding that the selling party will buy back a specific amount of goods from the buyer in return.
3. *Buyback:*
This type of agreement typically involves industrial projects where a company supplies technology, equipment, or machinery to a foreign partner, and the partner agrees to pay back the supplier with goods produced by that equipment or technology.
4. *Offset:*
Common in government or military contracts, an offset agreement requires the seller to invest in the buying country, either through local production, technology transfer, or other economic activities, as part of the trade deal.

Challenges in Countertrade

While countertrade offers a viable solution for conducting IB in challenging economic environments, it also presents several challenges. One of the primary challenges is the complexity of negotiating and managing countertrade agreements. These deals often require extensive legal and financial expertise, as they involve multiple transactions, a complex valuation of goods and services, and careful coordination between parties. Another challenge is the potential for inefficiencies in the exchange process. Unlike cash transactions, which are straightforward and immediate, countertrade agreements can involve significant delays and logistical challenges, especially when the goods being exchanged are of different types or require different production timelines. This can lead to complications in fulfilling the terms of the agreement and can impact on the profitability of the deal. Countertrade also carries risks related to market fluctuations and changes in the value of goods or services. For example, if one party's products decrease in value over the course of the agreement, it could result in an uneven exchange that disadvantages one side. Additionally, the quality and reliability of the goods being traded are crucial to the success of the agreement; if either party fails to deliver as promised, it can lead to disputes and financial losses. Moreover, countertrade agreements can be more difficult to enforce compared to traditional trade agreements, particularly in countries with weak legal systems or where international arbitration mechanisms are not robust. Companies engaged in countertrade must therefore conduct thorough due diligence and establish clear contractual terms to protect their interests.

Case Snapshot: PepsiCo and the Soviet Union

One of the most famous examples of countertrade is the agreement between PepsiCo and the Soviet Union during the Cold War. In the 1970s, the Soviet Union faced significant challenges in obtaining hard currency, making it difficult to purchase goods from Western countries. PepsiCo, seeking to enter the Soviet market, negotiated a countertrade agreement that allowed the company to sell its soft drinks in the Soviet Union in exchange for vodka. Under the terms of the agreement, PepsiCo provided Pepsi syrup to the Soviet Union, which was bottled and sold domestically. In return, PepsiCo received Stolichnaya vodka, a popular Soviet brand, which it then sold in the United States and other Western markets. This barter arrangement allowed PepsiCo to establish a strong presence in the Soviet Union, despite the absence of hard currency, and provided the Soviet Union with a valuable export product. The PepsiCo–Soviet Union countertrade agreement not only facilitated trade between the two parties but also highlighted the flexibility and creativity that countertrade can offer in overcoming traditional trade barriers. The deal was highly successful, leading to an expanded agreement in the 1980s where PepsiCo received additional Soviet goods, including ships, in exchange for its products.

Case Snapshot: Boeing and Offset Agreements

Another prominent example of countertrade in action is Boeing's use of offset agreements in its international sales of commercial aircraft. Boeing, one of the world's largest aerospace companies, often negotiates offset agreements as part of its deals with foreign governments, particularly in countries with emerging or developing economies. These offset agreements require Boeing to invest in the local economy of the purchasing country, which can include setting up local production facilities, transferring technology, or engaging in JVs with local companies. For instance, when Boeing sells aircraft to India, it may agree to source certain components from Indian manufacturers or establish a technology training center in India as part of the deal. This approach not only facilitates the sale of aircraft but also supports the development of the local aerospace industry, creating jobs and building local expertise. By engaging in offset agreements, Boeing is able to navigate the regulatory and economic requirements of different countries, making its products more attractive to foreign buyers. At the same time, these agreements help Boeing secure contracts in competitive markets where governments often prioritize deals that provide economic benefits to their country.

3.1.12 International Mergers and Acquisitions (M&A)

International M&As are a powerful mode of IB that enables companies to achieve strategic growth by acquiring or merging with foreign companies. This approach allows businesses to rapidly expand their global footprint, gain access to new markets, acquire valuable assets and technologies, and enhance their competitive positioning on the global stage. While M&A can deliver significant benefits, it also involves complex challenges that require careful planning, due diligence, and integration strategies to ensure success. An international merger occurs when two companies from different countries combine to form a new entity, while an acquisition involves one company purchasing a controlling interest in another company. Both M&As are driven by strategic objectives such as market expansion, diversification, economies of scale, and the acquisition of complementary technologies or capabilities. International M&A allows companies to overcome barriers to entry in foreign markets, accelerate growth, and achieve synergies that would be difficult to realize through organic expansion alone. International M&A can take various forms, including horizontal mergers (between companies in the same industry), vertical mergers (between companies at different stages of the supply chain), and conglomerate mergers (between companies in unrelated industries). Each type of M&A presents unique opportunities and challenges, depending on the strategic goals of the companies involved.

Challenges in International Mergers and Acquisitions

While international M&A offers significant opportunities for growth and expansion, it also presents a range of challenges that companies must navigate to achieve successful outcomes. One of the primary challenges is the complexity of cross-border transactions, which involve navigating different legal, regulatory, and tax environments. Companies must conduct thorough due diligence to assess the financial health, legal compliance, and operational capabilities of the target company, as well as to identify potential risks and liabilities. Cultural integration is another critical challenge in international M&A. M&As often involve the integration of companies with different corporate cultures, management styles, and employee expectations. Failure to address these cultural differences can lead to miscommunication, employee dissatisfaction, and operational inefficiencies, which can undermine the success of the merger or acquisition. Companies must develop comprehensive integration plans that address cultural alignment, employee engagement, and leadership transition to ensure a smooth and successful integration process. Another challenge is the potential for regulatory hurdles, particularly in industries that are subject to stringent antitrust or foreign investment regulations. Governments may scrutinize international M&A transactions to ensure that they do not harm competition, lead to monopolistic practices, or compromise national security. Companies must work closely with legal and regulatory experts to navigate these challenges and obtain the necessary approvals for the transaction. Additionally, international M&A transactions can be financially demanding, requiring significant capital investment and potentially leading to increased debt levels. Companies must carefully evaluate the financial implications of the transaction, including the potential impact on their balance sheet, credit rating, and shareholder value. Effective financial planning and risk management are essential to ensure that the transaction enhances, rather than detracts from, the company's long-term financial stability.

Case Snapshot: Tata Motors' Acquisition of Jaguar Land Rover

One of the most successful examples of international M&A is Tata Motors' acquisition of Jaguar Land Rover (JLR) in 2008. Tata Motors, an Indian automotive company, acquired the British luxury car brands Jaguar and Land Rover from Ford Motor Company for $2.3 billion. At the time, JLR was struggling financially, and Tata's acquisition was seen as a bold move for the Indian company, which primarily produced economy cars. The acquisition provided Tata Motors with several strategic benefits. First, it allowed Tata to enter the global luxury car market, which was growing rapidly and offered higher profit margins compared to the economy car segment. Second, Tata gained access to JLR's advanced automotive technology, strong brand equity, and established distribution networks in key markets such as Europe, North America, and China.

This acquisition also helped Tata Motors diversify its product portfolio and reduce its dependence on the Indian market. Following the acquisition, Tata Motors invested heavily in JLR, focusing on product innovation, expanding manufacturing capacity, and enhancing global marketing efforts. The strategy paid off, as JLR became one of the most profitable divisions of Tata Motors, with a strong presence in the luxury car market. The success of this acquisition demonstrates how international M&A can transform a company's global positioning and drive long-term growth.

Case Snapshot: InBev's Acquisition of Anheuser-Busch

Another significant example of international M&A is InBev's acquisition of Anheuser-Busch in 2008 for $52 billion. InBev, a Belgian-Brazilian brewing company, pursued the acquisition to create the world's largest beer company, later rebranded as Anheuser-Busch InBev (AB InBev). Anheuser-Busch, the maker of Budweiser, was a leading player in the US beer market, and its acquisition provided InBev with a dominant position in North America, complementing its strong presence in Europe and Latin America. The acquisition allowed InBev to achieve significant economies of scale, particularly in procurement, distribution, and marketing. Additionally, InBev gained access to Anheuser-Busch's extensive portfolio of iconic beer brands, which further strengthened its global market leadership. However, the acquisition also presented challenges, including managing the cultural differences between the two companies and addressing concerns from regulators and stakeholders in the US. Despite these challenges, AB InBev successfully integrated Anheuser-Busch's operations, leveraging its global scale to drive cost efficiencies and expand market share. The acquisition has since been regarded as a strategic success, positioning AB InBev as a global beer powerhouse with a portfolio of brands that dominate the industry worldwide.

3.1.13 International Agents and Distributors

International agents and distributors play a crucial role in helping companies expand their reach into foreign markets without the need to establish a physical presence. This mode of IB involves partnering with local entities that have in-depth knowledge of the market, established networks, and expertise in selling and distributing products or services. By leveraging the capabilities of international agents and distributors, companies can efficiently navigate the complexities of new markets, accelerate market entry, and reduce the risks associated with international expansion. International agents and distributors serve as intermediaries between the export company and the end customers in a foreign market. While both agents and distributors facilitate market access, they operate under different business models and offer distinct advantages. *International*

Agents: Agents act on behalf of the exporting company, representing its products or services in the foreign market. They typically work on a commission basis, earning a percentage of the sales they generate. Agents do not take ownership of the goods; instead, they facilitate sales by negotiating contracts, managing customer relationships, and providing market intelligence. This arrangement allows the exporting company to maintain control over pricing, branding, and customer service while benefiting from the agent's local market knowledge. *International Distributors*: Distributors, on the other hand, purchase products from the export company and resell them in the foreign market. Distributors take ownership of the goods, handle inventory, and manage the entire sales and distribution process within their territory. They earn a profit by marking up the products before selling them to retailers or end customers. Distributors often provide additional services, such as warehousing, marketing, and after-sales support, making them valuable partners for companies looking to establish a strong presence in a new market. Both agents and distributors offer advantages, such as reduced market entry costs, faster access to new customers, and the ability to leverage local expertise. The choice between using an agent or a distributor depends on the company's strategic goals, the nature of the product or service, and the specific market conditions.

Challenges in Using International Agents and Distributors

While partnering with international agents and distributors offers numerous benefits, it also presents several challenges that companies must manage effectively. One of the primary challenges is ensuring alignment between the company's goals and those of the agent or distributor. Since agents and distributors often work with multiple brands or products, there is a risk that they may prioritize other clients or focus on higher-margin products, leading to suboptimal performance for the company's offerings. To mitigate this risk, companies must establish clear performance metrics, provide incentives for meeting sales targets, and maintain regular communication with their partners. Building strong relationships based on trust and mutual benefit is essential for ensuring that agents and distributors remain committed to promoting the company's products. Another challenge is maintaining control over brand identity and customer experience. When using agents or distributors, companies may have less direct control over how their products are marketed, sold, and serviced. This can lead to inconsistencies in branding, pricing, and customer support, which can negatively impact on the company's reputation and customer loyalty. To address this, companies should provide comprehensive training and resources to their agents and distributors, ensuring that they have the knowledge and tools to represent the brand effectively. Regulatory compliance is also a key consideration when working with international agents and distributors. Companies must ensure that their partners adhere to local laws and regulations, including those related to product labeling, advertising, and consumer protection. Noncompliance can result in legal penalties, product recalls, and damage to the company's reputation. Companies should conduct thorough due diligence when selecting agents and distributors and establish clear contractual terms that outline compliance requirements.

Case Snapshot: Coca-Cola's Use of Agents and Distributors for Global Expansion

Coca-Cola, one of the world's most recognizable beverage companies, exemplifies how international agents and distributors play a pivotal role in global market expansion. The company employs a mix of agents and distributors to reach diverse consumer bases across various regions, adapting its approach based on local market dynamics.

- *International Agents in Africa:*
  In certain African markets, Coca-Cola partners with local agents to facilitate market entry and build customer relationships. These agents, deeply embedded in the local business environment, provide critical insights into consumer preferences, negotiate contracts with retailers, and ensure regulatory compliance. By working on a commission basis, Coca-Cola benefits from the agents' local expertise while maintaining control over branding, pricing, and marketing strategies. This model has been particularly effective in smaller markets where direct investment in infrastructure might not be viable.
- *International Distributors in Latin America:*
  In Latin America, Coca-Cola relies heavily on its distribution partners to manage inventory, handle logistics, and ensure widespread availability of its products. One notable example is its partnership with Coca-Cola FEMSA, the largest Coca-Cola bottler in the world. Coca-Cola FEMSA acts as a distributor, purchasing concentrate from Coca-Cola and managing the production, bottling, and distribution of Coca-Cola products across the region. This distributor network allows Coca-Cola to penetrate even the most remote areas, ensuring that its products are accessible to a diverse range of consumers.

Case Snapshot: Procter & Gamble's Use of Agents and Distributors

P&G, a global consumer goods giant, relies heavily on international agents and distributors to market and sell its products in various countries around the world. P&G's extensive product portfolio, which includes household names such as Tide, Pampers, and Gillette, requires a robust distribution network to reach consumers in both developed and emerging markets. In many countries,

P&G uses a combination of agents and distributors to maximize its market coverage. For example, in sub-Saharan Africa, P&G partners with local distributors who have deep market knowledge, established retail relationships, and the logistical capabilities to navigate the region's challenging infrastructure. These distributors play a critical role in ensuring that P&G's products are available in both urban and rural areas, helping the company build brand loyalty and achieve sales growth in the region. In addition to distributors, P&G also works with agents who focus on specific product lines or customer segments. These agents help P&G tailor its marketing and sales strategies to local preferences, ensuring that the company's products resonate with consumers in different cultural and economic contexts. By leveraging the expertise of local agents and distributors, P&G can maintain a flexible and responsive approach to market entry and expansion, adapting its strategies to the unique conditions of each market.

3.2 The Need for Grouping IB Modes

As seen previously, in the rapidly evolving landscape of global business, companies face a myriad of options when it comes to choosing the appropriate mode of IB to expand their operations. The increasing complexity of global markets, coupled with the vast array of IB modes available, can often lead to confusion and misinformed decisions. Thus, there is the necessity of grouping IB modes to simplify decision-making processes, providing a structured framework that can guide companies in selecting the most suitable approach for their international expansion strategies.

The modern business environment offers an extensive range of IB modes, each with its own set of advantages, risks, and operational requirements. From exporting and licensing to JVs, mergers, and greenfield investments, the choices available to companies are both numerous and diverse. While this variety allows businesses to tailor their international strategies to specific goals and market conditions, it also poses significant challenges. Companies, particularly those with limited experience in international operations, may struggle to navigate the complexities of these options, leading to potential missteps in their global expansion efforts. One of the primary challenges lies in the fact that not all IB modes are equally suited to every business or market scenario. For instance, a company with limited financial resources may find it challenging to undertake a capital-intensive mode such as FDI, while a firm seeking rapid market entry might overlook the slower, but potentially more sustainable, approach of building a local presence through JVs or strategic alliances. The sheer number of modes combined with the varying levels of financial exposure, local engagement, and operational complexity they entail, can overwhelm decision-makers and obscure the most effective path forward. To address these challenges, it is crucial to introduce a method of categorization that simplifies the selection process. By grouping IB modes based on key dimensions that align with the strategic needs and capabilities of the company, businesses can more effectively assess their options and make informed decisions that support their long-term international objectives. The grouping of IB modes serves as a tool to provide clarity and structure to the IB decision-making processes. This approach is particularly valuable in helping companies align their capabilities (resources and know-how) with the pretended objectives in a simpler, yet effective manner.

3.2.1 The Rationale behind Grouping IB Modes

To group existing IB modes into a new set of categories, three specific common dimensions were identified: levels of financial exposure required (low, medium, or high), the need for a local company incorporation, and the need for a local production site. These dimensions were chosen based on three fundamental traits that are critical to any IB strategy: the resources needed to implement a strategy (financial risk), the levels of local engagement required (law compliance), and the need for a local manufacturing plant in the target market (competitive advantage). By evaluating IB modes against these three dimensions, companies can better understand the implications of each mode and how it fits within their broader strategic goals. The result is a more streamlined decision-making process that enables companies to visualize their international presence on a valuation scale, facilitating the creation of penetration strategies tailored to their specific needs.

1. *Levels of Financial Exposure Required to Operate*:
    Financial exposure is a critical consideration for any company looking to expand internationally. This dimension assesses the capital investment required to reach the objectives, ranging from low, medium, to high level of exposure. By understanding the financial commitment involved, companies can align their IB mode choice with their available resources and risk tolerance.
2. *The Need for Local Company Incorporation*:
    Some objectives necessitate the establishment of a local entity to operate effectively in the foreign market. This dimension evaluates whether local incorporation is necessary (by law, for competitive advantage, for fiscal optimization, etc.), influencing the level of control, compliance requirements, and potential for long-term operations in the market.
3. *The Need for a Local Production Site*:
    For businesses involved in manufacturing or production, the decision to establish a local production facility or production line is crucial. This dimension assesses whether local production is required,

impacting operational efficiency, cost structures, and responsiveness to local demand in search of competitive advantage.

Categorizing IB Modes: Four Main Groups

Based on the three dimensions outlined above, IB modes can be grouped into four main categories: Commercial IB, Service IB, Industrial IB, and Capital IB. Each category represents progression in terms of local engagement and financial exposure, providing a clear framework for companies to evaluate their IB strategies. Grouping IB modes based on the four dimensions provides several benefits that enhance strategic decision-making and operational planning for companies engaging in IB. These benefits include:

- *Clarity and Simplification*:
  By organizing IB modes into distinct categories, companies can more easily assess their options and identify the most suitable approach based on their strategic goals, resources, and risk tolerance. This clarity reduces the potential for confusion and missteps in the decision-making process.
- *Strategic Alignment*:
  The grouping of IB modes allows companies to align their international strategies with their broader business objectives. By understanding the implications of each mode in terms of financial exposure, local engagement, and operational requirements, companies can select the approach that best supports their long-term growth and competitiveness.
- *Enhanced Flexibility*:
  The categorization provides a flexible framework that can be adapted to different industries, markets, and business models. Companies can choose the group that aligns with their current capabilities and gradually progress to more complex and resource-intensive modes as they gain experience and confidence in the international arena.
- *Benchmarking and Evaluation*:
  The grouped IB modes serve as a benchmarking tool that companies can use to evaluate their international operations against industry standards and best practices. This benchmarking capability is valuable for developing long-term growth strategies, assessing the effectiveness of current approaches, and identifying areas for improvement.

3.2.2 Commercial IB

Table 3.1 Commercial IB traits

IB mode categorization	Financial exposure	Local incorporation	Production line
Commercial IB	Low	No	No

Commercial IB is a process where a company extends its commercial network beyond its national borders without permanently relocating resources abroad (Table 3.1). IB modes in this category typically suit consumer product businesses, where offshoring is not possible due to territorial dependencies. It is also particularly appealing to companies with a low-risk appetite, as it demands minimal initial and ongoing investment. However, this conservative approach also correlates with a lower potential for returns.

There are two primary methods for this IB category:

- *Indirect Mode*:
  This approach involves utilizing importers and/or distributors already established in the new market. By leveraging these existing channels, a company can introduce its products or services to foreign markets without establishing a physical presence. This method is cost-effective and reduces the company's direct involvement in the complexities of the new market. It allows for a more cautious and measured entry into international trade, minimizing risks such as cultural misunderstandings or noncompliance with local regulations. A negative aspect of the indirect mode is the lack of control over the relationship with the final customer, as are held by the third party.

- *Direct Mode*:
  In contrast, the direct mode involves the company promoting its products or services within the target market (via retail outlets, wholesale distribution, the Ho.Re.Ca. sector, etc.) from its central commercial office based in its home country. Typically, sales representatives make periodic visits to clients, operating on a "travel in – travel out" basis, rather than maintaining a permanent local presence. This method offers greater control over the brand, marketing strategies, and customer experience without having a constant presence in the country. It enables the company to build a direct relationship with the new market and its consumers. However, this approach requires a more significant commitment to resources and a deeper understanding of the local market dynamics.

Typically, Commercial IB is more suitable for businesses dealing with consumer products, where relocation is not an option due to dependency on the territory. Products that are deeply rooted in local culture, traditions, or resources are prime examples. Moreover, this mode is also well-suited for companies that are risk averse requiring an IB process. The low initial investment and ongoing costs make it an attractive option for businesses looking to expand internationally without the high stakes of establishing a full-fledged subsidiary or factory abroad. However, it's important to note that the lower risk is often accompanied by a lower potential for return. This trade-off between risk and reward is a critical consideration for companies contemplating this approach to international expansion. As observed, Commercial IB does not necessitate a permanent local presence, eliminating the need for a representative office or a production line in the country. This approach also avoids the requirement for incorporating a new venture, obliging the company to maintain its core business operations without incurring cross-industry sales. Such characteristics lead to a lower financial risk exposure, which is typically associated with a reduced potential for return on investment (ROI).

3.2.3 Service IB

Table 3.2 Service IB traits

IB mode categorization	Financial exposure	Local incorporation	Production line
Service IB	Medium	Yes	No

In this strategic approach, the focus is on establishing a consistent and robust presence in the targeted market. This typically involves the creation of a commercial representative office, which serves as the primary hub for identifying and nurturing various local opportunities. An integral part of this strategy is the appointment of a country manager, who is often selected within a company member. This individual is tasked with the crucial role of launching and overseeing the company's operations in that specific country, being the local face of the company. The subsidiary, in this context, functions as an extension of the company's commercial operations (Table 3.2).

The investment required for Service IB is primarily directed toward human resources and the administrative management of a branch. This includes the establishment and maintenance of necessary infrastructures such as offices and warehouses but does not comprise the installation of local production. In fact, it notably excludes the relocation of physical assets, making it a strategically lean approach. This IB mode categorization finds resonance with companies in the service sector, including those in fields such as engineering, architecture, and consulting. In these industries, the value of the service is often quantified in terms of the labor hours invested, rather than the physical goods produced. This necessitates a model where the human element (the service provider) is at the forefront, embodying the service offered. The success of Service IB heavily relies on the identification and collaboration of a suitable local partner, and this aspect becomes even more critical in emerging markets. A local partner's involvement is instrumental in significantly reducing various risks. These risks include, but are not limited to, challenges posed by cultural differences, potential corruption, and complex bureaucratic landscapes. A local partner's deep understanding of the market and cultural nuances can provide invaluable insights and guidance, facilitating smoother market entry and operations. Moreover, it allows for a more refined and culturally sensitive approach to IB. By having a dedicated team on the ground, accompanied by a local partner, companies can better adapt their strategies and operations to align local customs, business practices, and consumer preferences. This local presence also aids in building trust and credibility with local customers and stakeholders, which is crucial for long-term success in foreign markets. Additionally, this approach offers flexibility and scalability. Companies can adjust their level of investment and involvement based on market response and growth opportunities. This is particularly advantageous in dynamic and rapidly evolving markets, where agility and responsiveness are key to capitalizing on emerging trends and opportunities. Last, by limiting the investment to human resources and operational management, companies can maintain greater control over their international ventures with a relatively lower financial risk compared to modes that require significant capital investments in physical assets. This aspect of the mode is particularly appealing to companies looking to expand internationally while managing risk exposure.

In summary, with its emphasis on human resources and local partnerships, Service IB offers a strategic pathway for companies, especially in the service sector, to effectively navigate and establish themselves in foreign markets at controlled financial exposure (medium level of financial exposure). It combines the benefits of local market insight, cultural adaptability, operational flexibility, and controlled risk, making it a compelling choice for companies looking to expand their global footprint gradually. However, it requires the need to incorporate a new venture, and it does not comply with cross-industry penetration.

3.2.4 Industrial IB

Table 3.3 Industrial IB traits

IB mode categorization	Financial exposure	Local incorporation	Production line
Industrial IB	High	Yes	Yes

Industrial IB necessitates a substantial investment in resources, as it typically involves the construction of a production line in the target market (distinct from relocation). In this scenario, Industrial IB requires a detailed industrial plan, incorporating reliable market studies and econometric projections (such as ROI and Internal Rate of Return [IRR]) that justify the investment. This plan should not only focus on the immediate aspects of setting up the production line but also consider the long-term sustainability and growth potential in the target market (Table 3.3). Within the industrial plan, a key role is the development of a well-crafted financial strategy, which becomes an indispensable element for the successful implementation of this process. A meticulously planned financing strategy (a robust project finance), can significantly reduce risks and, consequently, enhance the likelihood of the project's success.

The financial strategy for such an endeavor is multifaceted. It involves securing adequate funding, which may come from a variety of sources including bank loans, equity financing, or even government grants, especially in regions keen to attract foreign investment. The strategy must also account for currency fluctuations, tax implications, and potential financial incentives offered by the host country. These factors can significantly impact on the overall cost and feasibility of the project. Moreover, the industrial plan should be rooted in a deep understanding of the target market. This includes not just the current demand for the product or service but also an analysis of future trends, potential competition, and regulatory environment. Market studies should provide insights into consumer behavior, preferences, and purchasing power in the target region, while econometric projections should offer a realistic view of financial performance and ROI over time. Another critical aspect is the assessment of operational risks, including supply chain management, logistics, and local labor market conditions. For example, establishing a production line in a foreign country often involves navigating complex supply chains and ensuring the availability of raw materials and skilled labor. Companies must also be cognizant of local laws and regulations, including labor laws, environmental regulations, and industry-specific compliance requirements. Cultural considerations are equally important. Understanding and adapting to the local culture can play a significant role in the success of the venture. This includes not only the consumer culture but also the business culture, which can influence everything from marketing strategies to day-to-day operations and employee management. It becomes evident the need for a local partner's support, someone who can guide the company in this intriguing scenario. The company's long-term commitment to the market becomes inevitable. Setting up a production line is not a short-term endeavor; it requires a sustained effort and continuous investment. This includes regular updates to the production technology, ongoing training for local staff, and continuous market research to stay ahead of market trends and shifts.

In summary, the process of setting up a production line in a foreign market as a means of industrial IB is a complex and resource-intensive strategy (high level of financial exposure). It requires a comprehensive approach that encompasses financial planning, market research, risk management, cultural adaptation, and long-term commitment. When executed effectively, however, it can lead to significant returns and a strong, sustainable presence in the target market. The incorporation of a new venture is implied, and a cross-industry penetration is not compatible.

3.2.5 Capital IB

Table 3.4 Capital IB traits

IB mode categorization	Financial exposure	Local incorporation	Production line
Capital IB	Medium/high	Yes	No

The concept of Capital IB refers to a categorization centered around acquiring stakes (partial or complete) in existing local entities. This can occur within the industry in which a company operates or in different fields (cross-industry penetration) as part of a diversification strategy (Table 3.4). This process carries significant risks, as it demands a thorough business evaluation that may not always accurately capture the real potential, and risks involved (the primary risk factor). Additionally, when acquiring a local company, cultural differences often emerge as a major barrier to communication between the parties, potentially hindering operational continuity. To increase the likelihood of success, accumulated experience is one of the few factors that can mitigate these risks. The variables involved are numerous and vary depending on the country, market, culture, industry, type of business, and other factors.

In this approach, the focus is on integrating into the local market through financial investments in existing businesses (only capital is moved). This could involve buying shares in local companies, either partially or wholly, and applies not just to the investor's primary industry but also to other sectors as a means of diversifying their portfolio. Regarding financial risk, the degree of exposure for companies engaging in Capital IB varies based on the value of the shares they purchase. Consequently, their financial exposure can range from low to medium or even high, depending on the extent of their investment in share acquisition. However, this strategy is fraught with challenges. One of the most significant is the need for a comprehensive and accurate assessment of the target company. This assessment must consider not only the financial health and potential of the business but also less tangible factors such as company culture, market position, and future growth potential. Misjudging these factors can lead to substantial risks and potential losses. For a company to succeed in this IB mode categorization, experience plays a crucial role. Experience in international acquisitions, understanding local business practices, and knowledge of the specific industry can all help in making more informed decisions and effectively managing the acquired company. Lastly, the variables involved in this approach are complex and diverse. They can vary greatly depending on the specific context, including the country's regulatory environment, the local market's dynamics, the industry's characteristics, and the specific type of business being acquired. Each of these factors can significantly influence the outcome of the investment.

In summary (Table 3.5), Capital IB is a complex and high-risk strategy that requires careful consideration and extensive experience. It involves not only financial investment but also a deep understanding of a range of factors, including cultural nuances, market dynamics, and industry specifics. While the potential rewards can be significant, the risks are equally substantial, making it a strategy best suited for companies with the requisite experience and resources to navigate these complexities. As seen, it does not require the incorporation of a new venture, as it implies the acquisition of shares of an existing company.

Table 3.5 The IB modes matrix

IB mode group	Financial exposure	Local incorporation	Production line	Associated IB mode
Commercial IB	Low	No	No	International Trade Licensing & Franchising International Agents & Distributors E-Commerce Strategic Alliances Consortiums Countertrade Piggybacking
Service IB	Medium	Yes	No	Licensing & Franchising International JVs Strategic Alliances Consortiums Piggybacking Countertrade Management Contracts
Industrial IB	High	Yes	Yes	FDI Turnkey Projects Management Contracts
Capital IB	Medium/high	No	No	International M&As Turnkey Projects Management Contracts

4 The 3Ws of Internationalization: When, Where, and What

"The power to create wealth and access resources is increasingly tied to global connections and partnerships." (Friedman, 2005)

As we progress on this journey, we are gradually shaping a methodology for companies looking to expand their horizons by entering new markets and developing a robust internationalization strategy. We have provided the tools to address three critical questions: "When" are we ready for internationalization, "Where" do we want to go (which market or markets do we want to penetrate), and "What" type of internationalization do we want, or can afford, to pursue. Now, let's understand how to use these tools.

4.1 "When"

In today's rapidly evolving global economy, driven by relentless technological innovation and shifting consumer demands, businesses face immense pressure to deliver higher-quality products at lower costs. As seen in previous chapters, this unrelenting pace of change demands adaptability as a cornerstone of corporate resilience and survival. For companies looking to remain competitive and relevant, internationalization has shifted from being a discretionary growth option to an inevitable step. The question is no longer "if" a company should internationalize but "when" and, crucially, how it should prepare for such a transformative move. The global marketplace offers immense opportunities, from access to new customer bases, to diversification of revenue streams, and exposure to innovative practices. However, these benefits are accompanied by significant challenges, including regulatory complexities, cultural differences, and operational hurdles. Successfully navigating these terrains requires meticulous planning, strategic foresight, and, most importantly, early preparation. Delaying the development of an internationalization strategy can lead to missed opportunities, loss of market relevance, and even failure to compete effectively in an interconnected world.

To navigate the internationalization process successfully, companies must recognize that the journey begins long before the decision to enter foreign markets. Preparation involves building the foundational elements that will enable a company to internationalize effectively when the time is right. This preparation should address three critical dimensions: resources availability, tolerance to risk, and degree of dependencies.

- *Resources Availability*
  Internationalization requires significant resources, not only in terms of finances but also operational capabilities, human capital, and IP. High levels of resource availability mean a company can afford to invest in a new market without jeopardizing its core operations, even in the event of failure. This degree of financial and operational resilience allows for the ability to experiment, innovate, and adjust as necessary.
- *Tolerance to Risk*
  Risk is an inherent part of any internationalization effort. A company's tolerance to risk reflects its ability to withstand uncertainties in foreign markets, such as fluctuating regulations, volatile currencies, and unfamiliar cultural landscapes. Companies with high-risk tolerance are willing to experiment and accept potential setbacks as part of their growth strategy. On the other hand, companies with low-risk tolerance may prefer cautious, incremental approaches, prioritizing stability over rapid expansion. Preparation for internationalization must include efforts to improve risk tolerance. This involves building a strong risk management framework, fostering a culture of adaptability, and acquiring deep insights into the target markets.
- *Degree of Dependencies*
  Dependency refers to how reliant a company is on external factors such as specific suppliers, patents, or regulatory approvals. High dependency can limit flexibility and increase vulnerability to disruptions in the internationalization process. For example, a company reliant on a single supplier for key raw material may face significant risks if supply chains are disrupted. Reducing dependency, or at least managing it effectively, is a critical aspect of preparation. This could involve diversifying suppliers, developing in-house capabilities, or establishing strategic partnerships to mitigate risks.

The internationalization process should not be a reaction to immediate pressures but rather an integral component of a company's long-term strategy. Whether a company plans to enter foreign markets within its first five years or sees internationalization as a goal for the distant future, the groundwork must be laid early. Companies must assess their current capabilities and identify gaps in resources, risk tolerance, and dependency, creating a roadmap that addresses these deficiencies over time. For instance, a startup with limited resources and low risk tolerance might initially focus on strengthening its domestic operations, building a strong financial foundation, and diversifying its supplier base. Over time, the company can pursue initiatives that improve its readiness for internationalization, such as acquiring international market knowledge, developing cross-cultural competencies among its workforce, and forming strategic alliances with global partners. As global markets evolve at breakneck speed, companies must develop IB strategies that are both proactive and dynamic. A rigid, static approach to internationalization is unlikely to succeed in today's complex and interconnected environment. Instead, strategies must be flexible, allowing companies to adapt to changing market conditions, new technologies, and shifting consumer preferences.

This adaptability also extends to the timing of internationalization. While early entry into foreign markets can provide competitive advantages such as brand recognition and customer loyalty, it is essential that the timing aligns with the company's readiness (resources availability, tolerance to risk, and degree of dependencies). Entering too soon, without sufficient preparation, can be just as damaging as delaying entry indefinitely. Internationalization is not merely a growth strategy; it is a necessity for survival in today's global economy. Companies must embrace it as an integral part of their long-term vision, preparing for it from the very beginning by addressing their resources availability, risk tolerance, and degree of dependency. By doing so, they can create a solid foundation for successful international ventures.

4.2 "Where"

How to select the right foreign market that will increase our chances of succeeding? This is the million-dollar question. Market Pareidolia offers a powerful selection tool, but it requires skillful application. As we've discussed, Market Pareidolia assigns a human age to a market, using the sensory illusion of pareidolia to convert complex and often confusing market variables into recognizable, human-like patterns. In this framework, markets are categorized into three main human stages: adolescence, adulthood, and seniority. Market Pareidolia will be utilized as the primary tool for this delicate and strategic activity.

Based on the characteristics of each market considered in Market Pareidolia, for a company to successfully expand into new markets, two critical factors must be considered: resources and risk tolerance. The levels of these two factors determine which markets a company can potentially enter with higher probabilities of success (or has the needed capabilities to penetrate). For instance, a company with limited resources may find it challenging to penetrate mature markets, as seen, these markets typically require significant financial exposure. On the other hand, a company with low tolerance for risk would be ill-advised to enter adolescent markets, where the potential for both risks and re-wards is high. These two variables, resources availability and risk tolerance, ef-fectively shape the range of market entry options available to a company. But what is really meant by resources availability and risk tolerance and how are they measured?

4.2.1 Resources Availability

When discussing a company's resources, it refers to the various assets and capa-bilities that a business can leverage to achieve its objectives, particularly in the context of expanding into new markets. These resources are fundamental to the company's ability to compete, grow, and sustain operations in an increasingly complex and globalized environment. A thorough understanding of a com-pany's resources is crucial for making informed decisions about internationali-zation and other strategic initiatives.

- *Tangible Resources*
  Tangible resources are the physical and measurable assets that a com-pany owns. These include things such as buildings, machinery, inven-tory, technology, and raw materials. Tangible resources are often the most visible and easily quantifiable assets on a company's balance sheet. For example, a manufacturing firm's production facilities and equip-ment are critical physical resources that enable it to produce goods on a large scale. These resources directly impact on a company's operational capacity and its ability to meet market demand.
- *Intangible Resources*
  Intangible resources, although not physically measurable, are equally important to a company's success. These include IP, brand reputation, patents, trademarks, and customer relationships. Intangible resources often provide a competitive advantage that is difficult for competitors to replicate. For instance, a strong brand can command customer loy-alty and allow a company to charge premium prices, while patents can protect innovative products from being copied by competitors. The value of intangible resources is often reflected in the company's market valuation and can be a decisive factor in its long-term success.
- *Financial Resources*
  Financial resources encompass the funds available to a company for in-vestment, operations, and growth. This includes cash reserves, lines of credit, and access to capital markets. Financial resources are the life-blood of a company's expansion efforts, as they determine the scale and scope of new projects, acquisitions, and market entries. A company with robust financial resources can afford to take on larger, more capital-in-tensive projects and can weather economic downturns more effectively.

Conversely, a company with limited financial resources may need to be more cautious, prioritizing smaller, less risky ventures.

- *Human Resources*
Human resources refer to the workforce that drives a company's operations, innovation, and customer engagement. This includes not only the number of employees but also their skills, experience, and overall productivity. Coproducts and resources are crucial for executing strategies, developing new products, and maintaining customer relationships. Highly skilled and motivated employees can significantly enhance a company's competitiveness, particularly in industries where knowledge and expertise are key differentiators. Human resources also encompass leadership and management, which play a vital role in guiding the company's direction and ensuring the effective use of all other resources.

- *Company's Solidity*
Company solidity refers to the overall strength and stability of a business, encompassing its financial health, market position, and operational resilience. A solid company is one that has strong fundamentals, such as consistent revenue streams, efficient operations, and a diversified customer base. Solidity is often measured by financial ratios, credit ratings, and other indicators of long-term viability. A solid company is better equipped to handle challenges such as economic downturns, competitive pressures, and regulatory changes. It also has greater access to credit and investment opportunities, allowing it to pursue ambitious growth strategies.

- *Credits and Debts*
Credits and debts are financial instruments that reflect a company's obligations and access to external funding. Credits, such as loans and credit lines, provide a company with the necessary capital to finance its operations and expansion efforts. However, these come with obligations to repay, often with interest, which can impact on a company's cash flow and financial stability. On the other hand, represent the amount a company owes to creditors. High levels of debt can strain a company's resources, limit its ability to invest in growth opportunities, and increase its financial risk. Conversely, well-managed debt can be a strategic tool for growth, allowing companies to leverage borrowed funds to achieve higher returns.

- *Other Resources*
In addition to the above, other resources may include partnerships, supply chain networks, and customer data. Partnerships can provide access to new markets, technologies, and expertise, while an efficient supply chain can reduce costs and improve service delivery. Customer data is increasingly valuable as companies seek to understand and anticipate

customer needs, driving more personalized and effective marketing strategies.

In summary, a company's resources (tangible, intangible, financial, human, and others) collectively determine its ability to execute its strategies, sustain operations, and grow over time (Figure 4.1). Understanding and managing these resources effectively is essential for making informed decisions about international expansion and other strategic initiatives. A well-rounded resource base not only enables a company to capitalize on opportunities but also provides the resilience needed to navigate the challenges of a dynamic global market.

Figure 4.1 Resources availability

Measuring Resources Availability

Assessing and defining a company's resource capacity for an internationalization strategy involves evaluating its ability to allocate the necessary financial, operational, and human resources to a new venture without compromising its core business operations. This assessment goes beyond simply having sufficient funds or assets; it also considers the company's resilience and ability to absorb potential setbacks if the venture does not succeed.

- *High Levels of Resources Availability*
  A company defined as having high resource availability is financially robust and has sufficient reserves or assets to absorb the complete loss of an international venture without significant impact on its ongoing operations. For such companies, international expansion becomes an opportunity to experiment with innovative strategies or test new markets without existential risks. MNCs with diversified revenue streams and strong cash flow, such as Amazon or P&G, often fall into this category. If their international venture fails, they can swiftly pivot or withdraw without destabilizing their core business. High resource availability provides the freedom to take bold steps in exploring high-potential markets.

- *Medium Levels of Resources Availability*
  Companies defined as having medium resource availability can afford to invest in internationalization but often need to secure external funding, such as loans or venture capital. While failure would not result in bankruptcy, it would cause financial strain and potentially delay other growth initiatives. These companies must adopt a calculated approach to internationalization, balancing ambition with caution. For instance, medium-sized firms expanding internationally for the first time may rely on securing financing while carefully selecting low-risk, high-potential markets to minimize their exposure. The recovery process after a failed venture might take years, impacting growth and market confidence.

- *Low Levels of Resources Availability*
  Companies with low resource availability are often risking their survival with international expansion. A failed venture could lead to insolvency or significant restructuring. Startups or small businesses that invest their limited capital in a single international market often fall into this category. For such companies, the stakes are exceedingly high, and failure is not an option. These companies must adopt highly conservative strategies, such as targeting geographically or culturally similar markets to reduce risks.

4.2.2 Risk Tolerance

Risk tolerance refers to the degree of variability in investment returns or the level of uncertainty a company is willing to accept in pursuit of its business objectives. It is a critical factor that influences decision-making, particularly when it comes to expansion into new markets, launching new products, or investing in innovative technologies. A company's risk tolerance is shaped by a combination of its leadership's mindset, financial health, industry conditions, and overall strategic goals. Understanding risk tolerance is essential for aligning business strategies with the company's capacity to absorb potential losses and handle unexpected challenges.

- *Financial Stability and Capital Reserves*
  One of the most significant factors influencing a company's risk tolerance is its financial stability. A company with strong financial reserves, consistent cash flows, and access to credit is generally more capable of taking on higher levels of risk. These financial buffers allow the company to absorb potential losses or withstand periods of low profitability without jeopardizing its overall viability. For example, a financially stable company might be willing to invest in a high-risk, high-reward project, such as entering a volatile emerging market or developing a disruptive new technology. In contrast, a company with tighter financial constraints may adopt a more conservative approach, focusing on lower-risk opportunities that offer steady, predictable returns.

- *Leadership and Corporate Culture*
  The mindset and attitudes of a company's leadership play a pivotal role in determining risk tolerance. Companies led by visionary leaders who are comfortable with uncertainty and eager to pursue bold strategies often exhibit higher risk tolerance. These leaders may prioritize innovation, market leadership, and long-term growth over short-term stability. For example, a CEO with a high-risk tolerance might advocate for aggressive expansion into new markets or the rapid adoption of cutting-edge technologies, even if these moves entail significant uncertainty. Conversely, a company with a more risk-averse leadership team may prioritize preserving capital, maintaining operational stability, and avoiding potential pitfalls. This approach is often reflected in a corporate culture that values caution, careful planning, and incremental growth. Companies are likely to favor strategies that minimize exposure to risk, such as expanding into familiar markets or investing in established technologies.

- *Industry Conditions and Market Dynamics*
  The industry in which a company operates also heavily influences its risk tolerance. Certain industries, such as technology, pharmaceuticals, or energy, are inherently more volatile and subject to rapid changes due to innovation, regulation, or market disruptions. Companies in these sectors may develop a higher tolerance for risk as a necessary response to the unpredictable nature of their business environment. For instance, a tech company may regularly invest in speculative R&D projects, understanding that some may fail while others could lead to groundbreaking

products. In contrast, companies in more stable industries, such as utilities or consumer staples, may exhibit lower risk tolerance. These industries typically experience slower, more predictable changes, and the companies operating within them often focus on steady growth, consistent dividends, and minimizing exposure to market volatility. As a result, these companies might avoid risky ventures that could disrupt their established business models.

- *Strategic Objectives and Long-Term Vision*
A company's strategic objectives and long-term vision are critical determinants of its risk tolerance. Companies with ambitious growth targets, such as becoming a global leader in their industry or doubling their market share, may need to embrace higher levels of risk to achieve these goals. This might involve entering new and untested markets, investing heavily in innovation, or acquiring competitors. These companies understand that taking calculated risks is essential for achieving significant rewards. On the other hand, companies with more modest objectives, such as maintaining market position or achieving steady, incremental growth, may prefer a lower risk tolerance. These companies might focus on optimizing existing operations, enhancing customer satisfaction, or improving efficiency, all while avoiding ventures that could introduce unnecessary uncertainty or volatility.

- *Regulatory and Legal Environment*
The regulatory and legal environment in which a company operates also impacts its risk tolerance. Companies operating in highly regulated industries, such as finance, healthcare, or environmental services, may face strict compliance requirements that limit their ability to take certain risks. The potential for legal repercussions, fines, or reputational damage may encourage these companies to adopt a more conservative approach to risk. For example, a pharmaceutical company may hesitate to launch a new drug without exhaustive testing and regulatory approval, even if the market demand is high. In contrast, companies in less regulated industries may have more flexibility to pursue risky strategies, such as rapidly scaling a new business model or entering emerging markets with less oversight. However, this greater freedom can also expose them to higher levels of uncertainty and potential challenges.

- *Operational Flexibility and Resilience*
Finally, a company's operational flexibility and resilience – its ability to adapt to changes and recover from setbacks – play a crucial role in shaping its risk tolerance. Companies that have built-in agility, such as diversified product lines, flexible supply chains, and robust crisis management plans, are generally better equipped to handle higher levels of risk. These companies can quickly pivot in response to market shifts, capitalize on emerging opportunities, and mitigate the impact of unforeseen

challenges. In contrast, companies with rigid structures, limited diversi-fication, or weak contingency planning may be less willing to take risks that could disrupt their operations. These companies may prefer to fo-cus on maintaining stability and continuity, even if it means forgoing potentially lucrative opportunities.

A company's risk tolerance is a multifaceted concept influenced by its financial stability, leadership mindset, industry conditions, strategic objectives, regula-tory environment, and operational flexibility (Figure 4.2). Understanding and accurately assessing risk tolerance is essential for aligning business strategies with the company's capacity to absorb potential losses and manage uncertainty. By carefully evaluating these factors, companies can make informed decisions about how much risk they are willing and able to take on, ensuring that their pursuit of growth and innovation is balanced with the need for stability and long-term success.

Figure 4.2 Tolerance to risk

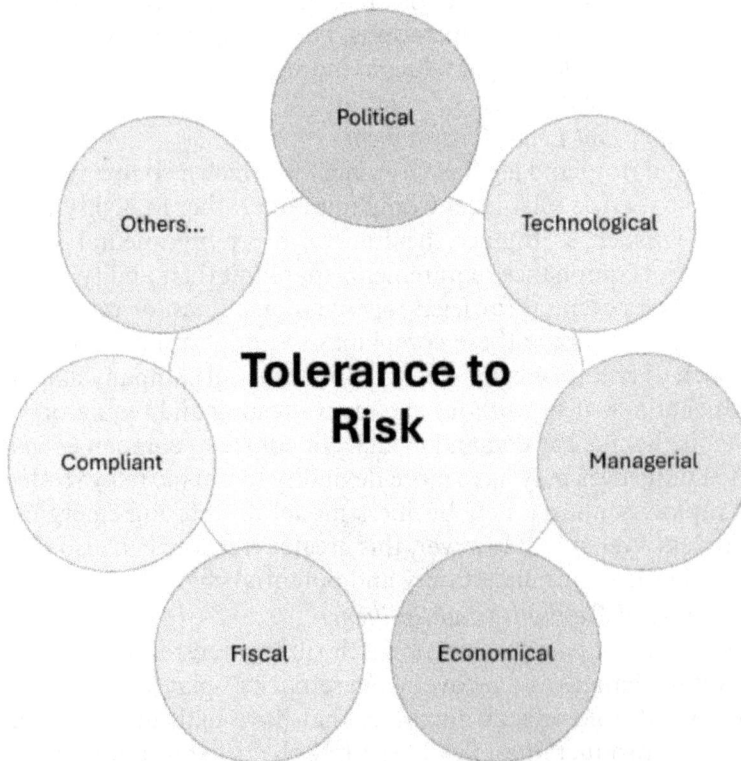

Entering a new market is a pivotal decision for any company, and selecting the right market is crucial for success. The repercussions of choosing the wrong market can be severe, leading to significant financial losses, wasted resources, and potential damage to a company's reputation. While entering any new market carries inherent risks, these risks can be mitigated by applying strategic tools and methodologies that increase the odds of success.

4.2.3 The "Where" Matrix

Following Market Pareidolia's principles, the first step in this process is for a company to clearly define its resources availability and tolerance to risk (Figure 4.3). Understanding these two factors is essential, as they serve as the foundation for making informed decisions about market entry. As seen, resources availability encompasses the financial, human, and operational capacities that a company can leverage when expanding into a new market. This includes capital investment, the ability to scale production, the availability of skilled personnel, and the technological capabilities necessary to compete in the target market (among others). On the other hand, tolerance to risk refers to the level of uncertainty a company is willing to accept in pursuit of its business objectives. Companies with high risk tolerance may be more willing to enter volatile young markets, while those with lower risk tolerance may prefer stable, mature markets where the potential for unforeseen challenges is minimized. Once a company has a clear understanding of its resources and risk tolerance, it can begin the process of filtering potential markets. This involves identifying markets that are not suitable for entry based on the company's specific constraints and capabilities. For example, a company with limited financial resources might rule out entering highly competitive markets that require substantial upfront investment (senior markets). Similarly, a company with low risk tolerance might avoid markets with political instability, economic volatility, or complex regulatory environments (adolescent markets). By systematically eliminating markets that do not align with the company's resources and risk tolerance, the focus can be shifted to those markets where the company is more likely to succeed.

By understanding and relating resources availability to tolerance to risk, companies can develop a more strategic approach to market selection. This approach not only helps in identifying markets where the company increases the probability to thrive but also in avoiding those where the odds of success are too low. The goal is to maximize the potential for success while minimizing exposure to unnecessary risks. The process of selecting the right market for expansion is a critical component of a company's overall strategy. By thoroughly assessing resources availability and risk tolerance, and by applying these insights to the market selection process, companies can increase their chances of successful market entry. This strategic approach ensures that resources are allocated effectively and that the company's expansion efforts are aligned with its long-term goals.

Figure 4.3 The "where" matrix – resources availability vs. tolerance to risk

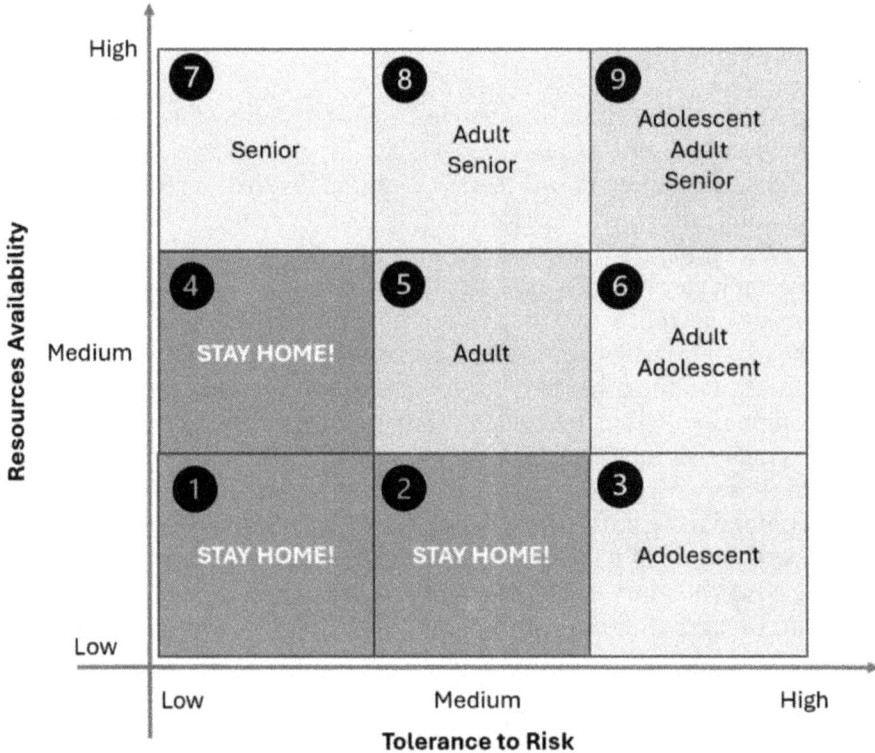

How to interpret the table:

- Areas 1, 2, and 4: Stay Home!
  Area 1: If a company possesses both low resources and a similarly low risk tolerance for new ventures, it is not yet ready to internationalize and should focus on domestic operations for the time being.
  Area 2: The same holds true for companies with low risk tolerance but medium resource availability; low risk markets are attractive and competitive; thus, they require high levels of engagement leading to the need for resources investment.
  Area 4: Similarly, for companies with a medium risk tolerance but low resources, the situation remains challenging, as markets that require an average level of risk tolerance also necessitate a comparable level of resources.

138

There are no foreign markets that align with companies having these characteristics, and the risk of failure in pursuing international expansion under these conditions is simply too high. Companies in this position should prioritize building their resources and gradually increasing their risk tolerance before considering any international ventures.

- *Area 3*: High Risk, High Reward
  Adolescent markets, as defined by Market Pareidolia, are risky yet speculative and typically low-budget markets. Companies with limited budgets but a natural predisposition toward risk-taking could find significant opportunities here. The potential for high returns in these markets could substantially boost a small company's turnover and quickly provide much-needed liquidity. For businesses willing to take on the challenge, these markets can offer rapid growth opportunities, against high levels of risk.

- *Area 5*: The Balanced Approach
  Adolescent markets are known for their high-risk levels, while senior markets are capital-intensive. Adult markets strike a balance between these two extremes. Companies with an average tolerance for risk and a moderate, though not vast, amount of capital to invest may find adult markets particularly suitable. These markets represent a strategic compromise for businesses that cannot commit large sums but are comfortable with a certain level of risk.

- Area 6: Expanding Horizons
  This area is similar to Area 3, but with the added benefit of greater resources. This opens the possibility of entering adult markets as well as adolescent markets, since adult markets require lower levels of risk tolerance and a moderate amount of resources availability. Companies in this category have a broader range of market opportunities to explore.

- Area 7: The Safe Bet
  As mentioned earlier, adolescent markets demand a high tolerance for risk, and even adult markets require some degree of risk acceptance. Companies with a low propensity for risk are automatically excluded from both adolescent and adult markets. However, if a company has abundant resources, it can confidently expand into senior markets, which are typically less risky but require significant capital.

- Area 8: Ready for Growth
  Area 8 consists of companies with an acceptable level of risk tolerance (though not enough for adolescent markets) and significant resources to invest. These companies are well-positioned to penetrate both adult and senior markets, where the risk tolerance required is lower, but substantial resources are necessary for success.

- Area 9: The Ideal Position
  This is the area where every company aspires to be: abundant resources and a high tolerance for risk. Companies in this position have the flexibility and adaptability to enter markets of all ages, giving them a wide array of opportunities to explore. These companies are typically healthy, robust, and well-equipped to thrive in diverse international environments.

4.3 "What"

What type of internationalization mode shall (can) a company use to internationalize? Previously, we explored how a company's resources and risk tolerance influence the markets it can realistically enter, with these factors guiding the selection of markets based on their Market Pareidolia developmental stage (whether adolescent, adult, or senior). However, identifying the right markets is only part of the equation. To successfully internationalize, a company must select the market (or markets) it shall penetrate, and the mode with which will operate. To correctly select the right mode, the company shall consider another critical variable: Levels of Dependency (Figure 4.4). Levels of dependency refer to the extent to which a company is reliant on specific external factors that could either facilitate or hinder its ability to expand internationally. These dependencies can arise from a variety of sources, including legal regulations, licensing agreements, supply chain constraints, and brand or product authenticity requirements, among others. Understanding these dependencies is essential because they can significantly influence which internationalization modes are viable and which might be problematic or even impossible to pursue.

4.3.1 Degree of Dependencies

- *Legal and Geographic Dependencies*
  One common form of dependency is legal or geographic constraints tied to the production or branding of a product. For example, in the food and beverage industry, certain products are legally required to be produced in specific locations to maintain their authenticity and branding. A notable case is the production of Prosecco in Italy. The name "Prosecco" is legally protected under geographic indication laws, meaning that only sparkling wine produced in the designated Prosecco region of Italy can bear this name. If a company wants to produce a similar product in another country, it can do so, but it cannot legally call the product Prosecco. This geographic dependency has practical business implications: transporting authentic Prosecco to distant markets such as Asia or the Americas incurs significant costs, and only markets with consumers willing to pay a premium for the genuine product may be

viable. As a result, the business model may not be sustainable in all regions. This kind of dependency forces companies to carefully consider their internationalization strategy. For example, instead of exporting the product globally, a company might explore forming strategic alliances or JVs in foreign markets to produce similar products under different branding that complies with local regulations.

- *Licensing and Intellectual Property Dependencies*
  Another crucial form of dependency involves licensing agreements and IP rights. Companies that operate under strict licensing arrangements may find their international expansion efforts constrained by the terms set by the licensor. For instance, a company selling Microsoft licenses in Denmark cannot expand its operations to other regions without Microsoft's explicit approval. This type of dependency can significantly limit the company's ability to scale its business internationally. Such dependencies necessitate a strategic approach to internationalization. The company might need to negotiate broader licensing agreements or seek partnerships that allow for more flexibility in expanding to new markets. In some cases, companies may decide to diversify their product offerings or develop new products that are not bound by such restrictive licensing terms, thereby gaining more control over their international growth.

- *Supply Chain and Resource Dependencies*
  In addition to legal and licensing constraints, supply chain dependencies can also play a significant role in determining the mode of internationalization. For example, a company dependent on specific raw material that is only available in certain regions may find its internationalization options limited. Similarly, companies relying on specialized technologies or manufacturing processes that cannot be easily replicated abroad may need to consider Service IB of Capital IB modes in new markets. Understanding these dependencies allows companies to better assess the feasibility of different internationalization modes.

Figure 4.4 Degree of dependencies

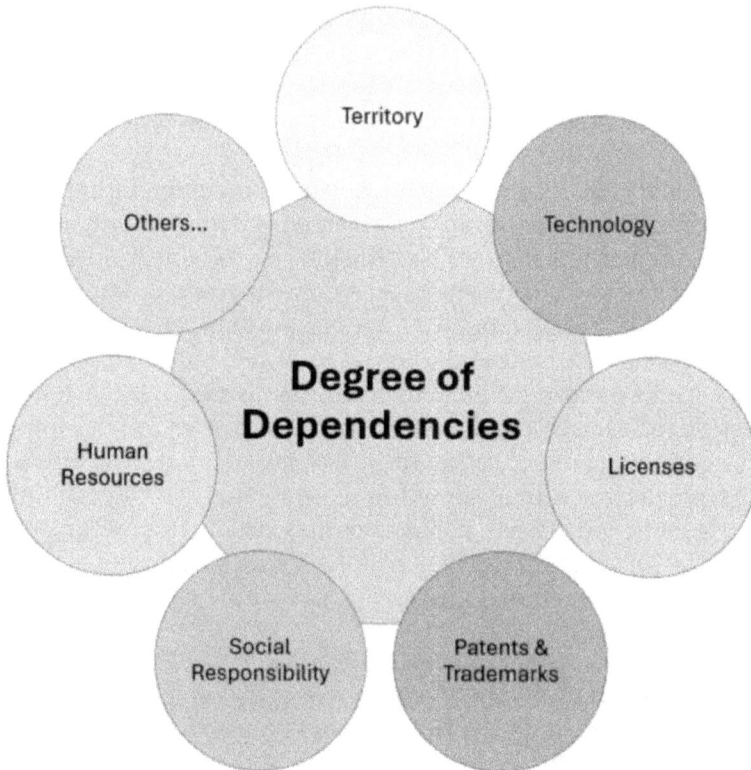

Ultimately, a company's critical dependencies negatively influence its flexibility and strategic options in internationalization. Dependencies, whether related to geography, raw materials, or technology, often involve factors beyond a company's direct control, limiting its ability to adapt to new markets. This inflexibility can result in competitive disadvantages, as it constrains the company's ability to respond to local market dynamics or competitive pressures effectively. For instance, reliance on specific raw materials available only in a limited region could compel the company to pay a premium for sourcing in new markets. In extreme cases, such geographical dependencies might render certain internationalization strategies economically unviable, as the costs of overcoming such constraints could outweigh the benefits of market entry.

4.3.2 The "What" Matrix

Identifying and evaluating critical dependencies is not just a preparatory step, it is a foundational aspect of strategic internationalization planning. A thorough assessment allows companies to foresee potential obstacles and adapt their approach to mitigate risks by defining the right internationalization mode. Dependencies do not inherently lead to negative outcomes; when strategically leveraged, they can become a source of competitive advantage. For example, a company possessing proprietary technology may find that its dependency on this specialized capability actually strengthens its negotiation position in licensing or partnership discussions. However, this requires a proactive approach to dependency management, including strategies to diversify supply sources, enhance process adaptability, or invest in innovation to reduce reliance on external factors. To ensure the feasibility and success of internationalization efforts and the selection of the right internationalization mode, companies must integrate dependency analysis into their decision-making frameworks. This involves several key steps:

- *Mapping Dependencies:* Companies should identify and categorize their critical dependencies, such as supply chain constraints, technological limitations, or regulatory challenges.
- *Assessing Impact:* For each dependency, assess its potential impact on the market. This includes evaluating cost implications, operational risks, and competitive pressures.
- *Exploring Mitigation Strategies:* Develop strategies to address dependencies. These could include diversifying suppliers, outsourcing production, or negotiating strategic partnerships, leading to selecting the correct internationalization mode.
- *Aligning with Strategic Objectives*: Ensure that the chosen internationalization mode aligns with the company's broader strategic goals, balancing dependency constraints with opportunities for growth and competitive differentiation.

Dependencies are an inherent part of any internationalization strategy. By proactively addressing these constraints and integrating them into the strategic planning process, companies can enhance their resilience and adaptability in global markets. While dependencies may pose initial challenges, recognizing them early enables companies to make informed decisions, safeguard against unforeseen risks, and position themselves for sustained success in an increasingly interconnected and competitive global economy.

However, the degree of dependency a company faces is not sufficient on its own to determine the appropriate mode of internationalization. The availability of resources also plays a crucial role, as each mode demands different levels of financial exposure (as seen in previous chapters). Therefore, to identify the most suitable mode (or modes) for a company to operate in international markets, it is essential to consider both the available resources and the degree of dependencies the company has (Figure 4.5).

Figure 4.5 The "what" Matrix - resources availability vs. degree of dependencies

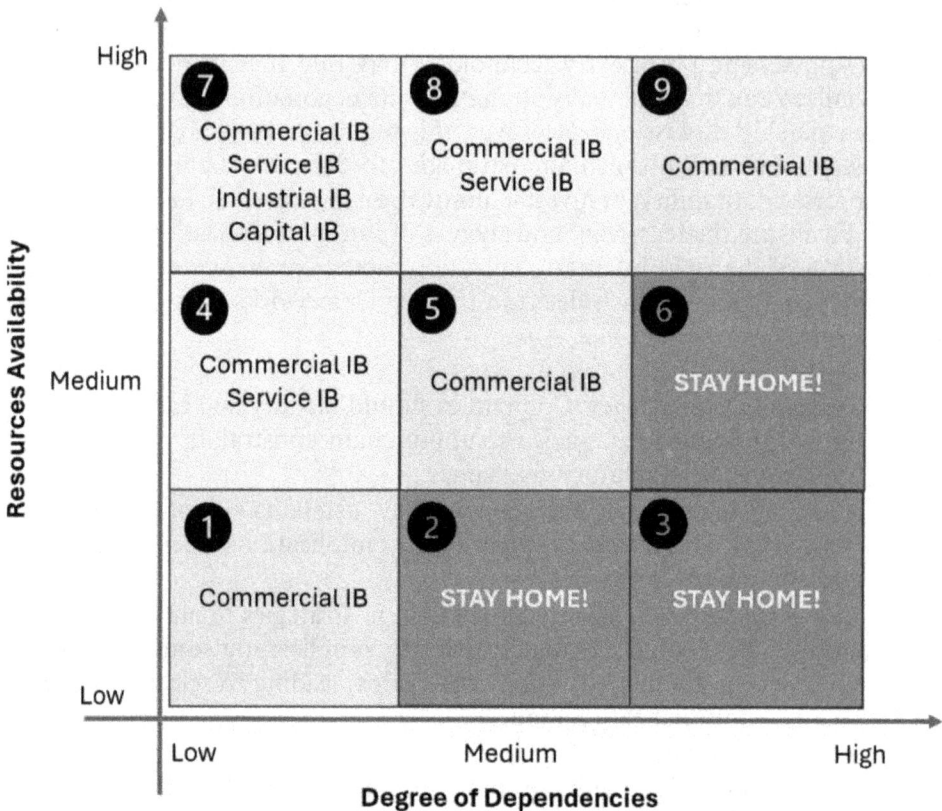

How to interpret the table:

- *Areas 2, 3, and 6: Stay Home!*
  The greater the degree of dependency, the more costly and resource-intensive it becomes to mitigate or reduce that dependency. When dependencies are tightly woven into a company's operation (whether through reliance on specific suppliers, technologies, or geographical factors), addressing them often demands significant investments in time, money, and strategic effort. Companies facing high levels of dependency may need to deploy substantial resources to develop alternative solutions, such as diversifying supply chains, adopting new technologies, or forming strategic partnerships, to remain competitive in their target markets. Moreover, even moderate levels of dependency require considerable re-

sources to manage effectively, as they may still pose risks that could disrupt operations or hinder internationalization efforts. In some cases, medium levels of dependencies might necessitate resource allocations on par with those for high dependencies, especially in volatile or complex markets where the risks of not addressing them are amplified. Before entering new markets, companies in these areas should reinforce their resources.

- *Areas 1, 5 and 9: Simple, but Effective*
Area 1: Having a low degree of dependencies means having a high degree of commercial freedom. This means having the possibility to choose within the four international modes. However, the selection is limited by the need for resources to implement the modes. In today's globalized world, where people are connected by definition, we have seen how Commercial IB requires low levels of resources for a company to internationalize. This leaves no room but for a Commercial IB.

Area 5: As the degree of dependency increases, a company's commercial freedom diminishes, which in turn undermines competitiveness and, in some cases, can jeopardize the viability of the entire internationalization effort. To address this issue, companies must allocate resources strategically to enhance their commercial freedom or develop alternative corporate strategies that enable effective market penetration despite these constraints. In situations where both the degree of dependency and the available resources are adequate but not optimal, companies face the challenge of balancing these limitations while still achieving commercial competitiveness. Under such conditions, resource investment becomes a necessity to maintain or regain competitive positioning. Among the various internationalization modes, Commercial IB stands out as the most feasible option when resource constraints are significant.

Area 9: Following the same reasoning outlined in Area 5, as dependency intensifies further, the need for resource allocation to counteract the decline in competitiveness grows proportionally. In such scenarios, companies are compelled to dedicate most of their substantial resources to maintaining market competitiveness, leaving limited resources available for exploring alternative internationalization modes. Under these circumstances, Commercial IB remains the only viable internationalization option. Its relatively low resource requirements make it the default choice, as companies must prioritize resource allocation toward preserving their competitive position in the market. While this approach may not allow for significant strategic flexibility, it ensures that the company can sustain operations and maintain a presence in the new market despite heightened dependency and constrained resources.

- *Areas 4 and 8: The Balanced Approach*
  Area 4: As resource availability increases while maintaining a low degree of dependency, the range of internationalization options begins to expand. In this scenario, the absence of a significant need to address dependencies for competitiveness allows resources to be allocated directly toward implementing the chosen internationalization mode. However, despite the availability of resources, their limited nature naturally excludes more resource-intensive modes such as Industrial IB and Capital IB. This leaves Commercial IB and Service IB as the most viable options, providing companies with flexible and efficient pathways to enter new markets while aligning with their operational capacities and strategic goals.
  Area 8: As observed in other areas, an increasing degree of dependency necessitates a proportional allocation of resources to counteract the resulting decline in competitiveness. Even when resource levels are high, a significant portion must be directed toward managing these dependencies, reducing the resources available for other strategic initiatives. This constraint limits the range of internationalization modes that remain feasible. In alignment with the dynamics of Area 8, Industrial IB and Capital IB, despite the availability of substantial resources, become unviable due to their intensive requirements. Consequently, companies are left with Commercial IB and Service IB as the most practical options. These modes balance the need to maintain competitiveness while aligning with the remaining resources, enabling companies to navigate their dependencies effectively and still achieve meaningful international market entry.
- *Area 7: The Safe Bet*
  This is the ideal position for any company: a combination of abundant resources and a low degree of dependency. In this scenario, commercial freedom reaches its peak, allowing companies to operate with minimal constraints. When coupled with a satisfactory or substantial amount of available resources, this position opens up a wide array of strategic options for internationalization. Companies in this advantageous situation are not only free from restrictive dependencies but are also well-equipped to adapt to market dynamics and seize opportunities in diverse environments. In this optimal area, businesses can strategically select from all four internationalization modes (Commercial IB, Service IB, Industrial IB, and Capital IB) without being hindered by resource limitations or dependency constraints. This freedom enables companies to align their chosen mode with their broader strategic goals, market characteristics, and operational strengths. Whether leveraging the simplicity and speed of Commercial IB, the client-centric focus of Service IB, the production capabilities of Industrial IB, or the resource-intensive but

high-impact approach of Capital IB, companies in this position can tailor their internationalization strategies to achieve maximum growth and competitive advantage.

4.4 Integrating the "Where & What" Matrix for a Comprehensive IB Strategy

We have explored how to select a new market based on risk tolerance using the Market Pareidolia approach (Where) and analyzed the modes of internationalization suitable for a company based on its degree of dependencies (What). Both aspects are intrinsically tied to the level of resources the company can allocate. By combining the "Where" and "What" (Figure 4.6) frameworks into a unified model, we construct a three-dimensional graph that encapsulates all possibilities and guides decision-making. This integrated "Where and What" graph positions the company across three key dimensions: the markets it can target, the modes of internationalization available, and the level of resources required to navigate dependencies and risks. Understanding where the company falls on this graph provides a strategic foundation for the internationalization process.

Figure 4.6 The "where & what" matrix

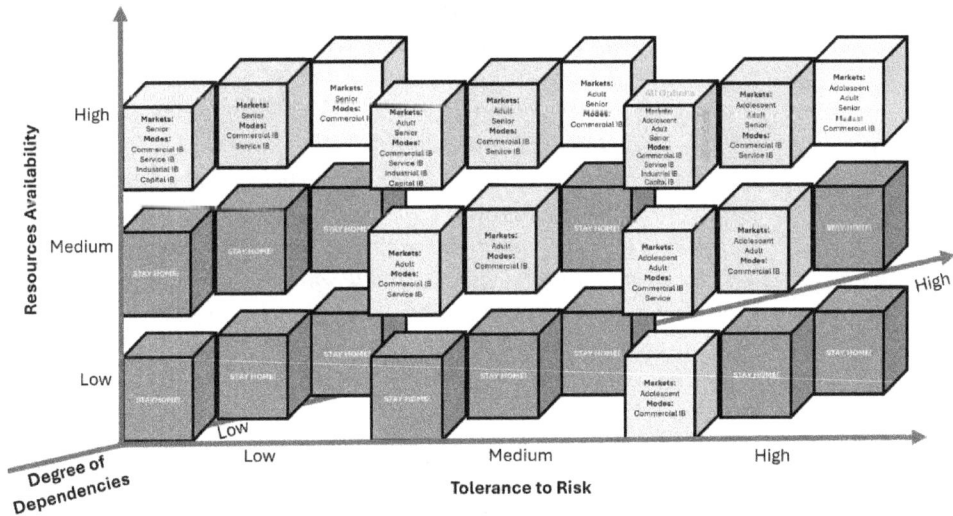

Where Does Your Company Stand on the "Where and What" Matrix?

The position of any company on this graph reveals critical insights into the readiness for internationalization and suggests actionable pathways forward. There are three primary scenarios such a company might face:

1. Located in the "Stay Home!" Zone
   - *What This Means:* Landing in this area indicates that the company is not yet ready for internationalization. The combination of high dependency, limited resources, and lower risk tolerance makes any immediate international expansion unfeasible.
   - *What It Should Do:* A pre-internationalization strategy is essential. This strategy should focus on addressing the company's weaknesses, whether that means increasing resources, reducing dependencies, or building resilience against market risks. Additionally, it must identify the specific section of the graph which aims to reach, targeting the efforts toward traits that will position the company in a more favorable area.
   - *Outcome:* This strategic preparation is intended to elevate the company to a point where internationalization becomes a realistic and viable option.
2. Located in a "Limited Options" Zone
   - *What This Means: The company is in a position where internationalization is possible, but the available options for markets ("where") or IB modes ("what") do not align with the strategic preferences of the company's vision. In this case there are two options:*
   - *Option A: Begin the internationalization process immediately with a mode or in a market which is not preferable but acceptable, leveraging the opportunities available while simultaneously working on the weaknesses to reposition the company in the desired section of the matrix and evolving with time. This approach allows to generate momentum and learn from real-world market engagement while improving the internal capabilities.*
   - *Option B: Develop and implement a targeted pre-internationalization strategy to address the gaps and reposition the company in the desired area of the graph before initiating the internationalization process. This path may take longer but ensures that the company enters the market on its own terms with a stronger foundation.*
   - *Outcome: Whether the company opts for immediate action or a preparatory phase, the goal is to transition to a zone that aligns with the internationalization objectives.*
3. Located in the "Ready to Expand" Zone
   - *What This Means:* Landing in this area signifies that the company has the needed resources, has a low dependency, and has a strategic alignment to pursue internationalization successfully. The company is positioned to choose between markets and IB modes proposed within the graphic area.

- *What the Company Should Do: Develop* a comprehensive internationalization strategy that takes full advantage of the company's strong position. This involves:
  - Selecting the most suitable foreign markets based on the "where" analysis.
  - Deciding on the appropriate IB mode (Commercial IB, Service IB, Industrial IB, or Capital IB) based on the "what" analysis and the resources available.
- *Outcome:* The company is ready to penetrate foreign markets confidently and effectively, maximizing the opportunities available while minimizing risks.

By understanding the company's position on the "where & what" matrix, the company gains a clear roadmap for navigating the complexities of internationalization. Whether it needs to prepare through a pre-internationalization strategy, refine the approach to align with its goals, or proceed directly to market entry, this framework empowers decision-makers to make informed, strategic decisions.

4.5 Moving Through the "Where & What" Matrix

Once a company has identified its position within the "where & what" matrix, this placement will determine which market age groups and types of IB modes the company can feasibly pursue to enhance its likelihood of success. However, the markets and IB modes deemed accessible based on this analysis may not align with the company's strategic goals, vision, or long-term internationalization objectives. In some cases, a company may find itself in the "Stay Home!" zone of the matrix, indicating that its current characteristics are insufficient to support a viable internationalization effort. This situation can be particularly discouraging, as it jeopardizes the feasibility of the entire project. When a company faces such limitations, the next step is not abandonment but preparation. The company must strategically plan to build the necessary capabilities and resources to reposition itself within the matrix. This involves identifying the desired block that aligns with its internationalization goals and crafting an actionable roadmap to transition toward that position. Such a roadmap will determine the "when," the timeline required to develop the attributes needed to achieve the desired matrix placement. This strategic preparation ensures that the company is not only ready to internationalize but does so in a manner consistent with its overarching business objectives. For example, consider Company X, which aspires to expand internationally but finds itself in Block 4 (Figure 4.7), the "Stay Home!" zone. This means that, even though it has a low degree of dependencies which provide the company with more freedom of choice, it currently lacks the resources or risk tolerance needed to successfully enter a foreign market. Rather than attempting an ill-fated internationalization effort, Company X must first address its deficiencies.

Figure 4.7 Company X position within the "where & what" matrix

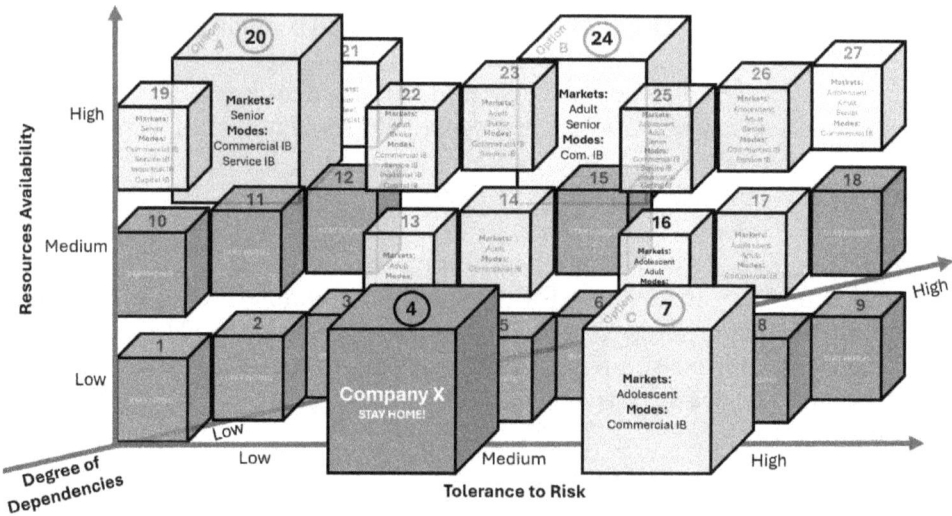

At this stage, Company X shall identify the nearest block (option) with the desired market age and IB mode and create a strategy to achieve these obligations (Figure 4.7). This could involve bolstering its financial reserves, developing internal capabilities, diversifying supplier relationships to reduce dependency, or gradually increasing its tolerance for risk through calculated domestic initiatives that mimic the complexities of international markets. By adopting this preparatory approach, the company can systematically enhance its readiness for internationalization. These steps will not only reposition the company within the "where & what" matrix but also provide a clearer timeline ("when") to sustainable international expansion. Ultimately, the matrix serves not as a barrier but as a diagnostic tool, helping companies identify gaps and create tailored strategies to overcome them. Through deliberate preparation and strategic action, even companies initially relegated to the "Stay Home!" zone can evolve into strong candidates for internationalization, entering the right markets with the right approach at the right time. However, shifting a company's position within the "where & what" matrix can be achieved through three distinct approaches (Figure 4.8), either independently or concurrently:

Figure 4.8 Approaches to shifting a company's position within the "where & what" matrix

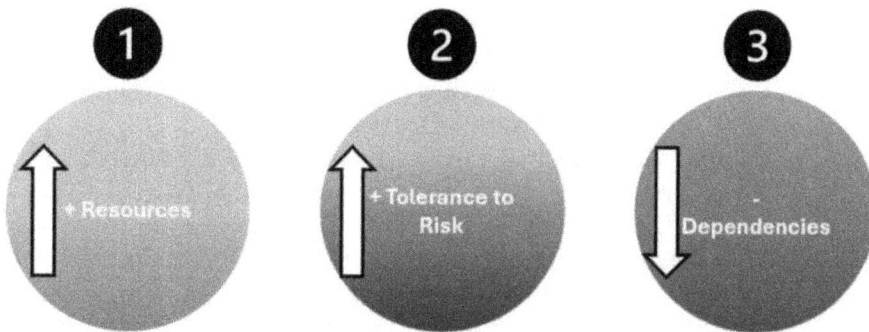

4.5.1 Adapting Resources Availability

Regardless of whether a company is pursuing an internationalization strategy, the need to bolster resource availability remains a constant imperative for sustained growth. Resources (financial, human, and operational) are the lifeblood of business expansion. Without adequate investments, growth becomes an unattainable goal. For companies that cannot afford to risk failure in an internationalization venture but still seek to grow their business, finding ways to enhance resource availability is not just an option but a necessity. Growing resource availability is a dynamic and ongoing process that involves a strategic blend of internal optimization, eventual external partnerships, and innovative approaches to financial management. There are many existing methods a business can employ to increase their resource availability and position themselves for growth:

1. *Increasing Share Capital*
   One of the most direct ways to enhance resource availability is by increasing share capital. By issuing new shares to existing or new investors, companies can secure additional funding without taking on debt. This approach is particularly suitable for businesses with strong growth potential and a compelling value proposition for investors.

2. *Securing Loans (Commercial or Noncommercial)*
   Loans remain a traditional yet effective way to raise funds. Commercial loans from financial institutions offer flexibility and scalability, while noncommercial loans, such as those from government programs or development funds, often come with favorable terms for specific industries or markets.

3. *Selling Noncritical Assets*
   Companies can free up capital by divesting nonessential or under-performing assets. This not only increases liquidity but also allows management to focus on core business operations.

4. *Finding a Strategic Partner*
   Forming a partnership with a complementary business can provide access to shared resources, reduce costs, and open new revenue streams. A well-aligned partnership brings more than just capital, it brings expertise, market access, and operational synergies.

5. *Selling Shares of the Company*
   While similar to increasing share capital, selling shares, particularly a minority stake, can be a targeted approach to bringing in strategic investors who add value beyond just funding. These investors often provide guidance, connections, and credibility.

6. *Finding a Sponsor*
   Sponsorship agreements can provide financial support in exchange for promotional opportunities. This approach is particularly effective for companies with strong brand recognition or those operating in industries with high public visibility.

7. *Fundraising*
   Fundraising campaigns, particularly for consumer-focused businesses, can tap into public support. Crowdfunding platforms have gained traction as a way to secure resources while building brand loyalty and awareness.

8. *Entering a Consortium*
   Joining a consortium allows companies to pool resources and share risks for large-scale projects. Consortia are particularly useful for high-cost ventures such as infrastructure development or research-intensive industries.

9. *Exploring Alternative Options*
   Beyond traditional methods, innovative solutions such as revenue-based financing, tokenization, or leasing arrangements can offer additional avenues for securing resources. These approaches can provide tailored funding solutions while preserving operational flexibility.

While increasing resource availability is essential, it is equally important to approach these methods strategically and with long-term sustainability in mind. Companies should consider their current financial health, strategic objectives, and risk tolerance before deciding which avenue to pursue. For instance, while taking on debt can offer immediate liquidity, it may not be the best option for a company already struggling with high leverage. Moreover, building a sustainable resource base often involves combining multiple approaches. For example, a company might simultaneously secure a loan for short-term needs while pursuing a strategic partnership to enhance market access. The key is to align these efforts with the company's broader vision and operational strategy.

For companies aiming to internationalize, the importance of resource availability cannot be overstated. International ventures often require significant investments in market research, infrastructure, compliance, and human resources. By proactively increasing their resource base, companies can better position themselves to handle the complexities of global markets. However, even companies not immediately pursuing internationalization should view resource optimization as a preparatory step. By building a strong foundation of resources, they can remain agile and ready to seize opportunities as they arise. This proactive approach not only enhances resilience but also ensures that the company is well-equipped to adapt to future challenges. In conclusion, increasing resource availability is not just a financial exercise, it is a strategic imperative that underpins a company's ability to grow, innovate, and compete in a rapidly changing global economy. By leveraging a combination of traditional and innovative methods, businesses can secure the resources they need to thrive in both domestic and international markets.

4.5.2 Change Tolerance to Risk through Perception

In the movie *After Earth* (Shyamalan, 2013), Will Smith's character poignantly tells his son, "Danger is very real. But fear is a choice." This underlines the role of perception in our understanding of reality. As Carl Rogers (1961) articulated, "Our interpretation of the world creates our reality." In essence, there exists a subjective reality, derived from our personal perceptions, and an objective reality, shaped by external events (Figure 4.9). The interplay between these realities profoundly influences how we assess risks and make decisions. This concept becomes especially evident when exploring how individuals perceive and react to risk.

Figure 4.9 The "Glass Half Full or Half Empty" Theory

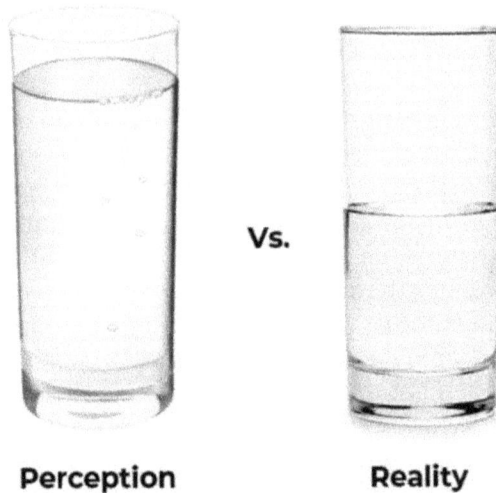

Vs.

Perception   Reality

Take, for instance, the case of a 16-year-old boy speeding down a road at 180 KPH on a bike without a helmet. Objectively, the risk in this scenario is extremely high, his life is in significant danger. However, from the boy's subjective reality, the perception of risk is minimal or even negligible. He might view the activity as thrilling or routine, dismissing its inherent dangers. In stark contrast, consider a senior lady contemplating a ride on a rollercoaster. While the actual risks involved in rollercoasters are statistically negligible due to stringent safety protocols, her subjective perception might amplify the danger to a point where the experience feels overwhelming and unacceptable. These examples highlight how the gap between reality and perception can create vastly different interpretations of risk. Crucially, perception isn't fixed, it can be reshaped. The question then arises: How can one align subjective perception more closely with objective reality to make informed decisions? The answer lies in information. By providing relevant, accurate, and context-specific information, perceptions of risk can be adjusted. For the boy on the bike, showing him statistics about the life-saving potential of helmets or discussing real-life consequences of reckless driving might make him reconsider his behavior. Equipping him with a helmet and good insurance not only addresses his perception of safety but also mitigates real risk, creating a safer environment while maintaining his freedom to ride. Similarly, for the senior lady, explaining the rigorous safety checks rollercoasters undergo or sharing data on their impeccable safety records might ease her anxiety and enable her to enjoy the ride. It's also worth noting that information doesn't merely bridge the gap between subjective and objective realities, it can serve as a tool to adapt to and manage risk. If the risks are genuine, strategies such as protective gear, insurance policies, or even behavior modification can be employed to lower them to an acceptable level. When risks are overestimated, providing evidence and clarity can recalibrate the individual's perspective, helping them engage with opportunities they might otherwise avoid.

The perception of reality within a business is often deeply tied to the company's primary objective: *creating wealth for its shareholders*. This revenue-driven focus can sometimes distort a company's risk perception. The allure of potential revenues can blind decision-makers to the risks inherent in their ventures, leading to critical missteps. History offers several cautionary tales of businesses and industries that underestimated risks, often with disastrous consequences:

- *The Carbon Dioxide Misconception (1950s)*
  In the mid-20th century, oil and gas companies actively promoted carbon dioxide as beneficial for plant growth, sidelining emerging evidence of its role in climate change. Blinded by the promise of continued revenue from fossil fuel sales, these companies dismissed the long-term environmental risks associated with increasing CO_2 emissions. The consequences of this misjudgment have been far-reaching, contributing significantly to today's climate crisis.
- *Thalidomide Tragedy (1960s)*
  Thalidomide was marketed as a safe drug for alleviating morning sickness in pregnant women. Despite its initial success, the drug caused severe fetal deformities, impacting thousands of families. This tragedy underscored how the drive for rapid market entry and revenue generation can lead to insufficient safety testing and catastrophic outcomes.
- *The Ulcer Misconception (Pre-1982)*
  For decades, ulcers were thought to be caused by stress and spicy food. Pharmaceutical companies profited from this narrative, developing treatments that managed symptoms rather than addressing root causes. It wasn't until Barry Marshall and Robin Warren discovered the role of Helicobacter pylori that this misconception was corrected, revolutionizing ulcer treatment.

These examples demonstrate the dangers of allowing revenue-driven perceptions to overshadow objective risk assessments. Misjudging or dismissing risks can lead to financial losses, reputational damage, and in some cases, irreversible harm to society.

So, how can companies improve their tolerance to risk while avoiding these pitfalls? The answer lies in equipping decision-makers with accurate, comprehensive information and employing systematic tools to evaluate and mitigate risks. By enhancing knowledge and awareness, companies can make informed decisions that balance opportunity with caution.

Key Steps to Enhance Risk Tolerance in Business:

- *Invest in Data and Research*
  Companies must commit to gathering and analyzing relevant data. This includes market trends, technological advancements, regulatory changes, and consumer behavior. By grounding decisions in empirical evidence, businesses can better understand potential risks and rewards.
- *Utilize Advanced Risk Assessment Tools*
  Implementing models and frameworks, such as Market Pareidolia, the OLI Model, or Transaction Cost Analysis (TCA), can provide structured approaches to identifying and mitigating risks. These tools allow companies to quantify and compare risks systematically, reducing subjective biases.
- *Encourage a Culture of Learning and Adaptability*
  Employees and managers must be encouraged to stay informed and adapt to evolving realities. Regular training, industry seminars, and internal knowledge-sharing sessions can foster a culture that prioritizes learning.
- *Simulate Potential Scenarios*
  Scenario planning and stress testing can help companies anticipate potential challenges and prepare contingency plans. By simulating different market or operational scenarios, businesses can better evaluate their resilience.
- *Seek Expert Advice and Partnerships*
  Engaging consultants, industry experts, or local partners can provide invaluable insights and help bridge knowledge gaps. Collaboration can also mitigate risks by sharing responsibilities and leveraging complementary strengths.
- *Focus on Transparent Communication*
  Transparent communication across all levels of the organization ensures that risks are not ignored or underestimated. Open discussions about potential challenges can lead to collective problem-solving and better decision-making.

As companies build their knowledge base and refine their risk assessment processes, their tolerance for risk naturally increases. When managers understand the real threats to revenue and how to mitigate them, they are more likely to pursue bold, calculated opportunities. This does not mean ignoring risks but rather approaching them with a clear-eyed understanding and a plan to manage them effectively. By increasing their knowledge and aligning perceptions with objective realities, companies can turn fear into action. This proactive approach not only minimizes the likelihood of failure but also positions businesses to cap-italize on opportunities that others might shy away from due to misplaced fears or insufficient preparation. In conclusion, risk tolerance is not an inherent trait, it is cultivated through knowledge, preparation, and strategic foresight. By ad-dressing perception gaps and equipping themselves with the right tools and in-formation, companies can navigate the complex landscape of internationaliza-tion and growth with confidence and clarity.

4.5.3 Reduce the Degree of Dependencies

As discussed previously, every company operates within a framework of de-pendencies that shape its ability and freedom to function effectively and expand into new markets. These dependencies can take many forms, including reliance on specialized workforce, raw material certifications of origin, licenses and per-mits, proprietary technology, and cultural alignment. The degree to which a company depends on these factors determines its level of flexibility (or freedom) to internationalize. The challenge for any company seeking to expand interna-tionally lies in mitigating these dependencies or finding adaptive solutions that allow for greater operational flexibility without compromising on core objec-tives. Addressing dependencies is not a one-size-fits-all endeavor; each situation requires a tailored approach to identify, understand, and resolve specific con-straints:

1. Territorial Dependency
   - *Challenge*: Products or services may be intrinsically tied to a spe-cific geographic origin, such as a certification of origin or a re-gional cultural association.
   - *Solution*: Where feasible, adapt the product to the new market while preserving its core attributes. This might include creating a similar product without violating territorial protection or em-phasizing alternative unique selling points.
2. Specialized Workforce Dependency
   - *Challenge:* Companies relying on highly skilled personnel may find it difficult to replicate operations in regions lacking the re-quired expertise.
   - *Solution:* Invest in comprehensive training programs tailored to local talent, enabling them to meet the company's standards.
3. Technology Dependency
   - *Challenge:* Dependence on proprietary or unavailable technolo-gies in certain markets can hinder expansion.
   - *Solution: Seek alternative technologies that meet similar stand-ards or partner with local firms offering comparable solutions.*

4. Raw Material Dependency
   - *Challenge:* Reliance on specific raw materials can lead to supply chain disruptions, especially when sourcing is geographically constrained.
   - *Solution:* Diversify suppliers to reduce risk or explore alternative materials that meet similar quality and performance standards.
5. Licenses and Permits Dependency
   - *Challenge:* Regulatory requirements for licenses and permits in foreign markets can delay or obstruct internationalization efforts.
   - *Solution:* Engage in proactive negotiations with local authorities to secure extensions or fast-track approvals, leveraging local legal expertise.
6. Cultural Dependency
   - *Challenge:* Products or services tied to specific cultural contexts may fail to resonate with international audiences.
   - *Solution:* Adapt products to align with local cultural preferences while maintaining brand identity.
7. Additional Dependencies
   - *Dependencies can vary widely,* including reliance on local infrastructure, political stability, or existing brand equity in the new market. Each requires a bespoke strategy to ensure successful internationalization.

For companies to decrease their degrees of dependency, they must begin by conducting a comprehensive dependency analysis. This involves identifying all critical dependencies, assessing their impact on internationalization, and prioritizing them based on their significance to the company's objectives. By understanding these constraints, companies can develop actionable strategies to address each dependency effectively. It is important to note that not all dependencies can or should be eliminated. Some may represent competitive advantages, such as patented technologies or unique cultural branding. The goal is not necessarily to remove all dependencies but to manage them in ways that enhance the company's flexibility and resilience. Addressing dependencies should be an integral part of a company's internationalization strategy. This process may require cross-functional collaboration, as different dependencies often span financial, operational, and cultural domains. By integrating dependency management into the broader strategy, companies can proactively mitigate risks and enhance their readiness for new markets.

While dependencies may initially seem like barriers to internationalization, they also present opportunities for innovation and growth. Companies that approach dependency management strategically can not only overcome constraints but also create new avenues for differentiation and value creation.

For instance, a company reliant on specific cultural branding might leverage this dependency to build stronger emotional connections with international consumers. By adopting a systematic and adaptive approach to managing dependencies, businesses can unlock greater freedom to explore new markets, capitalize on global opportunities, and achieve sustainable growth in an increasingly interconnected world.

5 International Business Processes (HOW)

"Internationalization is the process of making the world our marketplace while understanding that each market is uniquely complex." (Dunning, 1993)

Chapter 4 laid the groundwork for understanding the various models of internationalization, dissecting them into four main categories for a more comprehensive grasp. This chapter delves deeper, shifting the focus from the "what" to the "how" of international expansion. Once selected the IB model, there is the need to draft the action plan to achieve it. It is a journey into the intricate processes and decision-making frameworks within which companies navigate their operations beyond domestic borders. As the narrative unfolds, we will explore the existing paradigms and methodologies that businesses employ to project their presence onto the international stage. This exploration is not merely academic; it is a practical guide that dissects the operational aspects of internationalization. From the strategic imperatives that drive a company to seek global markets to the nuanced tactics they employ to penetrate them, each element will be examined. The chapter will articulate how companies, from multinational behemoths to dynamic startups, tailor their strategies to fit the diverse tapestry of global markets. By examining the models of international processes, the discussion will lay bare the complexities and challenges inherent in going global, setting the scene for a deeper understanding of IB strategy in the modern era.

5.1 Uppsala Model

In the Uppsala Internationalization Model, often referred to simply as the Uppsala Model (Figure 5.1), the process of internationalization is simple: Firms gradually intensify their activities in foreign markets. Developed by Johanson and Vahlne in the 1970s, it originates from the observation of Swedish firms and their process of going international. The model is grounded in the behavioral theory of the firm and is predicated on the notion of experiential learning and incremental commitment, which suggests that firms can internationalize by gradually increasing their involvement in foreign markets. It is particularly pertinent to companies with limited international experience, as it advocates a step-by-step approach to entering new markets. This operational model proposes a staged approach, beginning with no regular export activities (indirect commercial IB), followed by export via independent representatives (direct commercial IB), subsequently establishing a foreign sales subsidiary (service IB), and finally, other production facilities abroad (industrial IB). The Uppsala Model is utilized by firms to mitigate the uncertainties associated with internationalization, leveraging experiential learning to inform each successive entry into a new market.

Figure 5.1 Uppsala Model diagram

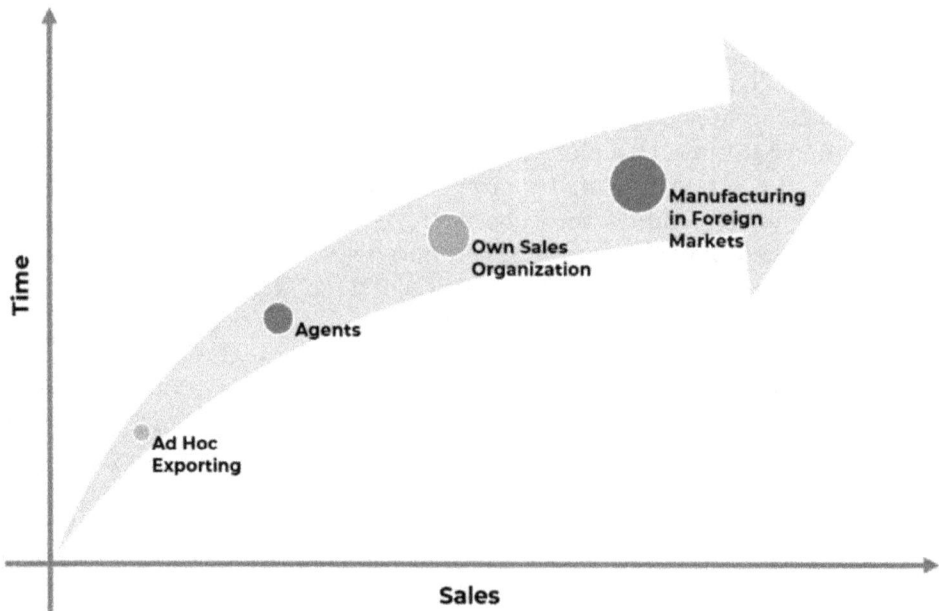

The rationale behind the Uppsala Model is risk minimization through the gradual accumulation of market knowledge and incremental investment. This staged approach allows firms to build their international operations organically, reducing the risk of large-scale failures due to inexperience or lack of market understanding (Table 5.1). The model suggests that as companies learn from their experiences in foreign markets, they are better equipped to make informed decisions and commit greater resources.

Table 5.1 Advantages and Disadvantages of the Upsala Model

Advantages	Disadvantages
Incremental Risk Management: The incremental approach helps firms manage risks gradually	*Slow Pace of Expansion:* An incremental approach may cause firms to miss timely opportunities in fast-moving industries.
Focus on Learning Curve: Emphasizes the importance of experiential learning for sustainable growth.	*Standardization Issues:* Does not account for benefits of standardized global strategies.
Precise Resource Allocation: Allows effective resource allocation, avoiding overextension.	*Missing Emerging Market Dynamics:* May not be as applicable in rapidly changing modern global markets.
Gradual Cultural Adaptation: Slow approach enables thorough adaptation to new cultures and business environments.	*Competitive Disadvantage Approach:* A cautious approach may lead to disadvantages against more aggressive firms.
Strong Relationship Building: Gradual expansion fosters long-term relationships with stakeholders.	*Slow Response to Market Changes:* May hinder quick response to market shifts or innovations.
Strategic Flexibility: Permits adjustments in strategy in response to market changes or new information.	*Resource Underutilization:* Potentially leads to underuse of a firm's capabilities and resources.

The Uppsala Model remains a seminal framework for internationalization processes, offering a cautious and methodical approach to international expansion. While it provides a robust structure for understanding the internationalization process, especially for firms with a conservative risk profile or those in stable and predictable markets, it may not fully encapsulate the dynamics of contemporary global business, where speed and agility are often paramount. Firms must weigh the benefits of a gradual approach against the potential costs of lost opportunities and competitive positioning, adapting the model as necessary to align with their strategic objectives and industry characteristics. This model is particularly well-suited for companies that operate in industries where the incremental accumulation of knowledge and gradual market entry can significantly reduce risks and enhance long-term success. These companies typically have a longer strategic horizon and place a high value on developing strong, enduring relationships with local partners, suppliers, and customers.

Industries that are characterized by complex and specialized products, such as advanced manufacturing, bespoke engineering, and high-tech sectors, often find the Uppsala Model advantageous. These sectors benefit from the model's emphasis on learning and adaptation, which is crucial when navigating the nuanced requirements and regulations of different markets. For instance, companies in the pharmaceuticals and medical devices industries must adhere to stringent regulatory standards that vary greatly between countries, making the careful step-by-step approach advocated by the Uppsala Model highly relevant. Furthermore, businesses in traditional industries such as agriculture, food production, and textiles, which may experience fewer rapid technological changes, can also benefit from this model, as they often require time to understand local consumer preferences and establish a reliable supply chain, which the Uppsala Model supports through its incremental internationalization process. In contrast, industries that operate on fast-paced innovation and rapidly changing consumer trends, such as technology and fashion sectors, may find the slow progression of the Uppsala Model less suitable due to the potential for missed opportunities and the need for swift action to capitalize on market trends.

Example of industries using Uppsala Model for internationalization:

- *Manufacturing Industry*:
  Companies with complex products that require adapting to local regulations, such as those in the automotive or machinery sectors, often use the Uppsala Model to carefully navigate foreign market entries.
- *Professional Services:*
  Firms offering legal, accounting, and consulting services where local market knowledge and relationships are paramount for business, often employ a gradual internationalization strategy.
- *Banking and Financial Services*:
  Banks and financial institutions use this model to incrementally understand and adapt to the regulatory environment of new markets.
- *Pharmaceuticals*:
  The highly regulated nature of pharmaceuticals means companies must learn about different countries' healthcare systems and regulations, making the Uppsala Model a good fit.
- *Heavy Engineering and Construction:*
  These industries involve large-scale projects that require a deep understanding of local construction codes, labor laws, and political climates.
- *Consumer Goods:*
  Particularly those with long product life cycles, where understanding local consumer preferences is essential for adaptation and success.

Example of industries NOT using Uppsala Model for internationalization:

- *Technology and Software*:
  Companies in the tech sector often adopt a "Born Global" approach due to the digital nature of their products, which allows for immediate global reach without the need for incremental steps.

- *Fashion and Apparel*:
  The fast fashion industry is driven by quickly changing trends and demands immediate response to consumer preferences, often requiring a more aggressive and less incremental market entry strategy.

- *Consumer Electronics*:
  With product life cycles becoming shorter and global demand for the latest technology, companies in this sector tend to enter multiple markets simultaneously to maximize their competitive edge.

- *E-commerce*:
  Online retailers and platform-based companies can instantly access global markets without the need for a physical presence, making the gradual approach less relevant.

- *Entertainment and Media*:
  The global distribution of content often happens simultaneously to capture audiences worldwide, bypassing the gradual steps outlined in the Uppsala Model.

- *Telecommunications*:
  The rapid global expansion of telecom companies to capture market share and establish networks is generally not conducive to the slow, sequential approach of the Uppsala Model.

5.2 Born Global Model

The Born Global Model (Figure 5.2) deviates from traditional internationalization theories by focusing on businesses that adopt a global perspective from their inception. This model, which gained traction in the 1990s through the work of scholars such as Oviatt and McDougall (1994, 1996, 2018), pertains to firms that, from or near their founding, seek to derive significant competitive advantage from the use of resources and the sale of outputs in multiple countries. Often driven by entrepreneurial vision and enabled by advancements in technology and communication, these firms are characterized by a borderless approach to markets, seeking immediate entry into the international arena. This model is most applicable to startups and new ventures that operate in rapidly evolving industries such as IT, biotechnology, and advanced manufacturing. These firms typically have a unique set of resources, innovative products, or services that provide them with global reach from the outset. The model is used to describe and strategize the internationalization process of these entities, emphasizing speed and spread rather than the incremental stages of traditional models. It addresses why certain firms are predisposed to internationalize early, often driven by niche markets, global scalability, or the transnational networks of their founders.

Figure 5.2 Born Global Model diagram

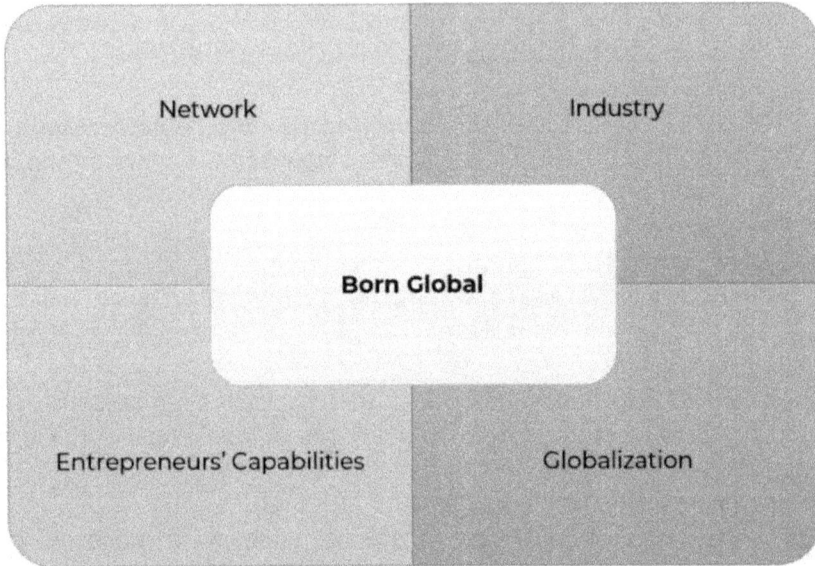

The Born Global Model showcases the potential for firms to be global players from or near their outset. This approach reflects the modern business landscape, where technological advancements and global networks have made immediate international presence a feasible goal for many startups. While the model emphasizes speed and innovation, it also brings to light the challenges of rapid global scaling (Table 5.2). For firms adopting the Born Global pathway, a careful balance of ambitious global vision and strategic market engagement is crucial to achieving sustainable international growth.

Table 5.2 Advantages and Disadvantages of the Born Global Model

Advantages	Disadvantages
Speed to Market: Capitalizes on swift entry into multiple markets, often outpacing competitors who internationalize more gradually.	*Resource Constraints*: Early-stage ventures may face resource limitations, making it difficult to sustain a presence across multiple markets.
Innovative Approach: These firms are agile, innovative, and responsive to changes in the global market landscape.	*Market Overextension*: Rapid expansion can lead to overextension, where the firm cannot effectively manage its international operations.
Global Reach: Born Globals leverages global networks, technological advancements, and cross-	*Cultural and Regulatory Challenges*: Born Globals might underestimate the complexity of navigating diverse cultural, regulatory, and legal environments.

border transactions to maximize their market presence.

Cost Efficiency: Early and rapid internationalization allows firms to quickly achieve economies of scale and spread costs over a larger market base.	*Strategic Vulnerability*: The focus on rapid internationalization may lead to strategic missteps due to a lack of deep market knowledge
Flexibility in Strategy: Ability to pivot and adapt strategies quickly in response to international market feedback.	*High Initial Costs*: Despite cost efficiencies, the initial outlay for establishing multiple international operations can be substantial.
Attractiveness to Investors: Demonstrating a global vision and early international success can attract investment and partnerships.	*Risk of Dilution*: Rapid global expansion may dilute brand identity and core values if not managed carefully.

As stated, the Born Global Model for internationalization is a distinctive approach that suits companies with a vision to penetrate and operate in multiple international markets right from or near their inception. This model is particularly fitting for businesses that operate in sectors where the barriers to international entry are low, and where products or services have a global appeal without significant adaptation. Industries such as technology and software, digital media, biotech, and specialized consumer goods are prime examples where companies often adopt a Born Global strategy. These sectors benefit from the rapid dissemination of innovations and the global digital infrastructure that allows for immediate international reach and operations. Companies that thrive as Born Globals typically possess innovative products or solutions with a universal demand, high levels of entrepreneurial orientation, and the ability to leverage digital platforms for marketing, sales, and distribution. The agility to adapt to different market needs quickly and the foresight to build international networks from the outset are also crucial traits. These firms are usually led by globally minded entrepreneurs who understand the importance of cross-cultural competence and have a clear vision for their international footprint.

On the other hand, industries that are heavily regulated require significant capital investment for market entry or have a strong dependency on localized business relationships and practices might find the Born Global Model challenging. For instance, traditional manufacturing, large-scale agriculture, and utilities may not fit well with this model due to the high costs of establishing operations abroad and the slower pace of entering foreign markets. Similarly, businesses that rely heavily on understanding nuanced local consumer behavior, such as certain segments of the retail and food and beverage industries, may benefit more from a gradual internationalization strategy that allows for in-depth market learning and adaptation. The Born Global Model favors industries and companies that are innovative-driven, operate on digital or global platforms, and can manage the complexities of operating in diverse cultural and regulatory environments from an early stage. Companies outside these criteria may need to evaluate alternative internationalization strategies that better suit their operational, financial, and market-specific characteristics.

Example of industries using Uppsala Model for internationalization:

- *Technology and Software*:
  Companies in this sector often target global markets immediately, leveraging digital distribution.
- *Digital Marketing and Social Media Services*:
  The universal appeal and digital nature allow for immediate global reach.
- *Biotechnology and Pharmaceuticals*:
  Start-ups in this field frequently aim for global markets due to the universal need for healthcare innovations.
- *E-commerce*:
  Online retail platforms can serve global customers from day one without the need for physical presence.
- *Mobile Applications and Gaming*:
  The digital distribution of apps and games enables developers to target a worldwide audience instantly.
- *Renewable Energy Technology*:
  Innovators in clean energy often seek global partnerships and markets to scale up quickly.

Example of industries NOT using Uppsala Model for internationalization:

- *Traditional Manufacturing*:
  Companies may face challenges in scaling production and navigating trade barriers quickly.
- *Local Retail and Food Services*:
  These businesses often depend on physical presence and local tastes, making global scaling more complex.
- *Utilities and Infrastructure*:
  High capital investment and heavy regulation make rapid international expansion challenging.
- *Real Estate*:
- Market-specific knowledge and regulatory environments limit the ability to go global from inception.
- *Heavy Industry and Construction*:
  The need for substantial physical assets and adherence to local regulations complicate immediate global operations.
- *Agriculture*:

Local climate conditions, regulatory environments, and supply chain complexities often necessitate a more localized approach.

5.3 Network Process Model

The Network Process Model (Figure 5.3) of internationalization represents a paradigm shift from traditional models, focusing on the establishment and development of relationships within networks as the primary driver of international expansion. This approach, emerging prominently in the 1980s and 1990s, particularly through the work of researchers such as Johanson and Mattsson (1989), suggests that firms are embedded in networks of relationships which influence and enable their internationalization processes. Unlike the Uppsala Model, which emphasizes incremental market entry based on experiential learning, the Network Process Model considers the firm's position within interorganizational networks as crucial to its international endeavors.

Figure 5.3 Network process model diagram

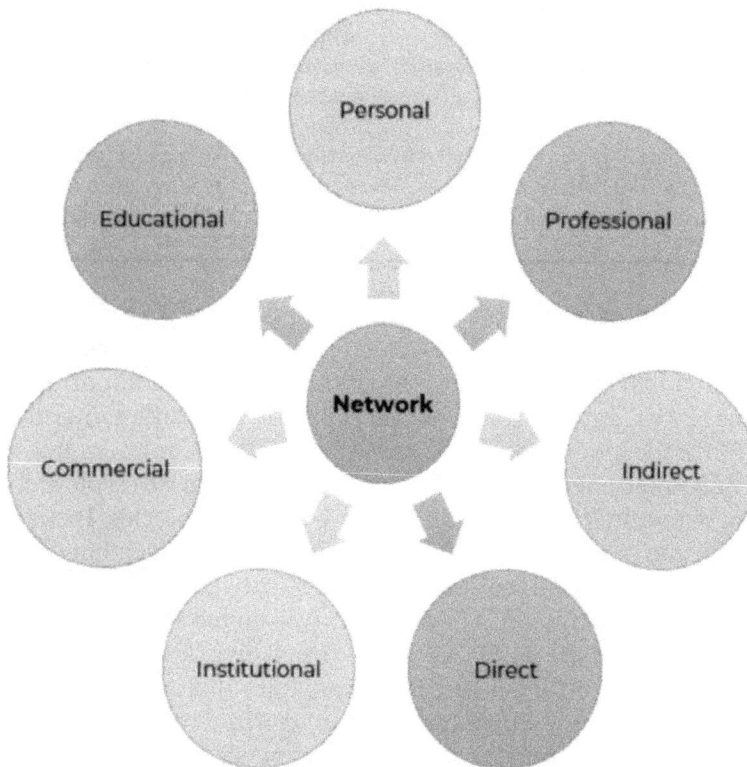

This model is used when a firm is looking to leverage existing relationships or form new ones to facilitate entry and expansion in foreign markets. It is especially relevant in industries where business networks are complex and well-established, such as manufacturing or B2B services. Firms with strong network positions can utilize their connections for support, information, and resources, which can lower the entry barriers in new markets (Table 5.3). The model is also applied in situations where informal structures, trust, and interfirm collaborations are decisive factors for successful internationalization.

Table 5.3 Advantages and Disadvantages of the Network Process Model

Advantages	Disadvantages
Resource Leverage: Firms can leverage resources and capabilities of network partners, reducing the need for direct investment.	*Dependence on Relationships*: Overreliance on networks can lead to vulnerability if relationships falter.
Reduced Uncertainty: Networks provide access to localized knowledge, reducing market uncertainty.	*Network Rigidity*: Existing networks may resist change, limiting adaptability to new market conditions.
Speed of Market Entry: Strong network ties can accelerate market entry and establishment.	*Limited Control*: Firms may have limited control over internationalization, influenced by network partners' actions.
Innovation and Learning: Networks facilitate the flow of new ideas and innovation, aiding competitive advantage.	*Exclusivity and Access Issues*: New entrants may struggle to penetrate established networks, creating entry barriers.

The Network Process Model offers a nuanced understanding of internationalization, highlighting the significance of relationships and networks in today's interconnected global economy. This model underscores the importance of strategic alliances, JVs, and the role of social capital in facilitating international expansion. While the model provides a robust framework for leveraging collective resources and knowledge, firms must navigate the complexities of inter-firm dynamics and maintain flexibility within their network strategies. In an era where collaboration and connectivity define competitive advantage, the Network Process Model serves as a vital lens through which firms can strategize their global growth initiatives. The model is particularly well-suited for companies that operate in sectors where strategic alliances, partnerships, and relational networks play a crucial role in business success. Companies that benefit the most from this model typically operate in industries characterized by high levels of innovation, complex value chains, and a significant dependence on specialized knowledge or technologies. These include the technology and software industry, biotechnology, renewable energy, and advanced manufacturing sectors. In these fields, the ability to leverage resources, share knowledge, and accelerate market entry through established relationships can provide a substantial competitive advantage. Firms that thrive on innovation and continuous learning find the network model especially advantageous as it facilitates the flow of new ideas and best practices across borders.

Conversely, companies that might not fit well with the Network Process Model are those in industries with less emphasis on collaborative innovation and more on direct competition or where the market entry and expansion strategies are heavily regulated and standardized. Such industries might include traditional manufacturing, where competitive advantage is often based on cost leadership or scale rather than innovation or flexibility. Similarly, sectors such as mining and utilities, which are capital-intensive with long investment cycles and are often subject to stringent regulatory requirements, may find the network model less applicable due to the limited scope for partnership-driven market entry. Additionally, industries that are highly sensitive to brand identity and consumer perception, such as luxury goods and consumer brands, might also be cautious in employing the Network Process Model. In these sectors, the potential dilution of brand identity through extensive networking and reliance on partners can pose a significant risk, making a more controlled and direct approach to internationalization preferable.

Example of industries using the Network Process Model for internationalization:

- *Technology and Software*:
  Rapid innovation cycles and the global nature of the tech market encourage collaboration.
- *Biotechnology and Pharmaceuticals*:
  Partnerships are crucial for R&D, clinical trials, and navigating regulatory landscapes.
- *Renewable Energy*:
  Collaborations help in sharing technology, research, and accessing new markets.
- *Consulting and Professional Services*:
  Networking builds client bases and partnerships for specialized knowledge exchange.
- *Digital Media and Entertainment*:
  Content sharing, coproduction, and distribution benefit from strong networks.
- *Fashion and Apparel*:
  Fast fashion and luxury brands alike leverage networks for trends forecasting, manufacturing, and global distribution.

Example of industries NOT using Uppsala Model for internationalization:

- *Extractive Industries (Mining, Oil & Gas):*
  Capital-intensive with long investment cycles, often regulated with a focus on direct investments.
- *Utilities and Energy Infrastructure:*
  Heavily regulated with significant capital and operational requirements, limiting the effectiveness of network-based strategies.
- *Heavy Manufacturing:*
  Competitive advantage often lies in scale, cost leadership, and operational efficiencies rather than networking.
- *Agriculture and Basic Food Production:*
  While there are exceptions, much of this sector is characterized by traditional practices and direct market access.
- Transportation and Logistics:
  Large-scale infrastructure and regulatory compliance often necessitate direct investment and control.
- *Telecommunications:*
- High capital expenditure and regulatory barriers create an environment where direct investment is often preferred over networking strategies.

5.4 Eclectic Paradigm (OLI Model)

The Eclectic Paradigm (Figure 5.4), also known as the OLI Model, digs into a specific internationalization model: FDIs. It presents a comprehensive framework for understanding the factors that influence a company's decision to engage in an FDI and the choice of market entry modes. Introduced by John Dunning in the late 1970s (Dunning, 1980), this model posits that three distinct advantages must converge for a firm to successfully internationalize: Ownership (O), Location (L), and Internalization (I) advantages.

- *Advantages of Ownership:*
  Ownership advantages refer to the firm-specific assets that a company possesses, which could include proprietary technologies, IP rights, organizational competencies, or unique products and services. These advantages make it possible for a firm to compete in foreign markets despite the additional costs associated with operating at a distance.
- *Location Advantages:*
  Location advantages are the benefits a firm gain by doing activities in a particular foreign market. These benefits may arise from factors such as favorable economic policies, access to natural resources, skilled labor, technological clusters, or proximity to customers.

- *Internalization Advantages*:
  Internalization advantages are the gains obtained from transferring a firm's unique assets across borders within the organization rather than through partnerships or licensing. This dimension of the paradigm emphasizes the value of controlling and coordinating activities to maximize efficiencies, protect proprietary knowledge, and better respond to foreign market conditions.

Figure 5.4 Eclectic Paradigm (OLI Model) diagram

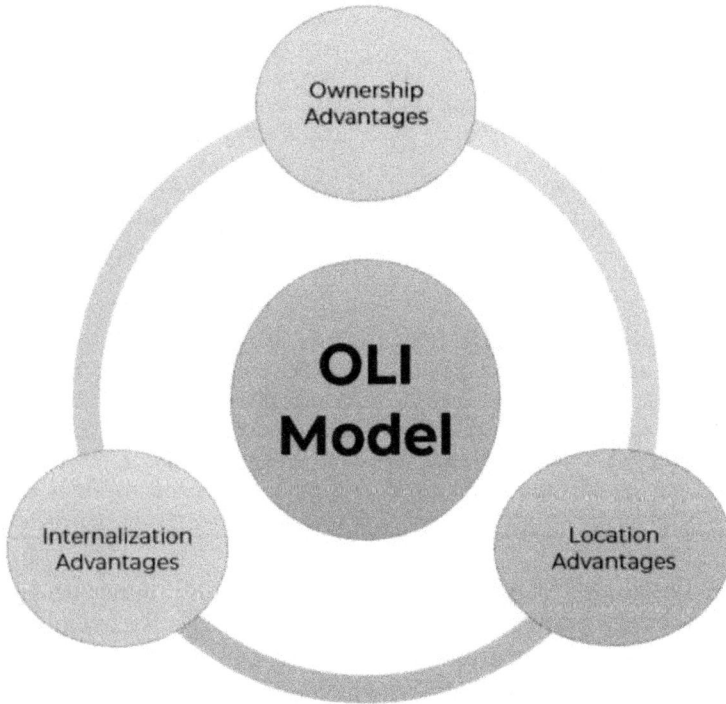

The Eclectic Paradigm is used when a firm is considering FDI as a method of internationalization. It is a strategic tool to evaluate the benefits and costs of entering specific markets and the modes of activity that could range from wholly owned subsidiaries to JVs or strategic alliances. The model serves as a comprehensive guide for firms to assess their readiness and the potential for success in international ventures (Table 5.4).

Table 5.4 Advantages and Disadvantages of the OLI Model

Advantages	Disadvantages
Comprehensive Framework: Offers a holistic view of internationalization, integrating ownership, location, and internalization factors.	*Complexity*: The model's comprehensive nature can make it complex and challenging to apply in practice.
Strategic Flexibility: Enables firms to assess various internationalization strategies (e.g., exporting, FDI, licensing) based on OLI advantages.	*Dynamic Market Conditions*: May not fully account for rapid changes in global market conditions and the digital economy.
Risk Mitigation: By considering OLI factors, firms can better identify and mitigate risks associated with international markets	*Overemphasis on Large Firms*: Initially focused more on the capabilities of large MNCs, potentially overlooking the nuances of smaller firms or startups.
Competitive Advantage: Facilitates the identification of firm-specific advantages that can be leveraged internationally.	*Static Analysis*: While offering deep insights, it can be perceived as static, not always capturing the evolving nature of IB.
Market Selection: Helps in determining the most suitable markets for entry or expansion based on location advantages.	*Resource Intensive*: Thorough analysis of OLI factors requires significant resources and expertise, which may be a barrier for some firms.
Adaptation and Learning: Encourages adaptation and learning, as firms assess internal and external factors affecting international operations.	*Potential for Oversimplification*: The need to categorize complex internationalization decisions into three broad categories can lead to oversimplification.

The Eclectic Paradigm (OLI) Model remains a vital tool in the strategic arsenal of firms considering internationalization through FDI. By examining ownership, location, and internalization advantages in concert, the model helps firms make informed decisions about where, when, and how to establish a presence in foreign markets. Despite some limitations, particularly in rapidly changing sectors, the Eclectic Paradigm's comprehensive approach provides valuable insights into the complex interplay of factors that drive IB strategy. This model is particularly well-suited for companies that possess unique competitive advantages, such as proprietary technology, patents, or specialized knowledge that can be leveraged internationally. It caters to businesses that are evaluating FDIs as a mode of international expansion, allowing them to systematically assess their internal strengths, the potential of various locations, and the benefits of controlling their international operations versus licensing or exporting. Industries where the OLI Model finds significant applicability include high-tech sectors, pharmaceuticals, manufacturing, and services with a strong IP component. Companies in these fields often have clear ownership advantages that can be exploited globally. Furthermore, firms looking to expand in countries with distinct location advantages, such as low labor costs, specific resource availability, or strategic market access, will find the OLI framework useful in aligning their internationalization strategies with these geographic benefits.

Conversely, the OLI Model might be less fitting for companies operating in highly dynamic or digital-centric industries where the physical location is less relevant to their business model. For example, digital services, online platforms, and e-commerce businesses may find the location aspect less critical, given their virtual presence. Similarly, startups and SMEs with limited resources and international experience might struggle with the comprehensive analysis required by the OLI Model, especially if they lack clear ownership advantages or face challenges in internalizing their operations abroad. Industries heavily reliant on rapid market changes, such as fashion retail or consumer electronics, might also find the model's structured approach less accommodating to their need for agility and flexibility in international markets. For these businesses, models emphasizing network effects, digital strategies, or lean internationalization approaches might be more appropriate. The OLI Model serves as a powerful tool for firms that can clearly identify and leverage their unique assets in a structured international expansion but may be less applicable for businesses whose competitive edge is less dependent on proprietary advantages or those operating in rapidly evolving digital marketplaces.

Example of industries using OLI Model for internationalization:

- *Manufacturing*:
  Firms with proprietary technologies or production processes that confer ownership advantages.
- *Pharmaceuticals*:
  Companies that rely on patents and high R&D investments as ownership advantages to enter foreign markets.
- *Energy*:
  Especially in oil, gas, and renewable energy sectors where location advantages are crucial.
- *Banking and Financial Services*:
  Firms leveraging ownership advantages in brand reputation and proprietary algorithms, considering location advantages for regulatory reasons.
- *Automotive*:
  Companies that integrate advanced technologies and brand reputation (ownership advantages) with strategic manufacturing and assembly locations worldwide.

- *Agribusiness*:
  Firms exploiting location advantages related to specific agricultural conditions, along with proprietary technology in seed genetics or farming techniques.

Example of industries NOT using OLI Model for internationalization:

- *Digital Services and E-commerce*:
  These sectors often transcend geographical boundaries, making location advantages less relevant.
- *Startup Tech Companies*:
  Especially those in the app development or SaaS sectors, where rapid scalability often depends more on digital infrastructure than on traditional OLI factors.
- *Fashion Retail:*
  Fast-changing market trends and consumer preferences may not align well with the static analysis of OLI advantages.
- *Local Service Providers*:
  Such as restaurants or local retail, where business models are inherently tied to specific locations without a clear path to internationalization.
- *Content Creation and Media*:
  Where the digital distribution of content can bypass traditional location and ownership considerations.
- *Professional Services (Small Firms):*
  Small consultancy or legal practices might not have distinct ownership advantages that can be leveraged internationally without substantial adaptation.

5.5 Transaction Cost Analysis (TCA) Model

The TCA Model (Figure 5.5) is a pivotal economic theory that describes a firm's rationale behind the choice of market entry strategies based on the concept of minimizing transaction costs associated with IB activities. Developed by Ronald Coase in the 1960s (Coase, 1960) and expanded by Oliver Williamson in the 1970s (Williamson, 1979) and 1980s (Williamson, 1989), TCA posits that firms will seek to internalize operations when external transaction costs are higher than the costs of internal governance.

Figure 5.5 Transaction Cost Analysis (TCA) Model diagram

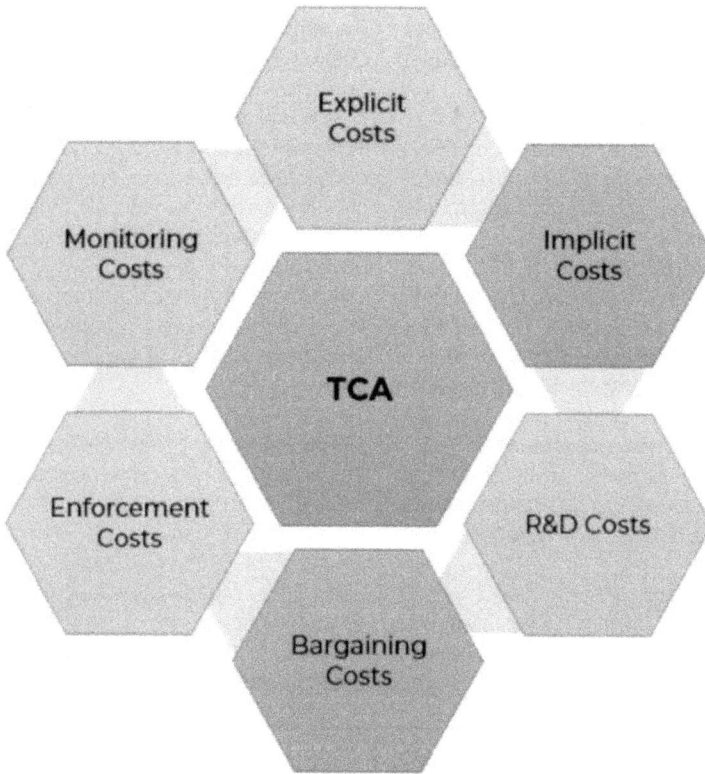

The TCA Model is utilized when firms are determining whether to engage in foreign markets through exports, contractual agreements, or by establishing subsidiaries; decisions primarily influenced by the costs of negotiating, monitoring, and enforcing contracts in the international context. The core idea is to optimize the efficiency of operations by considering costs such as search and information costs, bargaining costs, and enforcement costs (Table 5.5). When these external market transaction costs are prohibitive, a firm may opt for direct investment to internalize operations and minimize these costs.

Table 5.5 Advantages and Disadvantages of the TCA Model

Advantages	Disadvantages
Cost Efficiency Focus: TCA helps firms focus on cost efficiency in international operations, promoting	*Assumption of Rationality*: TCA assumes that all parties are rational and that costs can be accurately measured,

careful analysis of various market entry costs.

Strategic Decision-Making:
It provides a structured approach to strategic decision-making regarding market entry and mode of operation.

Risk Management:
By considering the transaction costs, firms can better manage risks associated with contractual uncertainties and market imperfections.

Flexibility in Approach:
TCA allows firms to choose the most efficient governance structures for their international operations, be it through market transactions or hierarchical control within the firm.

Informed Outsourcing Decisions:
TCA aids in deciding whether to outsource or keep activities in-house by analyzing transactional costs associated with outsourcing.

Enhanced Contractual Efficiency:
Encourages the creation of more efficient contracts by focusing on the minimization of transaction costs.

which may not always reflect real-world complexities.

Potential for Over-Internalization:
Firms might overestimate external transaction costs, leading to unnecessary internalization and potential inefficiencies.

Neglect of Strategic Variables:
TCA may overlook strategic variables such as competitive advantage, firm capabilities, and industry forces that can also influence internationalization decisions.

Static Nature of Analysis:
The model may not adequately account for the dynamic nature of international markets and the evolution of transaction costs over time.

Underestimation of Non-transactional Costs:
There can be an underestimation of non-transactional costs like quality control and the impact on company culture when using TCA.

Difficulty in Measuring Intangible Assets and Costs:
TCA often struggles to measure intangible assets and the costs of social relationships, which can be crucial in IB.

The TCA Model offers a compelling lens through which to examine internationalization decisions, emphasizing the importance of understanding and managing the costs associated with cross-border operations. It provides a pragmatic framework that prioritizes economic efficiency in the face of complex international market structures. Despite certain limitations, such as its somewhat static and rationalistic assumptions, TCA remains an influential model that can guide firms in navigating the cost implications of their global expansion strategies.

Example of industries using TCA for internationalization:

- *Franchising (Fast Food Chains):*
  TCA is critical in determining whether to operate through franchising or company-owned outlets, balancing costs of monitoring franchisees with operational efficiency (e.g., McDonald's, Domino's, and Subway).

- *Manufacturing*:
  Manufacturing firms assess whether to outsource production or set up their own plants abroad, weighing transaction costs like contract enforcement against the costs of internalizing operations (e.g., Nike evaluating contract manufacturing vs. owned factories).
- *Automotive*:
  Automotive companies often rely on TCA to decide between in-house production of components or outsourcing to suppliers in foreign markets, evaluating risks like opportunism or quality control (e.g., Toyota's supplier integration).
- *Retail Supply Chains*:
  Retailers such as Walmart use TCA to assess whether to manage supply chains internally or rely on local third-party distributors in foreign markets.
- *Oil and Gas*:
  Companies evaluate transaction costs in international JVs for oil exploration, ensuring they mitigate risks associated with partner opportunism and asset specificity (e.g., ExxonMobil in joint operations).
- *Technology Hardware*:
  Firms such as Apple use TCA to determine the costs and risks of outsourcing hardware manufacturing versus establishing foreign subsidiaries (e.g., Foxconn partnerships vs. direct Apple factories).

Example of industries NOT using TCA for internationalization:

- *Digital Services and SaaS*:
  These industries often operate globally without significant transaction costs tied to location-specific factors, relying on digital platforms instead (e.g., Zoom or Dropbox).
- *Content Creation and Streaming Media*:
  Platforms such as Netflix expand internationally without heavy reliance on TCA, as digital distribution minimizes asset specificity and contract enforcement costs.
- *Fashion and Luxury Brands*:
  Brands such as Zara often expand using wholly owned subsidiaries or licensing agreements without deep analysis of transaction costs, as their decisions are driven by market responsiveness.
- *E-commerce*:
  Companies such as Amazon rely on scalable digital infrastructure rather than transaction cost calculations to decide on market entry, focusing on consumer demand and logistics optimization instead.

- *Consulting and Professional Services*:
  Small firms or niche consulting practices internationalize by leveraging reputation or partnerships, where TCA's focus on asset specificity and monitoring costs is less relevant.
- *Independent Artists or Small Content Creators*:
  These entities often reach global audiences through digital platforms (e.g., YouTube or Etsy), bypassing the need for TCA in decision-making.

5.6 Porter's Diamond

Porter's Diamond Model (Figure 5.6), developed by Michael E. Porter in 1990, is a framework designed to analyze the competitive advantage of nations and regions in the context of IB. The model provides insights into why certain industries within specific countries are more competitive on a global scale than others. By examining the factors that contribute to a country's competitive edge, the Diamond Model helps businesses understand the potential opportunities and challenges of internationalization in specific markets. Porter's model is especially valuable for companies looking to expand internationally, as it offers a structured approach to assess how well-suited a country is for supporting and sustaining industry competitiveness. Porter's Diamond Model comprises four interrelated components that together shape the competitive environment within a country. These components are:

1. *Factor Conditions*:
   This refers to the nation's endowments in terms of natural resources, skilled labor, infrastructure, and technological capabilities. Factor conditions play a crucial role in determining the competitive advantages of a country's industries. For instance, a country rich in natural resources might have a competitive edge in industries like mining or agriculture, while a country with a highly educated workforce might excel in technology or financial services.
2. *Demand Conditions*:
   This component looks at the nature of home-market demand for a particular industry's products or services. A sophisticated and demanding local customer base can drive companies to innovate and improve their offerings, thereby enhancing their global competitiveness. For example, a country with a high demand for cutting-edge consumer electronics can foster a competitive electronics industry.

3. *Related and Supporting Industries*:
   The presence of supplier industries and related sectors that are internationally competitive can enhance a country's competitive advantage. When related industries cluster together, they can benefit from synergies, shared technologies, and a skilled labor pool. For instance, the automotive industry benefits from strong steel production and advanced engineering services.

4. *Firm Strategy, Structure, and Rivalry*:
   This dimension examines how companies are organized, their management practices, and the nature of domestic competition. Intense local competition can drive innovation and efficiency, leading to stronger global competitiveness. For example, a country with numerous competing firms in a particular industry might see those firms continuously pushing for improvements, thereby enhancing their global standing.

Figure 5.6 Porter's Diamond Model diagram

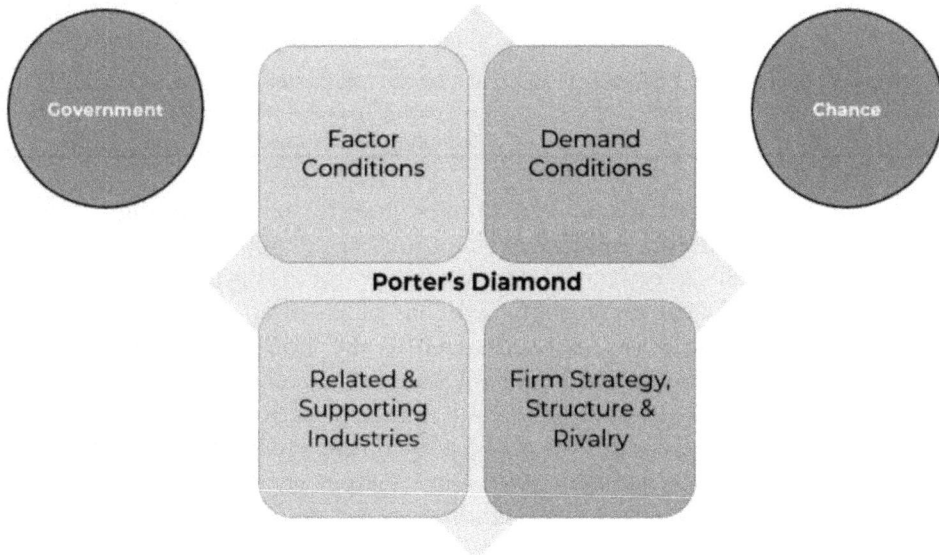

In addition to these four components, Porter also identified two additional factors that can influence the diamond:

1. *Government:*
   Government policies can either enhance or hinder the national competitive advantage by affecting the four components mentioned above. For example, government investments in education can improve factor conditions, while trade policies can influence demand conditions.

2. *Chance:*

    External events that are beyond the control of firms, such as natural disasters, major technological innovations, or geopolitical shifts, can also impact the competitive advantage of nations.

Table 5.6 Advantages and Disadvantages of the Porter's Diamond Model

Advantages	Disadvantages
Provides a comprehensive framework for analyzing national competitiveness.	May oversimplify complex global dynamics.
Emphasizes the importance of local conditions in shaping global success.	Assumes that national borders are key to competitive advantage, which may not always be the case in a globalized world.
Encourages companies to consider domestic factors before international expansion.	May not fully account for the influence of MNCs and global supply chains.
Helps identify the strengths and weaknesses of a country's industries.	Can be less effective in industries where global factors outweigh national conditions.
Useful for strategic planning and identifying areas for government intervention.	The model's focus on national competitiveness may not be applicable to all industries.
Can guide government policies to support competitive industries.	It may not adequately address industries that are highly dependent on international collaboration and resources.

While Porter's Diamond Model is a valuable tool for understanding the competitive dynamics within a country, it is not universally applicable across all industries. The model's effectiveness depends largely on the nature of the industry in question and how closely it aligns with the national conditions that Porter emphasizes. Some industries are well-suited to the model's framework, while others may not find it as useful. Porter's Diamond Model offers a powerful lens through which to view the competitive advantage of nations, particularly in industries where national conditions play a critical role. However, its applicability varies depending on the industry, with some sectors benefiting more from the model's insights than others. Understanding these nuances allows companies to better leverage Porter's Diamond Model when planning their internationalization strategies (Table 5.6).

Example of industries using Potter's Diamond for internationalization:

* *Automotive Manufacturing:*
  The industry benefits from strongly related and supporting industries such as steel production, engineering services, and advanced manufacturing technology.

- *Agriculture*:
  Countries with favorable natural resources and climate conditions can gain a competitive advantage in agriculture.
- *Consumer Electronics*:
  Demand conditions in technologically advanced countries can drive innovation and global competitiveness in this sector.
- *Pharmaceuticals:*
  Strong factor conditions such as skilled labor, advanced research facilities, and related industries like biotechnology can enhance competitiveness.
- *Financial Services*:
  Countries with sophisticated financial markets, regulatory frameworks, and a well-educated workforce can excel in this industry.
- *Aerospace*:
  The presence of advanced engineering, innovation-driven demand conditions, and supportive government policies can make certain countries globally competitive in aerospace.

Example of industries NOT using Potter's Diamond for internationalization:

1. *E-commerce*:
   Highly dependent on global digital infrastructure and less influenced by national boundaries.
2. *Oil and Gas*:
   Global market dynamics and international corporations play a more significant role than national conditions.
3. *Fast Fashion*:
   Relies heavily on global supply chains and international consumer trends, making it less tied to any single nation's competitive advantage.
4. *Telecommunications:*
   Global networks and technologies often outweigh the influence of national factor conditions.
5. *Outsourcing and Offshoring*:
   Driven by global cost arbitrage and international talent pools rather than domestic conditions.
6. *Software Development*:
   Frequently influenced by global demand and collaboration, with talent and resources distributed internationally.

6 The Local Partner: Importance and Selection Methodology

"The effectiveness of international business mentoring is significantly enhanced when mentors possess a deep understanding of the local context and culture, underscoring the importance of selecting partners with local expertise." (Purcell & Scheyvens, 2015)

As businesses expand beyond their home markets, the complexities of operating in foreign environments become increasingly apparent. Internationalization offers tremendous opportunities for growth, but it also presents significant challenges that can hinder success if not carefully managed. In previous chapters, we have analyzed tools for market selection (where), for mode selection (what) and models for how to internationalize. However, another effective strategy for mitigating these challenges is to establish a partnership with a local entity in the target market. Having a local partner can provide invaluable insights, resources, and support that are crucial for navigating the intricacies of a new market. Moreover, in today's global business landscape, having a local partner is becoming not just an advantage but a necessity, driven by both regulatory requirements and ethical considerations.

Every market has its unique characteristics, shaped by cultural, economic, legal, and political factors. Understanding these dynamics is essential not only for any company looking to succeed internationally, but to gain a competitive advantage over new entrants. A local partner brings firsthand knowledge of these market-specific factors, enabling a company to make informed decisions and avoid common pitfalls. Local partners understand the cultural nuances that influence consumer behavior, the regulatory landscape that governs business operations, and the economic trends that drive market demand. This deep understanding allows a company to adapt its strategies to better align with local conditions, thereby increasing the likelihood of success. For example, a company entering a new market may face challenges related to consumer preferences, which can vary widely from one country to another. A local partner can provide insights into these preferences, helping the company tailor its products or services to meet local needs. Similarly, understanding local business practices and regulatory requirements can be complex, particularly in markets with strin-gent legal frameworks. A local partner can guide the company through these complexities, ensuring compliance and reducing the risk of costly legal issues.

6.1 Strengths and Weaknesses of Having a Local Partnership

6.1.1 Navigating Regulatory and Legal Requirements

One of the most daunting aspects of internationalization is navigating the regu-latory and legal requirements of the target market. Each country has its own set of laws and regulations (both written and unwritten) that govern business activ-ities, from labor laws and tax codes to environmental regulations, IP rights, and social dynamics. Noncompliance with these regulations can result in severe pen-alties, including fines, legal action, discreditation, and even the loss of business licenses. For example, many countries are increasingly tightening their local content laws to incentivize or even mandate the involvement of local partners in business ventures. These regulations are designed to ensure that foreign compa-nies contribute to the local economy and that the benefits of international in-vestment are shared with local stakeholders. In many cases, having a local part-ner is no longer just an option but a legal requirement. This shift makes it im-perative for companies to establish strong partnerships with local entities, to comply with these regulations and to gain the necessary approvals to operate in these markets. Furthermore, a local partner, familiar with the legal landscape, can help a company navigate these regulations more effectively. They can assist with obtaining necessary licenses and permits, ensuring compliance with local laws, and managing relationships with government agencies. Additionally, a lo-cal partner can provide advice on best practices for structuring contracts, man-aging risks, and protecting IP in the target market. This support can be invalu-able for companies that lack the expertise or resources to manage these com-plexities on their own.

6.1.2 Building Relationships and Trust

Markets are created by people and managed by people (customers, suppliers, companies, governments, etc.), therefore, penetrating a market with success means understanding the human nature of markets leading operations to rely on relationships (this is more evident for adolescent and adult markets) and trust (mainly for senior markets). Building these interactions can be challenging for foreign companies, particularly in cultures where business is conducted based on personal connections and long-standing social embeddedness. A local part-ner can play a crucial role in facilitating these connections, leveraging their existing network to help the company establish credibility and trust with key stakeholders. For example, in markets where business is heavily influenced by government relationships (adolescent markets and some younger adult markets), a local partner with established connections can be instrumental in securing government contracts or navigating regulatory approvals. Similarly, in markets where consumer trust is paramount (older adult markets and senior markets), a local partner can help build brand credibility by endorsing the company's products or services and facilitating a positive word-of-mouth. Furthermore, a local partner can assist in managing public relations and communication strategies, ensuring that the company's messaging resonates with local audiences and aligns with cultural expectations. This is particularly important in markets where brand reputation can be easily influenced by public perception.

6.1.3 Overcoming Operational Challenges

Internationalization often presents a range of operational challenges, from establishing supply chains and distribution networks to managing local human resources and adapting to unfamiliar technologies. A local partner can play a pivotal role in addressing these challenges, offering invaluable on-the-ground expertise and resources that streamline operations and reduce costs. For example, a local partner can assist with sourcing materials and suppliers, managing logistics, and overcoming local infrastructure challenges. Additionally, they can recruit and manage local talent, ensuring access to skilled workers who possess a deep understanding of the local business environment. A significant advantage of partnering with an already established local entity is the ability to accelerate the operational setup. A local partner with an existing business infrastructure can reduce the foreign company's time to become operational, minimizing the risks and complexities of building operations from scratch. This can be especially beneficial in navigating bureaucratic hurdles, as local partners often have established relationships and an understanding of regulatory frameworks, expediting compliance with local laws and permits. Moreover, a local partner can offer insights into local technology trends and assist in adapting the company's operations to meet local standards and expectations. By leveraging the established networks, resources, and expertise of a local partner, a foreign company can not only reduce operational risks but also enhance its ability to integrate seamlessly into the new market. This collaborative approach increases the likelihood of success in the internationalization process while allowing the company to focus on strategic growth rather than operational difficulties.

6.1.4 Enhancing Competitive Advantage and Ethical Responsibility

In highly competitive markets, having a local partner can provide a significant advantage: It can offer insights into the competitive landscape, helping the company identify opportunities and threats that may not be immediately apparent, or hidden to a foreign eye. They can also assist in developing strategies to differentiate the company's offerings and position the brand effectively within the local market by correctly interpreting local cultures and traditions. Moreover, a local partner can provide access to local distribution channels, marketing networks, and customer bases, enabling the company to reach its target audience more effectively. This can be particularly valuable in markets where foreign companies may struggle to gain market share due to strong domestic competition or consumer preference for local brands. Beyond gaining a competitive advantage, partnering with a local entity reflects a commitment to ethical business practices and sustainable internationalization by enhancing local content policies. At the core of this approach lies the principle of knowledge transfer to local communities, a vital element in creating a mutually beneficial relationship between the guest (foreign company) and the host market. While companies reap the rewards of accessing new markets, they bear a responsibility to contribute meaningfully to the economic and social development of the regions they enter. Knowledge transfer involves more than simply training employees; it is about empowering local talent and stakeholders with the skills, tools, and expertise needed to thrive in a competitive global economy. This includes developing technical skills, managerial capabilities, and innovative approaches that can elevate the local workforce and strengthen the region's economic fabric. For instance, companies operating in industries such as manufacturing or technology can introduce advanced production techniques or IT systems, significantly enhancing local productivity and innovation capacity.

This ethical dimension of internationalization has tangible benefits for both the company and the local community. For the company, fostering knowledge transfer builds goodwill and trust among local stakeholders, including employees, partners, customers, and regulators. It positions the business as a socially responsible entity that values collaboration and shared growth. Such efforts can enhance the company's reputation and brand loyalty, creating a more stable and supportive business environment. Furthermore, skilled local employees can reduce the reliance on costly expatriates, while a well-trained workforce contributes to operational efficiency and long-term sustainability. On the community side, knowledge transfer ensures that the benefits of international expansion are not concentrated solely within the foreign company but are equitably distributed. By empowering local workers and businesses, the host market experiences economic growth, inequality reduction, and an increase in living standards. This creates a virtuous cycle, where the strengthened local economy, in turn, generates greater demand for the company's products and services. Additionally, this approach aligns with global sustainability and ESG principles, which are increasingly important to investors, customers, governments and grants access to sustainable finance. By actively participating in the development of local talent and infrastructure, companies demonstrate their commitment to the "social" pillar of ESG, strengthening their position within sustainable business practices. Ethical internationalization also involves creating policies that ensure cultural sensitivity and inclusiveness. Partnering with local businesses or individuals allows foreign companies to gain deeper insights into cultural dynamics, avoiding missteps that might alienate local communities or damage their reputation. When local stakeholders feel respected and valued, they are more likely to embrace the company's presence and support its growth in the region. In today's interconnected world, businesses can no longer afford to operate with a singular focus on profit. Sustainable and ethical internationalization strategies, such as prioritizing knowledge transfer, are key to building resilient businesses and thriving communities. By empowering local partners and communities, companies can achieve not only financial success but also a legacy of positive and lasting impact in the regions they serve. This dual focus on profitability and responsibility is not just a strategic advantage but a moral imperative in the modern globalized economy.

In conclusion, the importance of having a local partner when internationalizing cannot be overstated. A local partner brings essential knowledge, resources, and connections that are critical for navigating the complexities of a new market. By leveraging the expertise of a local partner, a company can better understand local market dynamics, navigate regulatory and legal requirements, build relationships and trust, overcome operational challenges, and enhance its competitive advantage. Moreover, in many regions, local partnerships are increasingly becoming a legal requirement, making them an indispensable part of the internationalization process. For example, in the UAE, companies are obliged to be incorporated with at least 51% of shares given to a local partner. This is an extreme case, but governments around the world are following this example and driving in that direction. Beyond legal compliance, these partnerships also reflect a commitment to ethical business practices, ensuring that local communities benefit from the presence of foreign companies through knowledge transfer and economic development. Ultimately, a local partnership can significantly increase the likelihood of success in international markets, providing a strong foundation for sustainable growth and long-term profitability. As companies expand their global reach, forming strategic partnerships with local entities should be considered a key component of their internationalization strategy.

6.1.5 Dangers of Having a Local Partnership

While having a local partner is often a critical component of successful internationalization, it is not without its risks. One of the primary dangers lies in the potential for misaligned interests. Even when both parties share the common goal of business success, differences in strategic priorities, operational approaches, and long-term objectives can lead to conflicts. A local partner may prioritize short-term gains or have different ethical standards, which could jeopardize the foreign company's reputation or lead to decisions that are not in line with the company's core values. Ensuring that both parties have a clear and aligned vision from the outset is crucial to mitigating this risk. Another significant danger is the potential for dependency on the local partner, which can create vulnerabilities for the foreign company. In some cases, the local partner might gain excessive control over key aspects of the business, such as customer relationships, supply chains, or regulatory compliance. This dependency can limit the foreign company's flexibility and decision-making power, making it difficult to operate independently or respond to changes in the market. Additionally, if the relationship with the local partner deteriorates, it can lead to significant disruptions in operations, loss of market share, or even legal disputes. To avoid these pitfalls, it is essential for companies to carefully structure their partnerships, with clear agreements that outline roles, responsibilities, and exit strategies to protect their interests.

Another important factor to account for requires companies to carefully evaluate the potential risk of reputational damage that could arise from the partner's activities. This is particularly critical in younger or emerging markets, where the prevalence of corruption, lack of transparency, and informal business practices may present significant challenges. While local partners often possess invaluable on-the-ground expertise and networks, these same networks can sometimes operate in ways that expose foreign companies to ethical, legal, and reputational risks. One of the primary concerns in such environments is the tendency for local partners to underestimate or disregard the risks associated with the exchange of favors. In markets where informal practices are deeply ingrained in the business culture, activities such as offering bribes, facilitating unfair advantages, or leveraging personal connections to bypass regulatory hurdles may be perceived as routine. However, for MNCs or businesses from highly regulated jurisdictions, such activities can have severe consequences. Foreign companies could inadvertently become implicated in corruption scandals, leading to investigations, penalties, or legal actions under international anti-corruption frameworks, such as the US Foreign Corrupt Practices Act (FCPA) or the UK Bribery Act. Local partners often rely on their networks to gain competitive advantages, such as fast-tracking approvals, securing contracts, or overcoming logistical barriers. While this network leverage can initially seem beneficial, it may also involve practices like "buying favors," offering gifts, payments, or other incentives to officials or key stakeholders to smooth operations. This practice not only poses legal risks but also jeopardizes the ethical standing of the foreign company, potentially tarnishing its reputation in the global marketplace.

Moreover, the reliance on informal or opaque methods to overcome com-petition or administrative bottlenecks can backfire if these practices come to light. In the age of heightened transparency and corporate social responsibility (CSR), stakeholders, including consumers, investors, and regulatory bodies, are increasingly scrutinizing companies for their ethical conduct and adherence to global standards. A misstep by a local partner can quickly spiral into a reputa-tional crisis for the foreign company, even if the company was unaware of or uninvolved in the partner's actions. To mitigate these risks, companies must adopt a proactive approach when selecting and managing local partners. Con-ducting rigorous due diligence is essential, including verifying the partner's busi-ness practices, reputation, and compliance track record. Companies should also implement clear guidelines for ethical conduct and establish robust monitoring systems to ensure compliance with international anti-corruption laws and inter-nal policies. Additionally, providing ethics training for local partners can help bridge the gap between informal local practices and the company's compliance requirements. By educating partners on the risks and implications of corruption, companies can foster a culture of transparency and accountability. Contractual agreements should also include clauses on compliance, allowing the foreign company to terminate the partnership if the local partner engages in unethical or illegal activities.

6.2 How to Negotiate with a Local Partner

As previously discussed, forming a partnership with a local entity when entering new markets is both a critical opportunity and a potential risk. Once the right local partner has been identified, the next step involves negotiating a collabora-tion agreement that ensures a *win–win outcome*. For a partnership to succeed, it is imperative that both parties feel satisfied with the agreement. If one party feels coerced or undervalued during the negotiation process, their long-term commit-ment to the partnership may waver, increasing the likelihood of failure. When negotiating a partnership, whether it involves a JV, distribution agreement, or operational collaboration, there are *three key dimensions* that must be ad-dressed: *finance* (who pays), *operations* (who executes), and *governance* (who de-cides and controls). Achieving alignment on these dimensions is the foundation of a successful and equitable partnership.

The Three Dimensions of Negotiation:

1. *Finance (who pays):*
   This dimension revolves around financial contributions and finan-cial risk-sharing. A successful partnership requires clarity on how costs will be distributed among the parties, whether through direct investments, ongoing operational expenses, or emergency funding. For example, who will finance the initial market research? Who will

invest in infrastructure development? These questions must be answered with precision to avoid future disputes.

2. *Operations (Who Executes):*

This dimension focuses on the distribution of roles within tasks. It requires both parties to agree on who will handle key operational aspects such as logistics, supply chain management, and local hiring. According to the age of the market and the nature of the local partner, these roles may vary consistently. For example, in an adolescent market, a local partner may guarantee a best-as-possible local distribution system that the international partner may find it hard to build due to the lack of local infrastructures, however, in a senior market, the international partner may guarantee a more efficient local distribution due to its economy of scale nature and the presence of good quality local infrastructures.

3. *Governance (Who Decides and Controls):*

Governance defines how decisions are made and who holds authority in critical areas of the partnership. This includes determining leadership structures, voting rights, and mechanisms for resolving disputes. Establishing clear governance structures ensures that neither party feels marginalized, and that the partnership operates efficiently over time.

Every new project can be broken into specific tasks, each of which must be allocated across finance, operations, and governance. For each task, the parties must decide:

- Who pays for it?
- Who is responsible for its execution?
- Who has decision-making authority and control?

While tangible responsibilities, such as financing or managing a supply chain, are relatively straightforward to quantify, intangible responsibilities like networking or local knowledge often pose a challenge. For example, maintaining a strong local network may be more critical than securing favorable loan terms from banks (or vice versa), how to measure or compare them? Or else, how can the value of local cultural expertise be compared to technical expertise? To address these challenges, tasks (both tangible and intangible) should be *economically quantified* for comparability. This involves assigning monetary values to the tasks required for a successful partnership's objectives, weighted based on the task's *importance* and *urgency* within the overall strategy. The more urgent a task is, the more we shall weigh in the negotiation process between the parties (and vice versa). The same is to be expected for tasks which are urgent, as more urgent tasks will have a greater weight in the negotiation phase than negligible ones (and vice versa). Two tasks requiring the same economical effort distinguish themselves by the degree of urgency and importance for their execution and can be traced within the *Urgency-Importance Matrix* (Figure 6.1).

Figure 6.1 Generalized Urgency-Importance Matrix

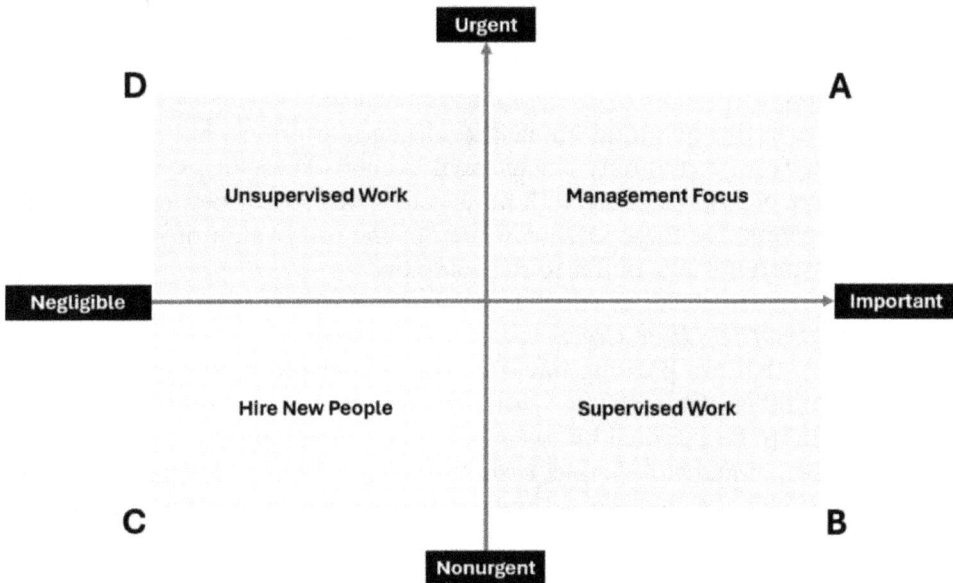

6.2.1 Using the Urgency-Importance Matrix

The *Urgency-Importance Matrix* is a powerful and useful framework but shall be adapted from its original form in order to be used as a guide to set the rules for a local partnership bargaining process. In its original form, this matrix is used internally by companies to allocate resources to different tasks and subtasks. Tasks are consequently classified based on their urgency and importance within the overall project and shall be placed within one of the four quadrants of the *Urgency-Importance Matrix*:

> *Quadrant A – High Urgency, High Importance*:
> Tasks belonging to this quadrant are important and urgent to successfully execute (e.g., bring in the needed finance). These critical tasks have a high degree of risk and responsibility requirements, where time and quality of delivery play a key role. For such tasks, no errors nor delays are allowed, raising the degree of ownership required, and demanding the assignments be given to trusted managers.

Quadrant B – Low Urgency, High Importance:
These are tasks that are essential but have a longer timeline (e.g., building local brand reputation). Tasks in this quadrant are negligible to execute in the short run, but the responsibility given by the nature of the task is high. This is a good task to test trustworthiness of internal HR, by assigning them the responsibility to successfully deliver the task under the supervision of an experienced manager.

Quadrant C – Low Urgency, Low Importance:
Tasks in this quadrant are neither urgent nor critical but may still add value (e.g., community engagement events). These tasks require a low degree of responsibility with no urgency, perfect for new entrants. Hiring people for these tasks can help in the integration of new HR and provide a mistake buffer to the company.

Quadrant D – High Urgency, Low Importance:
Tasks that are pressing but less critical in the long term are allocated within this quadrant (e.g., office furniture). Tasks in this quadrant are urgent to be executed but their outcome will not affect the performance of the company. A perfect condition to test internal HR resilience and independence. In this quadrant, companies usually seek the managers of the future.

By quantifying tasks and categorizing them within this matrix, the company can objectively assess each task's contribution and importance. This approach ensures that each task is correctly evaluated (quantified), prioritized, and understood, reducing potential risks and promoting transparency. Using the Urgency-Importance Matrix increases success rate and optimizes resource allocation.

6.2.2 Adapting the Urgency-Importance Matrix to a Local Partnership Negotiation

A new partnership can be viewed as a collaborative project, requiring the allocation of tasks and resources from each partner, much like the launch of an internal corporate initiative. Adapting the Urgency-Importance Matrix from its traditional internal use to the context of international partnership formation provides an objective and systematic framework for assessing and comparing the contributions of both parties. By applying this methodology, the Matrix transforms each task into a quantifiable tool that highlights each partner's role and effort within the new venture. This structured approach not only establishes clear ground rules for negotiation but also fosters transparency, equity, and mutual understanding. At its core, this method emphasizes that the partner assuming greater responsibilities (whether in terms of financial contributions, operational execution, or governance oversight) will naturally command a proportionally larger share of the partnership. To ensure fairness, both tangible tasks (such as financing infrastructure) and intangible tasks (such as leveraging a well-established local network) must be economically quantified and categorized within the Matrix. For example, consider a partner who has spent years cultivating a robust local network. This network provides access to key stakeholders, accelerates the permitting process, and ensures smoother entry into the local market. While this network represents an intangible asset, it has a measurable economic value if based on its capacity to generate income, attract clients, or reduce market entry barriers. Given its high relevance with a nonurgent nature, this task could be appropriately placed in Quadrant B (Low Urgency, High Importance). Conversely, tasks such as securing immediate financing or ensuring compliance with urgent local regulations might be placed in Quadrant A (High Urgency, High Importance), reflecting their critical and time-sensitive nature. By assigning monetary values to these tasks, the Matrix allows for an objective comparison of responsibilities (Figure 6.2).

Figure 6.2 Adapted Urgency-Importance Matrix

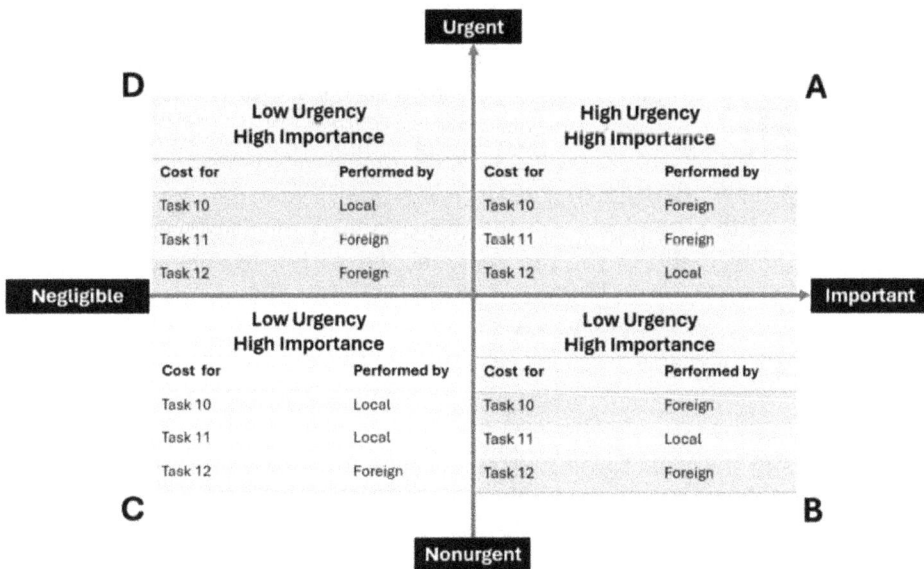

Tasks in different quadrants cannot have the same weight, as the levels of risk, importance, and timing vary significantly. Companies performing tasks in Quadrant A are much more exposed than those handling tasks in Quadrant C, necessitating the assignment of weights (levels of exposure) to each quadrant based on a task's urgency and importance. This approach provides an objective measurement of the exposure a company assumes by performing a specific task. By applying these weights, tasks across the entire project can now be compared equitably. To enable this comparison, the economic value of each task is multiplied by the weight assigned to the quadrant in which it operates. This quantification ensures that even intangible contributions, often undervalued or overlooked, are properly recognized. Furthermore, this systematic method moves the negotiation process beyond subjective judgments, fostering a results-oriented discussion centered on shared goals and equitable contributions. Based on this approach, and using a logic of "higher exposure means higher value," the following weights are applied to each quadrant:

Quadrant A: Weight Allocated 100%
Tasks in this quadrant are of high urgency and high importance, making them critical to the project's success. These tasks often involve significant financial, operational, or reputational risk and require immediate attention. Examples include securing regulatory compliance or finalizing urgent financial arrangements.

Quadrant B: Weight Allocated 75%
Tasks in this quadrant are low urgency but high importance, essential to the long-term success of the project. While not immediately pressing, their strategic value makes them a priority. Examples include building a strong local brand reputation or cultivating long-term stakeholder relationships.

Quadrant C: Weight Allocated 25%
Tasks in this quadrant are low urgency and low importance, contributing marginally to the project's success with a low level of company exposure. These tasks often add value incrementally and are suitable for lower-priority efforts. Examples include community engagement events or office aesthetics.

Quadrant D: Weight Allocated 50%
Tasks in this quadrant are high urgency but low importance, requiring immediate action but carrying relatively low long-term impact. These tasks intrinsically carry a lower level of company exposure if compared to tasks performed in quadrant B, but higher than those in quadrant C. Examples include managing logistical challenges like securing temporary office supplies or addressing minor operational disruptions.

This weighting system ensures a balanced and transparent approach to task evaluation, promoting fairness and clarity in partnership negotiations (Figure 6.3).

Figure 6.3 Adapted Urgency-Importance Matrix with weights

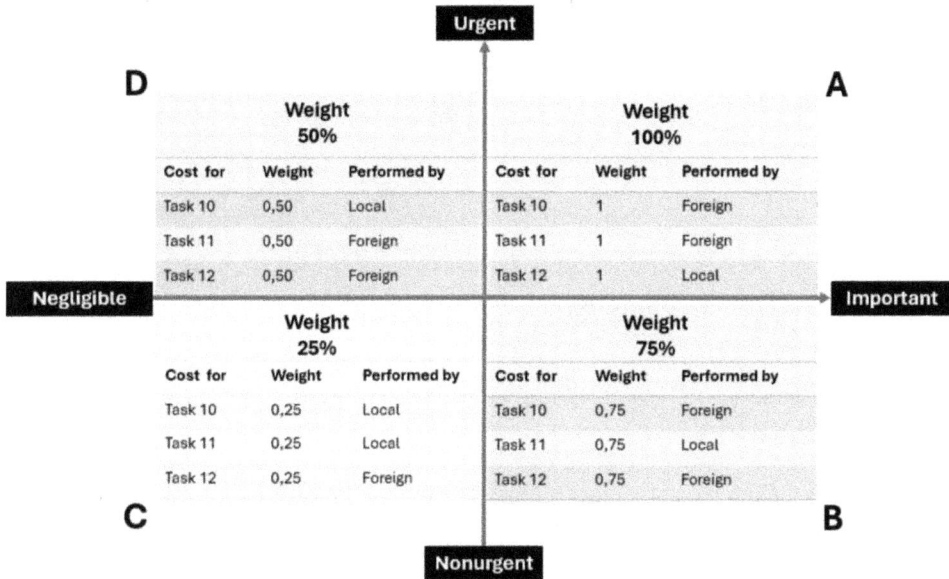

Lastly, all parties calculate their contribution to the partnership by summing up the weighted, monetary valued tasks they perform. The total contribution of each party will collectively represent 100% of the partnership, with each party's share determined by their respective contributions. The formula used is as follows:

1. **Calculation of each party's weighted contribution**

Local Partner Contribution $= Q.\ A_{Local} + (Q.\ B_{Local} \times 0,75) + (Q.\ D_{Local} \times 0,50) + (Q.\ C_{Local} \times 0,25)$

Foreign Partner Contribution $= Q.\ A_{Foreign} + (Q.\ B_{Foreign} \times 0,75) + (Q.\ D_{Foreign} \times 0,50) + (Q.\ C_{Foreign} \times 0,25)$

2. **Assignment of each party's share in the new partnership**

$$\%\ \textbf{Local Partner} = \frac{\text{Local Partner Contribution}}{(\text{Local Partner Contribution} + \text{Foreign Partner Contribution})} \times 100$$

$$\%\ \textbf{Foreign Partner} = \frac{\text{Foreign Partner Contribution}}{(\text{Foreign Partner Contribution} + \text{Local Partner Contribution})} \times 100$$

This weighted approach ensures that each party's tangible and intangible contributions are fairly represented in the partnership agreement, promoting transparency and equity in the allocation of shares. For a practical example, please refer to the next chapter. It is important to underline that the negotiation process should be guided by a commitment to fairness, open communication, and mutual respect. By clearly defining roles, responsibilities, and engagement levels and ensuring that these are proportionately valued, companies and their local partners can establish a partnership that is not only equitable but also primed for long-term success.

7 Developing a Roadmap to Build an IB Strategy

"In theory there is no difference between theory and practice, in practice there is." (Yogi Berra, n.d.)

Crafting a robust and effective IB strategy is both an art and a science. It requires a delicate balance between theoretical frameworks and practical applications, ensuring that companies can navigate the complexities of global markets while leveraging their unique strengths. As we conclude this book, it is vital to transition from theory to practice, offering readers actionable insights into how the concepts discussed can be applied to real-world scenarios. This chapter aims to serve as a bridge between the foundational methodologies presented throughout the book and their tangible implementation through detailed case studies. Internationalization is a multifaceted endeavor; from assessing market potential and categorizing markets to negotiating with local partners and managing operational risks, the journey is rife with opportunities and challenges. Companies embarking on this path must contend with diverse factors such as cultural differences, regulatory landscapes, resource allocation, and competitive dynamics. While theoretical models provide a solid foundation for understanding these complexities, it is the application of these theories in real-world contexts that truly determines success.

The purpose of this chapter is to provide practical guidance for readers interested in developing their IB strategy by showcasing two real-life case studies. These examples have been carefully selected to demonstrate how the methodologies outlined in this book can be applied across different industries, markets, and strategic objectives. Each case study illustrates a unique aspect of internationalization, offering valuable lessons that can be adapted to suit the specific needs of any organization. Together, these case studies offer a comprehensive roadmap for developing an IB strategy. They demonstrate how companies can transform theoretical knowledge into actionable strategies, navigating the complexities of international markets with confidence and precision. By studying these examples, readers will gain a deeper understanding of how to apply the principles of market categorization, resource allocation, partnership negotiation, and risk management in real-world scenarios. As we delve into these case studies, it is essential to approach them with an open mind, recognizing that each organization's journey is unique. The goal of this chapter is not to provide a *one-size-fits-all* solution but to inspire and empower readers to adapt the methodologies presented in this book to their own contexts, ultimately paving the way for successful internationalization.

7.1 AguaClara's Dilemma: Turning ESG Challenges into Global Opportunities

7.1.1 Context

A Spanish multinational company, which for the sake of this analysis is referred to as "AguaClara S.A.," is specialized in the production and distribution of water treatment chemicals for municipal use. Among their flagship production lines is a facility dedicated to manufacturing Ferric Chloride; a compound highly effective in removing fine particles during the water treatment process. The product has historically been a cornerstone of their business, allowing the company to maintain a competitive edge in this specialized sector. However, the company now faces a significant challenge. With the European Union enforcing increasingly stringent ESG policies, AguaClara is compelled to reform its production processes to align with updated regulations. These new standards prioritize energy efficiency, a reduced environmental footprint, and enhanced worker safety measures. The company's administrative department has issued a stark warning to the board of directors: if the production line does not become ESG-compliant within two years, the company will face substantial penalty taxation for noncompliance. These penalties would dramatically increase the cost of their Ferric Chloride, rendering it uncompetitive in the market and threatening the sustainability of this business line.

Compounding the problem is the financial burden associated with achieving compliance. A thorough analysis reveals that retrofitting the existing machinery to meet ESG standards would cost significantly more than investing in a new ESG-compliant production line. This creates a paradoxical dilemma, as the current machinery is in excellent condition, capable of producing Ferric Chloride efficiently for many more years with minimal maintenance costs. Despite this, retaining the existing machinery would lock the company into a scenario where escalating production costs and punitive taxation would make continued operation untenable. The company finds itself at a critical juncture: a "cul-de-sac" situation with no apparent easy solution. Continuing operations "as-is" guarantees financial decline, yet the high upfront investment required for new ESG-compliant machinery poses a daunting challenge. The decision is not merely a financial one; it has strategic implications for the company's long-term viability and alignment with regulatory trends and market expectations. How can AguaClara navigate this precarious position? Should they take the bold step of investing in new machinery, find alternative markets or uses for their existing equipment, or explore innovative business models to mitigate the financial risks of transitioning to ESG compliance? This case study delves into the strategic decision-making process required to address these pressing questions, offering insights into how companies can turn existential challenges into opportunities for growth and innovation.

AguaClara's board of directors identified three potential courses of action to address their predicament:

1. *Sell the Existing Machinery and Purchase ESG-Compliant Equipment*

   This approach involves selling the current production line and using the proceeds to partially fund the purchase of new ESG-compliant machinery. While this option aligns with EU regulations and secures compliance, it comes with notable limitations. The existing machinery cannot be sold within the EU due to its noncompliance with ESG standards, and, additionally, selling it to markets such as India would yield a relatively low price, insufficient to meaningfully offset the cost of new machinery. This would result in AguaClara parting with a functional and reliable asset without significant financial relief, leaving the company to bear most of the replacement costs independently.

2. *Operate "As-Is" for Two Years and Transition Gradually*

   Under this option, AguaClara would continue using the current machinery for two more years, leveraging the interim period to generate as much revenue as possible before the ESG penalties take effect. Simultaneously, they would initiate the sale of the machinery closer to the compliance deadline, using the proceeds to contribute toward the purchase of new equipment. However, this strategy presents significant risks. The lead time for ordering, manufacturing, and delivering new ESG-compliant machinery is approximately 18 months, which would require substantial upfront capital from AguaClara. Additionally, the resale value of the old machinery is likely to depreciate further over the two-year period, eroding the financial benefits of this approach.

3. *Relocate the Ferric Chloride Production Line*

   The third option entails relocating the current production line to a market outside the EU, where ESG restrictions are less stringent. By leveraging the company's expertise and the reliability of its machinery, AguaClara could penetrate a new international market and capitalize on the existing production line's capacity. Concurrently, the company would invest in a new ESG-compliant production line for its EU operations, potentially accessing green finance from the EU

Just Transition Fund. This dual strategy would enable AguaClara to maintain its market share in its home region while diversifying its operations and tapping into new revenue streams abroad. However, this approach requires a larger initial investment and involves a longer implementation timeline, with added complexities related to market research, local partnerships, and logistical planning.

After careful deliberation, AguaClara's board of directors chose option three as the most strategic path forward. This decision reflects their commitment to sustainability, innovation, and long-term growth. While this option demands greater upfront investment and meticulous planning, it aligns with the company's vision of maintaining its competitive edge in the EU while exploring opportunities in new markets. The board has tasked the business development department with creating a tailored internationalization strategy to execute this ambitious plan. This strategy will not only address the operational and financial logistics of relocating the production line but also ensure that the new market entry is aligned with AguaClara's corporate values and long-term goals. The next steps for the company include conducting market analysis, identifying suitable relocation destinations, and crafting a robust roadmap to manage this complex transition effectively.

7.1.2 Selecting the "Where"

The business development department initiated its analysis by focusing on internal factors, starting with a comprehensive evaluation of AguaClara's capacity to invest abroad. As outlined in Chapter 2, identifying a market that aligns with the company's profile requires a thorough understanding of two critical dimensions: resource availability and risk tolerance. In terms of resource availability, AguaClara possesses a significant advantage, as by utilizing its existing production line (the core of this new venture), the company effectively covers a substantial portion of the initial capital expenditure (CapEx). Although this contribution is provided in kind rather than in cash, it still represents a high level of available resources for the project, giving AguaClara a solid foundation for international expansion. Regarding risk tolerance, AguaClara's position is nuanced. While the company is prepared to deploy its production line in the new market, a notable risk in itself, it remains cautious about exposing the asset to scenarios that could lead to its complete loss. This indicates a moderate level of risk tolerance: AguaClara is neither highly conservative nor excessively risk-seeking in its approach. With these internal factors in mind, AguaClara's options for international expansion are naturally constrained to adult and senior markets.

Figure 7.1 AguaClara's positioning in the "where" matrix

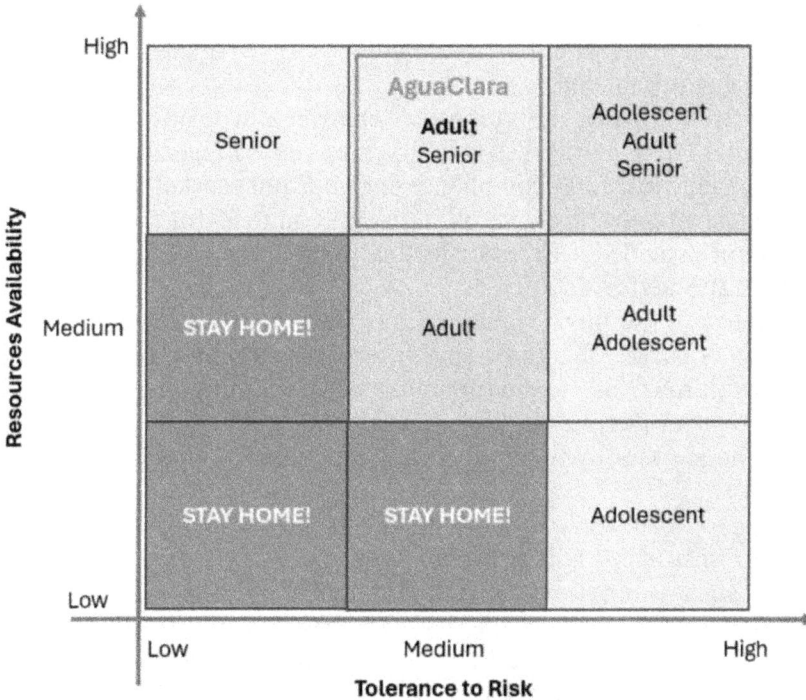

Markets that demand extreme risk tolerance or lack sufficient infrastructure to support the proposed venture are unsuitable. However, even within these market categories, selecting the optimal target requires further in-depth analysis. The choice must balance market potential with AguaClara's strategic priorities, ensuring a robust and sustainable internationalization strategy (Figure 7.1).

To identify the correct country, there is the need to start by identifying markets with a significant demand for Ferric Chloride. This chemical, essential for purifying municipal water supplies, is a key component in providing clean water services to residents, a responsibility typically managed by governments. As a commodity sold in large volumes with narrow margins, profitability in Ferric Chloride production relies heavily on market size and consistent demand. However, applying Market Pareidolia principles, not all countries have comprehensive water infrastructure to support widespread usage of Ferric Chloride. Apart from being not eligible markets for AguaClara as seen previously, adolescent markets often lack extensive water treatment systems, with infrastructure limited to major urban areas. Rural regions in these markets frequently lack access to treated water or any water infrastructure at all. For these countries, importing Ferric Chloride is often more practical than establishing a local production facility, as the limited market size would not justify capital investment.

Conversely, senior markets face similar ESG compliance challenges to those in the European Union, as these nations adhere to stringent environmental standards under agreements such as the 2016 Paris Agreement. Relocating production to a senior market would therefore fail to resolve AguaClara's core issue of meeting ESG requirements.

This left the business development department with a clear path: targeting adult markets. These markets strike a balance between infrastructure development and manageable ESG compliance levels. Adult markets fall within the 35 to 59 age range, presenting a pool of 112 viable countries for consideration. This categorization provided a focused starting point for AguaClara's strategic internationalization efforts.

To identify the most viable market for AguaClara's internationalization initiative (Table 7.1), additional filters were applied to refine the list of potential adult markets. These filters helped ensure alignment with the company's strategic objectives while addressing the challenges posed by stringent ESG compliance requirements. Below is a detailed breakdown of the selection process:

1. *Exclusion of European Countries:*
   European nations, including both EU member states and non-EU countries, were excluded from consideration due to their obligation to comply with the European Union's stringent ESG regulations. These requirements are akin to the challenges AguaClara seeks to mitigate through internationalization. This exclusion extends to Turkey, which, as a commercial bridge between Europe and the Middle East, adheres to similar ESG obligations to maintain trade relationships with its European neighbors. Relocating the production line to any of these regions would replicate the company's current obstacles rather than resolve them.

2. *Focus on Younger-Age Adult Markets*:
   Older adult markets, nearing senior status, often implement increasingly stringent ESG policies to align with senior markets' environmental standards. This trend poses risks similar to those found in the Euro Zone. To mitigate this, the focus was narrowed to markets within the 35–44 age range. These markets strike a balance between growth potential and manageable regulatory compliance, offering a more favorable environment for AguaClara's operations.

Table 7.1 Selected Adult Markets for AguaClara

Age	Country
59.41	Hungary
59.25	Slovenia
58.79	Thailand
58.07	Malaysia
57.08	Malta
56.48	Maldives
56.44	Estonia
56.26	Greece
55.68	Saudi Arabia
55.68	Lithuania
55.51	Slovakia
55.11	Bhutan
54.63	Croatia
54.39	Latvia
53.12	India
52.28	Romania
52.18	Sri Lanka
51.87	Uruguay
51.86	Barbados
51.77	Oman
51.39	Indonesia
51.16	Bulgaria
50.78	Dominica
50.73	Chile
50.47	Argentina
50.21	Vietnam
50.08	Mexico
49.99	Jamaica
49.64	Suriname
49.39	Brazil
49.02	Fiji
48.59	Kazakhstan
48.58	Belarus
48.04	Ukraine

Age	Country
47.95	Mauritius
47.80	Zambia
47.74	Mongolia
47.59	Trinidad and Tobago
47.20	Ghana
47.11	Kuwait
47.05	Panama
47.04	Cuba
47.03	Bahamas
47.02	Laos
46.74	Brunei
46.59	Cabo Verde
46.11	Peru
45.87	Serbia
45.84	Philippines
45.50	Seychelles
45.13	Azerbaijan
44.93	Myanmar (formerly Burma)
44.72	Costa Rica
44.49	Ecuador
44.39	Moldova
44.23	Uzbekistan
44.19	Turkey
44.17	Morocco
44.11	Vanuatu
43.54	Georgia
42.93	Dominican Republic
42.72	Senegal
42.59	Belize
42.25	Cambodia
42.19	Gambia
42.08	Paraguay
41.99	Albania
41.98	Armenia
41.67	Tanzania
41.67	North Macedonia

Age	Country
41.55	Bolivia
41.19	Saint Lucia
41.11	Papua New Guinea
40.99	Benin
40.98	Timor-Leste
40.90	Eritrea
40.78	Côte d'Ivoire
40.23	El Salvador
40.22	Kyrgyzstan
40.03	Malawi
39.98	Iran
39.86	Algeria
39.67	Montenegro
39.48	Saint Vincent and the Grenadines
39.03	Kenya
38.82	Colombia
38.61	Togo
38.54	South Africa
37.89	Bangladesh
37.84	Mozambique
37.83	Angola
37.69	Liberia
37.54	Samoa
37.43	Venezuela
37.26	Egypt
36.95	Nigeria
36.80	Guinea-Bissau
36.52	Burkina Faso
36.23	Guatemala
36.18	Solomon Islands
36.14	Nicaragua
35.92	Tunisia
35.85	Guyana
35.75	Mauritania
35.43	Pakistan
35.38	Bosnia and Herzegovina

Age	Country
35.26	Gabon
35.19	Jordan
35.12	Niger
34.91	Madagascar
34.79	Mali
34.76	Libya

3. *Population Size as a Key Indicator:*
   Population size serves as a critical proxy for the potential demand for Ferric Chloride, a key component in large-scale water treatment. Larger populations often require more extensive water purification systems, directly correlating to market potential. After applying the first two filters, the six most populated countries were shortlisted as follows:
   a. *Pakistan* – approximately 240 million
   b. *Nigeria* – approximately 223 million
   c. *Bangladesh* – approximately 171 million
   d. *Egypt* – approximately 111 million
   e. *Iran* – approximately 89 million
   f. *South Africa* – approximately 64 million

4. *GDP per Capita as a Refining Filter*
   While population size indicates potential demand, it does not account for a country's ability to pay for water treatment services. To refine the selection, GDP per capita was introduced as a key metric to gauge a country's capacity to invest in and sustain water infrastructure projects. The GDP per capita rankings are as follows:
   a. *Egypt* – approximately $16,691
   b. *Iran* – approximately $15,912
   c. *South Africa* – approximately $13,690
   d. *Nigeria* – approximately $5,286
   e. *Pakistan* – approximately $5,126
   f. *Bangladesh* – approximately $4,390

The first three countries exhibit significantly higher GDP per capita, indicating greater purchasing power and scalability for Ferric Chloride production. Consequently, Nigeria, Pakistan, and Bangladesh were excluded due to their lower economic capacity.

Evaluating the Final Three Candidates

1. *Egypt,* while it offers a substantial market size and the highest GDP per capita among the shortlisted countries, its water sourcing is highly centralized around the Nile River. This geographic dependency creates a bottleneck in commercial opportunities, as the majority of water treatment demand is concentrated in limited areas. This constraint reduces the scalability of a production facility and diminishes the overall attractiveness of the market.
2. *Iran*, while the population size and GDP per capita is appealing, international embargos and complex geopolitical constraints could significantly hinder operations, particularly when dealing with Italy.
3. *South Africa* stands out as a highly viable candidate. It boasts diverse water sources, a relatively high population, high enough GDP per capita, and limited local Ferric Chloride production, making it a less competitive market. Additionally, South Africa's membership in the Southern African Development Community (SADC) significantly enhances its appeal. The SADC region, comprising 16 member countries, offers duty-free trade for goods produced within the bloc. This creates a unique opportunity for AguaClara to access not only the South African market but also an additional 15 countries such as Angola, Botswana, Madagascar, Mozambique, and Zambia via efficient rail, road, and sea networks.

After a thorough evaluation, *South Africa* emerged as the optimal choice for AguaClara's internationalization project. Its strategic position within the SADC region, coupled with favorable trade conditions and market dynamics, provides AguaClara with a gateway to multiple new markets. This expanded reach not only maximizes the utility of the existing machinery but also aligns with AguaClara's long-term growth and internationalization objectives.

7.1.3 Selecting the "What"

AguaClara faces limited options regarding the type of internationalization strategy it can adopt. The decision to internationalize was driven primarily by the need to address a pressing issue: the use of an EU non-ESG-compliant production line. This industrial challenge inherently defines the nature of the internationalization process, making it an industrially focused venture by necessity. However, the question remains: does AguaClara possess all the necessary attributes to execute such a strategy effectively, or are there other options? As discussed in Chapter 3, two key dimensions must be assessed when planning an internationalization process: resources availability and degree of dependency. AguaClara's existing production line, as previously mentioned, serves as the cornerstone of the venture, and represents a substantial resource contribution. By leveraging this machinery as the company's primary investment in the internationalization process, the financial exposure for AguaClara can be considered high, reflecting robust resource availability. When evaluating dependency, Ferric Chloride production demonstrates minimal constraints. The process requires five key raw materials, all of which are widely available on the global market:

1.   Iron (Fe) or Iron Scrap – readily accessible in most regions.
2.   Chlorine Gas (Cl_2 – produced extensively in industrial hubs worldwide.
3.   Hydrochloric Acid (HCl) – often a byproduct of other industrial activities, ensuring consistent availability.
4.   Oxidizing Agents (Optional) – easily sourced if required for specific production needs.
5.   Water – universally accessible and abundant.

None of these raw materials' present supplier constraints or significant dependencies. Furthermore, the production process for Ferric Chloride is straightforward and does not rely on specialized manpower, proprietary technology, or patents. These factors collectively position the venture (Figure 7.2) as having a low dependency profile, reducing operational risks and increasing the feasibility of implementing the internationalization strategy.

Figure 7.2 AguaClara's positioning in the "what" matrix

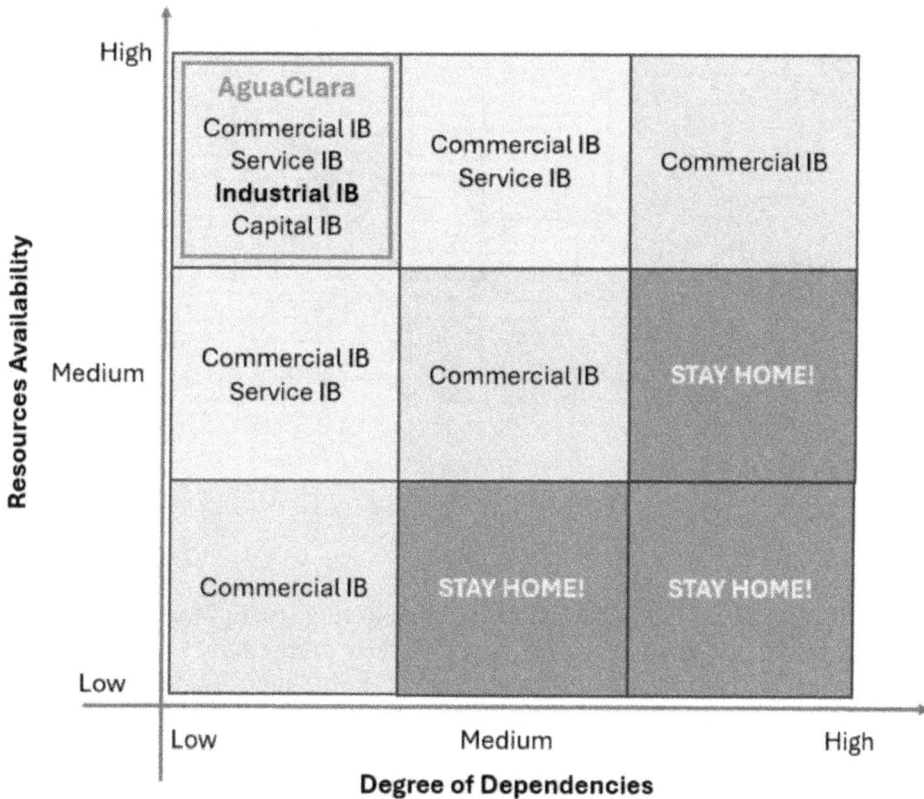

By combining high resource availability with low dependency traits, AguaClara is well-positioned to undertake its industrial internationalization project, ensuring the company can navigate the complexities of entering a new market with confidence.

In conclusion, AguaClara's robust resource availability, low dependency profile, and moderate risk tolerance position the company for success in mid-aged adult markets, where these attributes align closely with market requirements (Figure 7.3). However, if the company aims to venture into younger, higher-risk markets, it must substantially increase its risk tolerance to effectively address the complexities and uncertainties inherent in such environments.

Figure 7.3 AguaClara's positioning in the "where & what" matrix

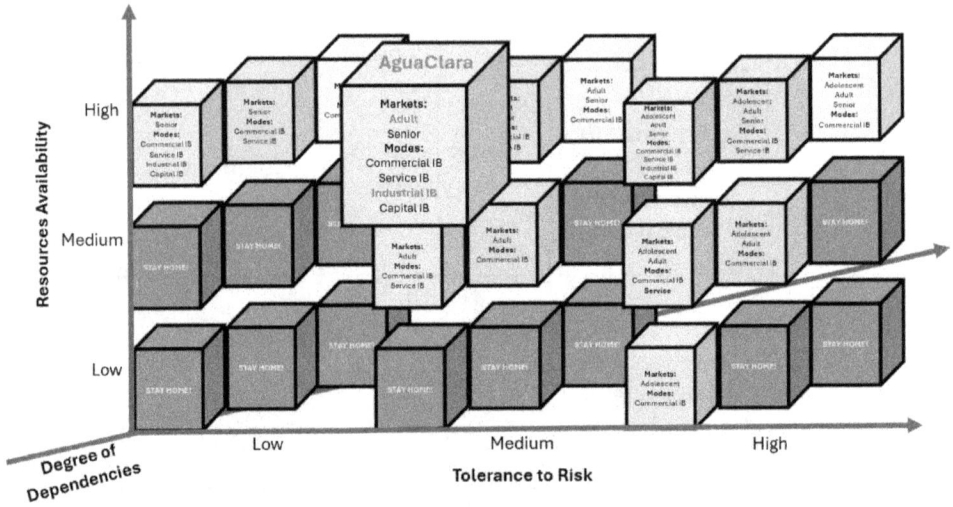

7.1.4 Selecting the "How"

When venturing into international markets, selecting the right strategic framework is crucial for ensuring alignment between a company's objectives, resources, and the dynamics of the target market. For AguaClara , the decision to internationalize stems from a strategic necessity: leveraging its existing non-ESG-compliant production line in a market with favorable conditions while expanding its global footprint. This decision is not merely about entering a new territory but involves carefully navigating complex variables such as regulatory environments, resource availability, operational efficiency, and long-term growth potential. With a range of internationalization models available, each offering unique perspectives and tools, AguaClara must evaluate which approach best suits its goals. The Uppsala Model emphasizes gradual learning, the Born Global Model focuses on rapid expansion, and the Network Process Model highlights leveraging relationships. Meanwhile, the Eclectic Paradigm (OLI Model) examines ownership and location advantages, the TCA Model centers on minimizing operational inefficiencies, and Porter's Diamond explores national competitive advantages. For the company, the choice of model is not just an academic exercise but a practical tool to guide its strategy. It must take into account South Africa's unique characteristics as the selected market, its regional advantages throughout the SADC bloc, and the company's internal capabilities. By analyzing these factors considering the available models, Porter's Diamond emerges as the most fitting framework, offering a comprehensive lens to evaluate external market conditions, internal strengths, and the broader strategic landscape. Let's see why, starting by analyzing the alignment with AguaClara's Context and Goals:

1. *Industry Context and National Competitive Advantage*:
   The Ferric Chloride market is tied to infrastructure and municipal water treatment systems, which are heavily influenced by national conditions such as government policies, local infrastructure, and economic stability. Porter's Diamond emphasizes the competitive advantage of nations, helping AguaClara identify South Africa's favorable conditions, such as access to regional markets (SADC), local demand, and potential synergies.
2. *Focus on External Factors*:
   AguaClara is seeking to leverage external market conditions (e.g., South Africa's infrastructure, trade agreements, and strategic regional advantages). Porter's Diamond allows a structured evaluation of factors such as demand conditions, factor conditions, related industries, and government influence, which are pivotal for industrial ventures.
3. *Strategic Adaptability*:
   AguaClara's decision to internationalize stems from the need to capitalize on non-ESG-compliant machinery while expanding to new markets. Porter's Diamond helps analyze the regulatory landscape and regional growth potential in ways other models do not.

Why Other Models Are Less Suitable:

- *Uppsala Model*:
  While it emphasizes gradual internationalization based on market familiarity, AguaClara is not entering a new market cautiously to "learn." Instead, it's relocating a production line based on external strategic factors, making Uppsala less relevant.
- *Born Global Model*:
  This model targets companies aiming for rapid global expansion, typically smaller firms in high-tech sectors. AguaClara is focusing on entering one specific market (South Africa) with an existing asset rather than pursuing a wide-reaching, rapid global strategy.

- *Network Process Model*:
  Though it could help leverage local partnerships and networks, the model prioritizes relational approaches. AguaClara's strategy focuses on internal capabilities and external market opportunities, where local networks are important but not the central driver.

- *Eclectic Paradigm (OLI Model):*
  While OLI is strong for explaining FDI decisions through ownership, location, and internalization advantages, its static structure does not address South Africa's broader regional influence and infrastructure. Porter's Diamond offers a more holistic, national-level view.
- *Transaction Cost Analysis (TCA) Model:*
  TCA focuses on cost efficiency in transactions. While AguaClara's relocation strategy considers operational costs, the decision to expand is driven more by strategic market access and regulatory considerations than cost minimization.

Why Porter's Diamond Is Best:
Even though OLI Model could be considered as a good fit, Porter's Diamond helps AguaClara holistically analyze South Africa's market conditions while positioning the company for broader regional success. By examining:

- *Factor Conditions:* Access to infrastructure, skilled labor, and raw materials.
- *Demand Conditions:* Growing regional need for water treatment chemicals.
- *Supporting Industries:* Regional supply chains within SADC.
- *Government Role:* Trade agreements like SADC's duty-free policies.

AguaClara can build a strategy that aligns with both local conditions and regional opportunities, ensuring a competitive and sustainable entry into South Africa. This comprehensive approach uniquely addresses AguaClara's dual goals of capitalizing on its existing assets and leveraging a new market's strategic advantages.

7.1.5 Negotiating a Local Partnership

AguaClara believes it has identified a promising local partner, which, for the sake of this exercise, will be called LocalChem. This potential partner brings several strategic assets to the table, including established office space, available land for the installation of the production line (though a warehouse would still need to be constructed), a robust commercial network within the local market, a strong political network to navigate regulatory landscapes, and access to non-specialized local human resources. However, LocalChem lacks prior experience in the production of Ferric Chloride, which poses a potential challenge. To ensure a structured approach to the partnership, all activities necessary to bring the project to fruition must first be identified and categorized. Each activity should be evaluated for its urgency and importance, allowing it to be placed in the appropriate quadrant of the urgency-importance matrix. Once categorized, these tasks should be monetarily quantified (in US dollars), with their respective costs weighted according to their urgency and importance. This process will provide a clear and objective basis for assessing each party's contributions and responsibilities, facilitating a transparent and equitable negotiation (Table 7.2). These are the results:

Table 7.2 Prioritized Cost Assessment of Key Activities between AguaClara and LocalChem

Activity	Responsibility	Urgency	Importance	Quadrant	Weight	Cost ($)	Weighted Cost ($)
Incorporation of the NewCo	LocalChem	High	High	A	1	10,000	10,000
Marketing (1 year)	LocalChem & AguaClara	Low	Low	C	0.25	30,000	7,500
Ferric Cholide Production Line	AguaClara	High	High	A	1	3,000,000	3,000,000
Transportation and assemblement of the Production Line	AguaClara	High	High	A	1	150,000	150,000
HR training	AguaClara	Low	High	B	0.75	45,000	33,750
Wharehose construciton	AguaClara	High	Low	D	0.5	850,000	425,000
Licences and permits	LocalChem	High	High	A	1	5,000	5,000
Commercial Local Network (on potential new contracts)	LocalChem	Low	High	B	0.75	500,000	375,000
Political Local Network (on potential new contracts)	LocalChem	High	Low	D	0.5	1,500,000	750,000
One year OpEx (office rent, HR, mobility, maintainance etc.)	AguaClara	Low	High	B	0.75	550,000	412,500
Certifications	LocalChem	Low	Low	C	0.25	25,000	6,250
Land for Wharehose	LocalChem	High	Low	D	0.5	400,000	200,000

These are the key activities grouped by macro areas. On demand, each of these activities can be broken down into numerous sub-tasks. The deeper and more detailed the activity analysis, the more accurate and realistic the assessment of each party's effective exposure and contributions will be. A granular approach ensures that no aspect of the partnership's responsibilities is overlooked, promoting transparency and fairness in negotiations. As illustrated in the table, certain activities stand out due to their urgency and importance. For example, the production line is classified as both highly important and highly urgent, as without it, there is no product to sell, making it the cornerstone of the project. Conversely, the commercial local network, while undeniably important for long-term success, is not immediately urgent. Until the production line becomes operational, there is no product to market or sell, reducing the immediate need for commercial efforts. On the other hand, the political local network presents a different scenario. While it is not critically important in the grand scheme of operations (licenses and permits could potentially be obtained without a local network, albeit with longer timelines), it is highly urgent, as delays in securing these approvals could push back the entire project timeline. Finally, marketing activities are neither urgent nor particularly important in this context. The primary clients for Ferric Chloride are municipalities, where personal networks and political connections tend to play a more significant role than traditional marketing campaigns.

By quantifying and assigning weights to these contributions (Table 7.3) for both the local and foreign partners, a clear picture of the shared responsibilities emerges. This systematic approach enables an equitable calculation of each party's weighted input, forming the basis for determining a fair and transparent share distribution in the partnership.

Table 7.3 Direct Contribution to Key Activities between AguaClara and LocalChem

	LocalChem Weighted Contribution ($)	AguaClara Weighted Contribution ($)
Total Weighter Investment	1,350,000	4,025,000
Shares	25%	75%

7.1.6 Conclusions

The case study of AguaClara and its decision to relocate its Ferric Chloride production line highlights the strategic considerations and complexities involved in internationalization. Faced with the dual challenge of complying with stringent ESG regulations in its home market and optimizing the utility of its existing production line, AguaClara demonstrated a methodical approach to identifying the most suitable market and structuring its partnership with LocalChem. This journey encapsulates the essence of how businesses can transform operational constraints into opportunities for growth and market expansion. AguaClara's decision-making process underscores the importance of aligning internal capabilities, such as resources availability, risk tolerance, and dependency levels, with external market conditions. By applying the principles of Market Pareidolia, the company effectively narrowed its focus to mid-aged adult markets that align with its strategic traits. This targeted approach not only reduced the risks associated with entering unsuitable markets but also optimized the use of its existing assets, ensuring that its investment would yield sustainable returns. The selection of South Africa as the target market was informed by a blend of quantitative analysis and strategic foresight. By leveraging the country's membership in the SADC region, AguaClara opened avenues to an extended market of 16 neighboring countries, transforming local investment into a regional opportunity. This decision highlighted the importance of evaluating regional synergies and trade agreements when assessing market potential.

The partnership with LocalChem also demonstrated the critical role of local partners in facilitating internationalization. LocalChem's strengths in political and commercial networks provided AguaClara with invaluable on-the-ground expertise, while AguaClara's operational and technical expertise balanced the partnership. The use of the Urgency-Importance Matrix to quantify and evaluate each partner's contributions ensured transparency and equity in structuring the partnership. This methodological approach not only minimized potential disputes but also fostered mutual trust and commitment, laying a strong foundation for long-term collaboration. Ultimately, this case study illustrates how strategic planning, data-driven decision-making, and collaborative partnerships can drive successful internationalization. AguaClara's ability to integrate its internal strengths with external opportunities serves as a model for businesses navigating the complexities of expanding into new markets. By transforming a regulatory challenge into an avenue for growth, the company not only safeguarded its operations but also positioned itself for long-term success in a competitive and evolving global landscape.

7.2 Éclat d'Olive: Crafting a New Era of Health-Conscious Beauty

7.2.1 Context

Sun&Shine LLC (referred to for ease of reference in this case study), a US-based company with headquarters in Miami, specialized in sunscreens and mid-tier women's makeup, is at a critical juncture in its growth trajectory. Despite sustained efforts over the past four years, the company has struggled to achieve significant growth in its key markets. Annual sunscreen sales increased by only 2%, mirroring the US Sun Protection market's modest growth average of 1.61% (Statista, n.d.), while the makeup segment posted a mere 0.23% annual growth rate, falling far short of the projected 3.38% growth for the US Cosmetics market (Statista, n.d.). This sluggish performance indicates a loss of market share despite incremental revenue gains, signaling stagnation in an increasingly saturated market. The company's leadership has exhausted traditional avenues for revitalizing sales, ranging from targeted local campaigns and national TV promotions to product rebranding and a focused e-commerce push. None of these strategies have yielded meaningful results. Recognizing the inevitability of market saturation, the board of directors concluded that diversification and a bold shift in product targeting were necessary for the company's continued growth. Under the guidance of the CEO, Sun&Shine's executive team proposed an innovative approach: a premium product line that seamlessly integrates beauty and health. This concept involves developing a range of products that merge high-quality cosmetics with scientifically backed health benefits, effectively catering to the growing consumer preference for wellness-oriented beauty products. Their market analysis revealed that the US Vitamins and Minerals market, with its projected annual growth rate of 4.58% (Statista, n.d.), offered a promising benchmark for this hybrid approach.

The cornerstone of this new product line would be a powerful anchor that conveys both quality and healthfulness. Research pointed to two globally recognized symbols of excellence: the French reputation for premium cosmetics and Italy's association with a healthy lifestyle. After careful consideration, the team proposed leveraging the cultural cachet of both nations. The product line, named "*Éclat d'Olive*" (translated as "Radiance of Olive"), would feature virgin olive oil as its star ingredient, a nod to its rich history as a beauty enhancer and health elixir. Italian olive oil, known for its purity and health benefits, would serve as the foundation of the product line, ensuring a strong association with wellness. Meanwhile, the products would be manufactured in France to capitalize on the perception of French-made cosmetics as the pinnacle of luxury and quality. The innovative concept, while promising, presents a series of challenges for Sun&Shine. For one, their current product line does not align with the proposed Éclat d'Olive philosophy. Existing makeup products, such as primers, are known to clog pores, which contradicts the health-first narrative of the new brand. Additionally, rebranding the entire makeup line under this new concept could alienate their existing customer base and risk disrupting the gains achieved in their current markets.

The solution? Establish Éclat d'Olive as an entirely separate brand under the Sun&Shine umbrella. This approach would allow the company to maintain its existing market share while targeting a new, health-conscious demographic through the new line. However, the question of market entry strategy loomed large:

- Should Sun&Shine launch Éclat d'Olive in the US, leveraging its existing distribution network?
- Should the company prioritize France or Italy, given their cultural ties to the new brand's identity?
- Are there other markets where the hybrid beauty-health concept might resonate even more strongly?

Producing in France provides clear benefits for the new brand's luxury positioning, while sourcing virgin olive oil from Italy ensures the authenticity of its health-focused narrative. Italian olive oil, accompanied by a certificate of origin, would reinforce the product's credibility in delivering wellness benefits. The duality of French quality and Italian health heritage provides a compelling brand story that can differentiate Éclat d'Olive in competitive markets. However, the choice of the pilot market is far from straightforward. The US, with its established distribution network, might seem an obvious choice, but market saturation and intense competition in the beauty sector could limit the brand's initial impact. France and Italy, as cultural homes to the brand's essence, offer potential advantages but may also present challenges related to consumer familiarity and differing retail landscapes. Alternatively, other markets with burgeoning middle classes and rising demand for premium wellness products might provide fertile ground for experimentation.

7.2.2 Selecting the "Where"

To identify the most suitable market age for piloting the new product offering under the Market Pareidolia framework, it is crucial to first evaluate Sun&Shine's resource availability and tolerance for risk, two critical dimensions when selecting "where." These factors will shape the decision-making process, ensuring that the chosen market aligns with the company's operational capacity and risk appetite. Sun&Shine has demonstrated a robust financial foundation, with sufficient assets to support this ambitious venture. The company's balance sheet shows not only solid liquidity but also stability, enabling it to sustain the capital expenditure required for the project. Importantly, the company's resources are substantial enough to support market entry efforts in more than one foreign market if necessary. This flexibility allows for experimentation and diversification, reducing the dependency on the success of a single market. Furthermore, even in the unlikely event of a project failure, the company is well-insulated from catastrophic financial repercussions. While losses would undoubtedly impact on short-term growth projections, they would not undermine the company's core operations or its ability to serve existing markets with standard products. This positions Sun&Shine as a company with high resource availability, ready to take calculated risks in pursuit of long-term strategic goals.

Despite its financial strength, Sun&Shine faces a critical limitation: a lack of prior experience in operating outside its domestic market. The company's current operations are deeply entrenched within the United States, and its leadership has limited exposure to the complexities of foreign market dynamics, such as navigating regulatory landscapes, cultural differences, and supply chain intricacies. This lack of experience translates into low familiarity with international markets, elevating the perceived risks of venturing abroad. Risk perception is further heightened by the company's unfamiliarity with the diverse consumer behaviors and competitive environments of foreign markets. For instance, the nuances of establishing a premium brand like Éclat d'Olive in a culturally distinct market could present unforeseen challenges. These considerations indicate that, while Sun&Shine is financially prepared for internationalization, its risk tolerance remains low, driven by its inexperience and apprehensions about the uncertainties of foreign expansion (Figure 7.4).

Figure 7.4 Sun&Shine's positioning in the "where" matrix

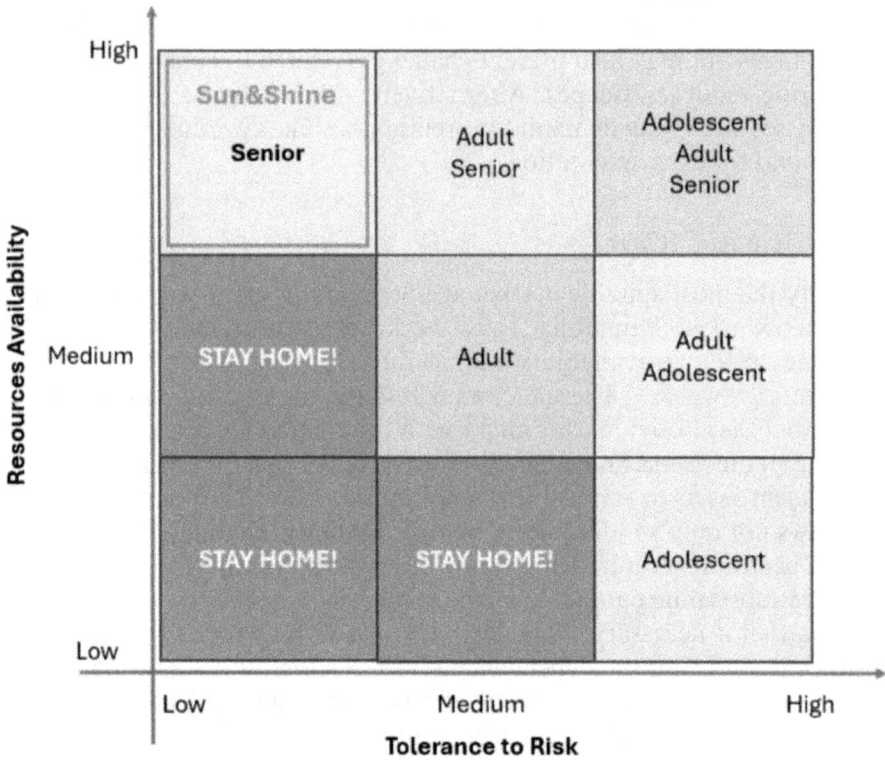

The combination of high resource availability and low risk tolerance suggests that Sun&Shine should target senior markets, which strike a balance between a large but competitive market with strong purchasing power, and limited risks. These markets typically offer stable political and economic conditions, an established middle class with disposable income, and a demand for premium wellness-oriented products, all characteristics that align with the aspirations of the Éclat d'Olive brand. By prioritizing senior markets, Sun&Shine can reduce the likelihood of cultural missteps or operational disruptions while maximizing the impact of its financial investments. This strategic focus will enable the company to leverage its strong resource base to build a foothold in a foreign market, even as it gradually develops the knowledge and capabilities needed to expand into younger, higher-risk markets in the future. The senior markets available are aged over 60:

Table 7.4 Selected Senior Markets for Sun&Shine

Age	Country
86.27	Japan
85.53	Singapore
79.38	United States of America
73.39	United Kingdom
73.04	Germany
71.76	Switzerland
71.05	South Korea
70.30	France
69.85	Italy
68.37	Netherlands
68.17	Ireland
67.59	China
67.46	United Arab Emirates
66.46	Qatar
66.20	Canada
65.97	Belgium
65.88	Norway
65.19	Finland
65.04	Australia
65.03	New Zealand
64.94	Denmark
64.41	Austria
63.96	Bahrain
63.93	Portugal
63.53	Sweden
63.06	Czechia (Czech Republic)
62.97	Israel
62.96	Luxembourg
61.87	Russia
60.90	Cyprus
60.83	Spain
60.81	Iceland
59.53	Poland

Poland, with market age approximating 60 years (rounded by excess), fall into the lowest range of senior markets. Despite this limited selection, these markets present intriguing possibilities. However, careful evaluation of multiple factors is essential to determine the optimal market for Sun&Shine's pilot project. Here are the critical considerations:

- *The Importance of French Market Presence*
A French identity is central to the brand's positioning, as "Éclat d'Olive" aims to leverage France's global reputation for high-quality cosmetics. Without a French market presence, the brand's authenticity could be questioned, undermining its ability to resonate with international consumers. While immediate strong revenues may not be expected, establishing a foothold in France will solidify the brand's French heritage and provide a foundation for credibility in future expansions.
- *Cultural Preferences in Italy*
Despite Italy being the origin of the brand's key ingredient, virgin olive oil, Italian consumers tend to favor domestic products over foreign alternatives when it comes to wellness and beauty. A French-branded product may face resistance, as Italians might perceive it as having a lower value for money compared to locally produced goods. This cultural nuance makes Italy a less favorable option for launching the pilot project, despite its proximity and familiarity with the product's ingredients.
- *Challenges of Distant Markets*
Markets such as New Zealand, Singapore, Australia, Japan, China, and South Korea are geographically distant and logistically challenging. High transportation costs could significantly inflate retail prices, making the brand uncompetitive as a newcomer. For a pilot project, such price sensitivities could discourage consumer adoption and lead to a premature failure, making these markets unsuitable for initial testing.
- *Cultural Challenges in Muslim Countries*
In many Arabic countries with a strong Muslim heritage, the cultural tradition of modesty has historically discouraged the use of makeup, particularly in public settings. Although societal norms are evolving, and the beauty industry is beginning to see growth in these regions, the potential market size for cosmetics remains relatively limited compared to Western or other global markets. Additionally, the local market's limited experience with makeup trends and preferences may not provide the robust insights or reliable feedback necessary for a successful pilot project. These factors collectively make such markets less ideal for launching innovative beauty products such as Éclat d'Olive.

- *Risk of Targeting the US for a Pilot*
  While the US is a critical market for long-term growth, launching a pilot there poses substantial risks. Failure could tarnish the company's reputation across its established product lines, leading to a ripple effect on other brands within Sun&Shine's portfolio. Protecting the company's existing US market share is vital, making it more strategic to approach the US market after validating the new brand's concept elsewhere.

- *Countries in Conflict*
  Countries undergoing some sort of political or economic conflict are against the company's low tolerance to risk. For this reason, Russia and Israel shall be excluded.

- *Exclusion of the other Eurozone Countries*
  While Europe could serve as a promising region for testing the new product line, the strategic aim of the pilot is to establish a strong foundation for eventually penetrating the US market. Since France will already serve as the production hub and home base for Éclat d'Olive, expanding the pilot to other European countries introduces unnecessary regional cultural nuances and barriers that could disrupt the consistency of results. Keeping the pilot outside the EU ensures that France maintains its position as the brand's cultural and geographic anchor, while avoiding complications associated with neighboring European markets.

After applying the above filters, the shortlist for the pilot project narrows to Canada and the United Kingdom. Both markets share characteristics that make them appealing testing grounds: cultural familiarity with European products, established middle-class consumers, and strong demand for premium wellness and beauty products. However, distinguishing factors tip the balance:

1. *Canada's European Heritage*
   Canada's European-influenced lifestyle and culture align closely with the brand's French identity and health-focused positioning. Canadian consumers are more likely to appreciate the natural and luxurious qualities of Éclat d'Olive, making it an ideal test market. Additionally, success in Canada could pave the way for entry into the larger US market, leveraging cultural and logistical proximity.

2. *The United Kingdom's Challenges*
   The UK, while a sizable market, does not have a reputation for prioritizing healthy lifestyles to the same extent as other European countries. This cultural disconnect could make it harder for the brand to resonate, especially given the focus on health and well-being that underpins the Éclat d'Olive concept.

Based on these considerations, France emerges as the optimal location to establish a foundational market presence, reinforcing the brand's French heritage. Simultaneously, Canada offers the best conditions for piloting the product line due to its cultural alignment, logistical feasibility, and potential as a gateway to the US market. Together, these two markets provide a strategic balance of credibility, growth potential, and manageable risk for Sun&Shine's ambitious new venture.

7.2.3 Selecting the "What"

With the "where" strategy firmly established, penetrating the French market and piloting the venture in Canada, the next critical step is addressing the "what" question: determining the most suitable internationalization mode for this ambitious endeavor (Figure 7.5). Sun&Shine has demonstrated high levels of resource availability, which positions it well to undertake substantial investments. However, the company also exhibits a significant degree of geographic dependency.

Figure 7.5 Sun&Shine's positioning in the "what" matrix

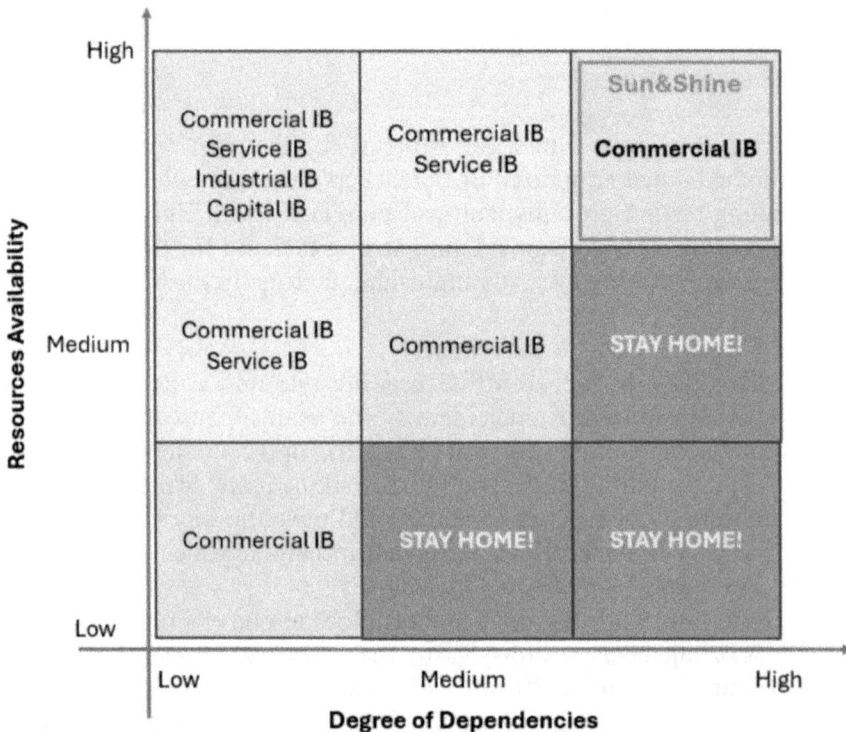

The "Made in France" branding is essential to establishing the product's perceived quality in cosmetics, while the main raw material, virgin olive oil, requires an authentic "Made in Italy" designation to underline its health benefits. This dual dependency on location strongly influences the type of internationalization strategy that can be adopted. Given these constraints, the company's only viable internationalization mode is adopting a Commercial IB approach, either directly or indirectly.

However, choosing between direct and indirect Commercial IB modes demands careful consideration.

- *The Limitations of Indirect Commercial IB*
  As a startup in the premium cosmetics segment, Sun&Shine cannot afford to rely on indirect Commercial IB, which typically involves distributing products through third-party channels. While this approach might reduce initial costs, it also significantly diminishes the company's ability to control branding, marketing, and customer engagement. Distributors often prioritize established products that guarantee returns, leaving new, untested offerings like Éclat d'Olive without the necessary attention and push to gain traction in competitive markets. This lack of motivation among third parties could severely hinder the brand's chances of success, especially in its critical early stages.
- *Direct Commercial IB: A Better Fit*
  To maximize its odds of success, Sun&Shine must maintain direct control over the brand and its operations. A direct Commercial IB strategy involves opening offices in both France (Paris) and Canada (Quebec City for its official French language). These offices will act as operational hubs, ensuring that the company retains control over marketing efforts, sales strategies, and customer relationships.

In France, the company can leverage the well-established network of independent laboratories and contract manufacturers specializing in high-quality cosmetics production. This allows Sun&Shine to avoid the significant risks and costs associated with setting up an Industrial IB operation (as seen in Figure 7.5, not an option), such as building and managing its own production facilities. Outsourcing production ensures access to pristine cosmetic manufacturing standards while reducing CapEx and operational complexities. The French office would also take charge of managing the domestic market. Its responsibilities would include coordinating with manufacturers, driving brand awareness, and ensuring product distribution aligns with the brand's luxury positioning. Meanwhile, a new Quebec City office would focus on penetrating the Canadian market. This office would oversee marketing campaigns, manage orders in coordination with the Paris office, and establish a strong presence in retail channels. Last, online sales will be managed by Sun&Shine HQ in Miami, in collaboration with the Quebec City and Paris offices. Canada's cultural alignment with European products and its position as a springboard for the US market make this step both strategic and necessary.

Figure 7.6 Sun&Shine's positioning in the "where & what" matrix

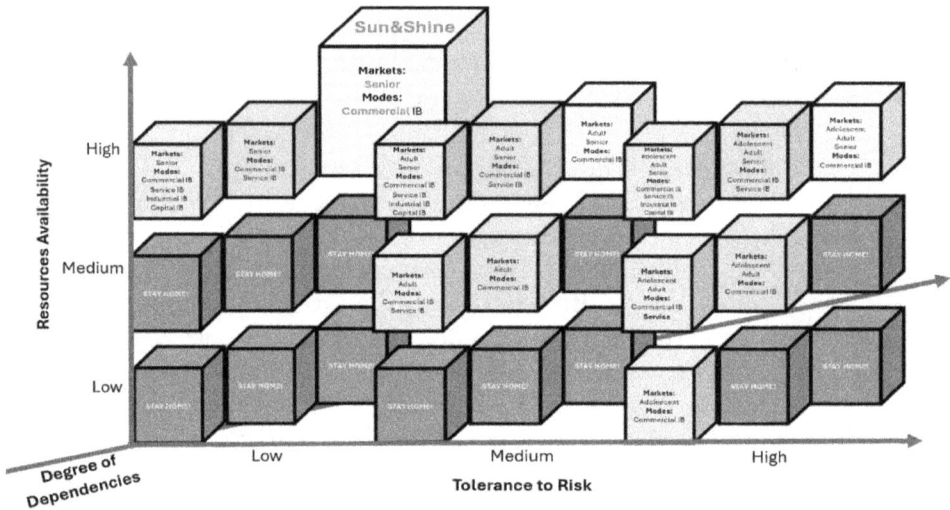

7.2.4 Selecting the "How"

The "where" and "what" strategies for Éclat d'Olive (Figure 7.6) have been clearly defined, establishing the target markets and internationalization approach. Now, it is essential to address the "how" – the implementation of these strategies. Among the various internationalization models explored in previous chapters, the Eclectic Paradigm (OLI Model) emerges as the most suitable framework for this venture. This model integrates three fundamental dimensions: Ownership advantages (O), Location advantages (L), and Internalization advantages (I), offering a comprehensive and strategic approach to guide the project's execution effectively. This comprehensive framework aligns seamlessly with the company's objectives, challenges, and strategic needs:

- *Ownership Advantages (O): Leveraging Brand Equity and Expertise*
  Sun&Shine's core strength lies in its well-established distribution network and extensive expertise in branding and product development within the makeup industry. While the company's current US-focused product lines face challenges in sustaining growth, the introduction of the Éclat d'Olive brand represents a transformative opportunity to capitalize on its existing operational capabilities and deep experience in the

cosmetics industry. Moreover, by maintaining full ownership and control of the Éclat d'Olive product offerings in the new markets, Sun&Shine ensures enhanced flexibility, stronger reputation management, and precise control over pricing strategies, positioning the brand for long-term success.

- *Location Advantages (L): Strategic Market Selection*
  The model's emphasis on location-specific advantages aligns well with Sun&Shine's dependency on geographic factors:
    - France offers unparalleled brand prestige in cosmetics. Setting up production here allows the company to capitalize on the "Made in France" label, a global marker of quality in this sector.
    - Italy's olive oil provides the health-focused foundation of the product line, reinforcing the brand's authenticity and aligning with the growing consumer demand for sustainable and wellness-oriented cosmetics.
    - Canada serves as a strategic pilot market due to its cultural alignment with European products and its potential as a springboard for US expansion.
- Internalization Advantages (I): Maintaining Control
  Sun&Shine's decision to opt for a direct Commercial IB model ensures that it maintains control over its brand and operations. This aligns with the Internalization advantage of the OLI Model:
    i. By managing production partnerships in France and directly overseeing operations in France and Canada, the company minimizes risks associated with third-party distributors.
    ii. Direct control ensures the brand image is meticulously crafted and communicated, essential for success in the high-end cosmetics market.

Why Other Models Are Less Suitable

- *Uppsala Model*
  The gradual, staged approach of the Uppsala Model is not well-suited to Sun&Shine's need for swift action to address stagnant growth. With the company's high resource availability, a more direct and ambitious strategy is possible, by passing the cautious incremental steps central to the Uppsala framework.
- *Born Global Model*
  The Born Global Model, while ideal for companies seeking rapid global expansion, does not align with Sun&Shine's geographic dependencies and targeted focus on high-value markets. Furthermore, Sun&Shine's lack of prior international experience makes a rapid, multi-market approach a risky endeavor that could jeopardize its success.

- *Network Process Model*
  This model, which depends heavily on leveraging preexisting relationships and networks, is similarly ill-suited for Sun&Shine, as the company currently lacks established networks beyond the US market. Without these connections, the model's primary advantage cannot be effectively realized.
- *Transaction Cost Analysis (TCA) Model*
  The TCA model, which emphasizes minimizing transaction costs and often advocates for third-party arrangements, would undermine Sun&Shine's goals. Outsourcing critical branding and marketing activities to distributors would weaken the company's ability to establish a strong market presence for the Éclat d'Olive brand and control its image and messaging.
- *Porter's Diamond*
  Finally, while Porter's Diamond could help Sun&Shine evaluate France's competitive strengths in the cosmetics sector, it does not provide a holistic framework for addressing the ownership advantages, location advantages, and internalization needs that are critical to the company's internationalization strategy.

Each of these models falls short in addressing Sun&Shine's unique combination of objectives, strengths, and market dependencies, reinforcing the conclusion that the OLI Model is the most appropriate framework for this venture. The OLI Model offers a balanced, strategic framework that aligns with the company's strengths and goals. It leverages the company's ownership advantages (brand expertise, product innovation), the location advantages of France and Italy (prestige and authenticity), and the internalization advantages of maintaining control over key aspects of the venture. By adopting the OLI framework, Sun&Shine can navigate the complexities of internationalization effectively, ensuring a robust foundation for Éclat d'Olive.

7.2.5 Negotiating a Local Partnership

Sun&Shine has established itself as a strong player in the US market, but its limited international experience leaves it unprepared to navigate the complexities of entering a sophisticated market like France (it would be easier with Canada as a neighboring country). Without prior exposure to the nuances of foreign markets or a robust local network, the risk of failure in such an ambitious venture increases significantly. To mitigate these challenges, Sun&Shine recognizes the critical importance of partnering with a local entity. A local partner can provide invaluable insights into the market, leverage their existing networks, and help the company avoid costly missteps. The ideal partner for

Sun&Shine would be one that possesses a well-established commercial network, even if modest, and shares the same goals of innovation and growth. A partner who is eager to expand their own horizons while collaborating closely to ensure mutual success is essential for navigating the French market's competitive landscape.

After an extensive search spanning several months, Sun&Shine's leadership team identified a promising candidate for their French partnership. For the purposes of this case study, this company will be referred to as LVL SARL (an acronym for La Vie en Luxe, meaning "Life in Luxury"). LVL is a mid-sized French company specializing in the national distribution of luxury multi-brand products. Their distribution network extends across France, covering several high-end chains. However, despite their experience in the luxury segment, LVL faces challenges that have constrained their growth potential, as the company's current market penetration is limited primarily due to the fiercely competitive nature of the French luxury market. High-end brands rarely grant exclusivity to distributors, leaving LVL dependent on the performance and visibility of their retail clients, factors largely outside their control. This dependency has stifled their ability to gain a competitive edge, making them highly motivated to explore new opportunities. The prospect of collaborating with Sun&Shine on the Éclat d'Olive brand presents an exciting strategic advantage for LVL. By owning shares in a unique, niche product that aligns with the growing consumer demand for health-conscious and premium offerings, LVL can differentiate itself from competitors and secure greater autonomy in the market. For Sun&Shine, LVL's established distribution network and expertise in the French luxury market offer a vital foothold into this competitive terrain. The alignment between Sun&Shine and LVL extends beyond strategic objectives; both companies share a vision for growth, innovation, and market leadership. LVL's drive to expand and strengthen its market presence complements Sun&Shine's ambition to establish Éclat d'Olive as a premium global brand. This shared commitment to excellence and mutual benefit forms a strong foundation for a successful partnership in this venture.

First, the list of activities needed for this new venture (Table 7.5) is listed, monetarily quantified, assigned to each party, and weighted:

Table 7.5 Prioritized Cost Assessment of Key Activities between Sun&Shine and LVL

Activity	Responsibility	Urgency	Importance	Quadrant	Weight	Cost ($)	Weighted Cost ($)
Incorporation of Éclat d'Olive SARL (France)	LVL & Sun&Shine	High	High	A	1	10,000	10,000
Incorporation of Éclat d'Olive Corp. (Canada)	LVL & Sun&Shine	High	High	A	1	10,000	10,000
Marketing (1 year) for the French market	LVL & Sun&Shine	Low	High	B	0.75	500,000	375,000
Marketing (1 year) for the Canadian market	LVL & Sun&Shine	Low	High	B	0.75	750,000	562,500
Research & Development for Éclat d'Olive	Sun&Shine	High	High	A	1	450,000	450,000
Production expenses for Éclat d'Olive	Sun&Shine	Low	High	B	0.75	1,500,000	1,125,000
French offices (1 year)	LVL	High	High	A	1	120,000	120,000
Canadina offices (1 year)	Sun&Shine	High	High	A	1	100,000	100,000
Licences and permits (France)	LVL	High	High	A	1	10,000	10,000
Licences and permits (Canada)	Sun&Shine	High	High	A	1	10,000	10,000
France commercial local network (on potential new contracts)	LVL	Low	High	B	0.75	900,000	675,000
Canada commercial local network (on potential new contracts)	Sun&Shine	Low	High	B	0.75	120,000	90,000
HR and logistics (France)	LVL & Sun&Shine	High	Low	D	0.5	250,000	125,000
HR and logistics (Canada)	Sun&Shine	High	Low	D	0.5	400,000	200,000
Certifications France	LVL	Low	Low	C	0.25	25,000	6,250
Certifications Canada	Sun&Shine	Low	Low	C	0.25	25,000	6,250
E-Commerce structural expenses	Sun&Shine	High	Low	D	0.5	600,000	300,000

LVL will take responsibility for overseeing logistics and operational activities within France, while Sun&Shine will manage logistics and operations in Canada. Additionally, Sun&Shine will lead R&D, manufacturing, and e-commerce operations for the Éclat d'Olive brand, including negotiations with Italian producers of virgin olive oil. Certain activities, such as marketing campaigns, will be collaborative efforts, leveraging the expertise and insights of both partners to maximize impact and market reach. Key activities are categorized and weighted based on their urgency and importance within the partnership. Tasks deemed highly urgent and highly important are those critical for establishing the foundation of the business. These include company incorporation (one entity in France and another in Canada), securing necessary permits and licenses, and conducting R&D for the Éclat d'Olive product line. These activities are fundamental to the feasibility and desirability of the new brand and require immediate and focused attention. Activities classified as low urgency, but high importance are those not essential in the initial stages but pivotal to the long-term success of the venture. For example, marketing campaigns and production processes can begin only after the R&D phase has been completed and the product is ready for launch. Tasks categorized as high urgency, but low importance are those necessary to kickstart operations but can be managed with less direct involvement from senior managers. For instance, initial HR recruitment and logistics can be outsourced temporarily, and given that Éclat d'Olive will rely on existing multi-brand retail outlets for its distribution, the creation of an e-commerce platform is urgent but not as critical as other foundational activities. Lastly, tasks with low urgency and low importance, such as obtaining certifications, can be outsourced entirely, as they do not immediately impact the business's core objectives or timelines.

By systematically quantifying and assigning weights to these contributions from both the local and foreign partners, a comprehensive understanding of the shared responsibilities emerges. This structured approach (Table 7.6) ensures that each activity is appropriately valued and accounted for, fostering clarity and transparency. The resulting calculations provide a solid framework for determining an equitable share distribution within the partnership, creating a fair and mutually beneficial collaboration.

Table 7.6 Direct Contribution to Key Activities between Sun&Shine and LVL

	LVL Weighted Contribution ($)	Sun&Shine Weighted Contribution ($)
Total Weighter Investment	1,397,500	2,822,500
Shares	33%	67%

7.2.6 Conclusions

The Sun&Shine case study exemplifies the complexities and opportunities inherent in internationalizing a business. Faced with stagnating growth in its domestic market, the company sought not only to expand geographically but also to redefine its product offering through the innovative Éclat d'Olive brand. This strategic pivot highlighted the importance of aligning internal capabilities with market opportunities, leveraging international partnerships, and employing sound internationalization models. The first critical step in Sun&Shine's journey was recognizing the need to diversify and innovate. The saturated US cosmetics and sunscreen markets posed limited growth potential, compelling the company to explore new segments. By merging cosmetics with health and wellness, the Éclat d'Olive concept offered a unique proposition. Grounded in the reputation of Italian olive oil for health benefits and the prestige of French cosmetics, the new brand effectively bridged two globally recognized standards of quality. This strategic decision underscored the importance of leveraging cultural and geographic associations to enhance product desirability in international markets.

In selecting target markets, Sun&Shine applied the principles of Market Pareidolia, identifying France as the primary market and Canada as the secondary pilot location. France, with its entrenched reputation for high-quality cosmetics, was an obvious choice to establish the brand's credibility and authenticity. Meanwhile, Canada, with its European heritage and cultural receptivity, provided an ideal springboard into North American markets. This dual-market approach balanced the need for credibility with the potential for scalability, demonstrating the importance of aligning market characteristics with corporate goals. The Éclat d'Olive venture also highlighted the value of the Eclectic Paradigm (OLI Model) in structuring the internationalization strategy. Sun&Shine's ownership advantages (its expertise in branding, R&D, and distribution) were pivotal in establishing the new brand. The location advantages of France and Italy reinforced the brand's narrative of quality and health, while internalization advantages ensured control over core activities such as marketing, production, and e-commerce. By aligning these dimensions, the company created a robust framework for entering and scaling new markets.

Partnership played a central role in mitigating risks and enhancing Sun&Shine's chances of success. Collaborating with LVL SARL in France provided critical on-the-ground expertise, local networks, and operational support. This partnership complemented Sun&Shine's strengths and addressed its lack of international experience, demonstrating the importance of selecting a partner with aligned goals and complementary capabilities. To ensure fairness and transparency, the collaboration was structured using the Urgency-Importance Matrix to quantify and weight each partner's contributions. This systematic approach not only facilitated equitable share distribution but also provided a clear roadmap for executing responsibilities, reducing the likelihood of conflicts and fostering mutual accountability. Ultimately, the Sun&Shine case demonstrates that successful internationalization requires a strategic blend of internal readiness, market analysis, and collaborative partnerships. By leveraging its existing strengths and adapting to new market dynamics, Sun&Shine positioned itself to expand its reach and revitalize its growth trajectory. The emphasis on innovation, strategic market selection, and partnership development provides a blueprint for other companies navigating the complexities of international expansion.

The Éclat d'Olive venture is not just a case of entering new markets but a testament to the importance of thoughtful planning, adaptability, and the strategic integration of cultural and geographic narratives. For Sun&Shine, this journey marks the beginning of a new chapter one where growth is driven not by conventional approaches but by bold, innovative strategies tailored to a global stage.

Note from the Author

As this book reaches its conclusion, I want to take a moment to reflect on the journey that brought these ideas to life. **Disrupting Internationalization: A Redefinition with Market Pareidolia** is more than just an exploration of global expansion strategies, it is a call to rethink how we perceive and categorize international markets, breaking free from traditional models that no longer serve the rapidly evolving world of business. Throughout this work, my goal has been to provide a structured, yet dynamic, framework that challenges conventional thinking and empowers businesses to make more informed, strategic decisions in their internationalization efforts. Market Pareidolia was born from the recognition that perception shapes reality, and in the complex world of global markets, how we categorize and interpret data can make the difference between success and failure.

I hope that the insights, methodologies, and case studies presented in this book serve as a practical guide for business leaders, strategists, and entrepreneurs looking to navigate the challenges of international expansion. But more importantly, I hope it inspires a shift in mindset, one that embraces adaptability, critical thinking, and the willingness to challenge established norms. Internationalization is not simply about expanding into new markets; it is about understanding them, respecting their nuances, and strategically positioning businesses to thrive within them. Whether you are an executive of an MNC, the founder of a growing startup, or an academic exploring global business dynamics, my hope is that this book provides value, clarity, and actionable strategies for your internationalization journey.

Thank you for joining me on this amazing journey.

Prof. Dr. Emiliano Finocchi, BE

Special Thanks

I would like to express my heartfelt gratitude to the individuals who have accompanied and supported me throughout this journey.

A special thank you to Dott. Luca Gatto, a dear friend, whose support has been invaluable across various aspects of this work.

To Dott. Alessandro Terzulli, I extend my sincere appreciation for his outstanding contribution through the remarkable preface he authored for this book.

My gratitude also goes to Dott. Valeriano Salciccia, a trusted friend, for his encouragement and endorsement.

Special thanks to Dott. Marco Lombardi, a loyal friend who stood by me in times of difficulty and generously offered his support and endorsement.

I am especially grateful to Dott. Pierluigi Aluisio for this endorcement, a true friend, whose presence and unwavering support during challenging times meant a great deal to me and my family.

Thank you all for being part of this journey.

Glossary of Acronyms

APEC – Asia-Pacific Economic Cooperation

AYS – Average Years of Schooling

BRICS – Brazil, Russia, India, China, and South Africa

CGD – Central Government Debt

COMESA – Common Market for Eastern and Southern Africa

CPI – Corruption Perceptions Index

EAF – Easiness to Attract Finance

EFI – Economic Freedom Index

ESG – environmental, social, and governance

FDI – Foreign Direct Investment

GCC – Gulf Cooperation Council

GDP – Gross Domestic Product

GIF – Global Influence and Financial Stability

GSP – Global Soft Power Index

IAU – Internet Access Usage

IMF – International Monetary Fund

JV – Joint Venture

LFA – Levels of Foreign Aid

LOD – Levels of Democracy

M&As – Mergers and Acquisitions

MINT – Mexico, Indonesia, Nigeria, and Turkey

NA – North America

OECD – Organization for Economic Cooperation and Development

OLI – Ownership, Location, and Internalization (Eclectic Paradigm)

PGR – Population Growth Rate

QOL – Quality of Life Index

RFE – Reserves of Foreign Exchange

RLI – Rule of Law Index

SADC – Southern African Development Community

SPE – Socio-Political and Economic

SPI – Social Progress Index

TAPI – Turkmenistan-Afghanistan-Pakistan-India (Pipeline Project)

TCA – Transaction Cost Analysis

UNDP – United Nations Development Programme

USMCA – United States–Mexico–Canada Agreement

WTO – World Trade Organization

References

Adams, R. B., Adams Jr, R. B., Ambady, N., Nakayama, K., & Shimojo, S. (Eds.). (2011). *The Science of Social Vision* (Vol. 7). Oxford University Press

Anderson, M., Vogels, E. A., Perrin, A., & Rainie, L. (2023). *Connection, Creativity and Drama: Teen Life on Social Media in 2022*. Pew Research Center

Benson, J. E., & Furstenberg Jr, F. F. (2006). Entry into adulthood: Are adult role transitions meaningful markers of adult identity?. *Advances in Life Course Research*, 11, 199–224

Burton, I. (1987). Report on reports: Our common future: The world commission on environment and development. *Environment: Science and Policy for Sustainable Development*, 29(5), 25–29

Carson, R. (1962). *Silent Spring III*. New Yorker, 23

Carruthers, B. G., & Stinchcombe, A. L. (1999). The social structure of liquidity: Flexibility, markets, and states. *Theory and Society*, 28(3), 353–382

Casasanto, D. (2015). All concepts are ad hoc concepts. In *The Conceptual Mind: New Directions in the Study of the Concepts* (pp. 543–566). MIT Press

Coase, R. (1960). The problem of social cost. *Journal of Law and Economics*, 3, 1–44.

Dunning, J. H. (1993). *Multinational Enterprises and the Global Economy*. Addison-Wesley

Dunning, J. H. (1980). Toward an eclectic theory of international production: Some empirical tests. In *The Eclectic Paradigm: A Framework for Synthesizing and Comparing Theories of International Business from Different Disciplines or Perspectives* (pp. 23–49). London: Palgrave Macmillan UK

Durand, R., Granqvist, N., & Tyllström, A. (2017). From categories to categorization: A social perspective on market categorization. In *From Categories to Categorization: Studies in Sociology, Organizations, and Strategy at the Crossroads*. Emerald Publishing Limited

Durand, R., & Paolella, L. (2013). Category stretching: Reorienting research on categories in strategy, entrepreneurship, and organization theory. *Journal of Management Studies*, 50(6), 1100–1123

Eden, L., Dai, L., & Li, D. (2010). International business, international management, and international strategy: What's in a name? *International Studies of Management & Organization*, 40(4), 54–68

Freund, A. M., & Smith, J. (1999). Content and function of the self-definition in old and very old age. *The Journals of Gerontology Series B: Psychological Sciences and Social Sciences*, 54(1), P55–P67

Friedman, T. L. (2005). *The World Is Flat: A Brief History of the Twenty-First Century*. Farrar, Straus and Giroux

Goleman, D. (2006). The Socially Intelligent. *Educational Leadership*, 64(1), 76–81

Granqvist, N., Grodal, S., & Woolley, J. L. (2013). Hedging your bets: Explaining executives' market labeling strategies in nanotechnology. *Organization Science*, 24(2), 395–413

Hannan, M. T., Pólos, L., & Carroll, G. R. (2007). Language matters, from logics of organization theory: Audiences, codes, and ecologies. Introductory Chapters

Hsu, G., Hannan, M. T., & Koçak, Ö. (2009). Multiple category memberships in markets: An integrative theory and two empirical tests. *American Sociological Review*, 74(1), 150–169

Johanson, J., & Mattsson, L. (1989). Strategic Action in Industrial Networks and the Development towards the "Single European Market." In IMP Conference (5th) (Vol. 5). IMP

Kim, A. B., Tyrrell, P., & Roberts, K. D. (2023). *2023 Index of Economic Freedom*. The Heritage Foundation

Kurzweil, R. (2001). The law of accelerating returns. In *Alan Turing: Life and legacy of a great thinker* (pp. 381–416). Berlin, Heidelberg: Springer Berlin Heidelberg

McDougall, P. P., Shane, S., & Oviatt, B. M. (1994). Explaining the formation of international new ventures: The limits of theories from international business research. *Journal of Business Venturing*, 9(6), 469–487

McDougall, P. P., & Oviatt, B. M. (1996). New venture internationalization, strategic change, and performance: A follow-up study. *Journal of Business Venturing*, 11(1), 23–40

Oviatt, B. M., & McDougall, P. P. (2018). Toward a theory of international new ventures. In *International Entrepreneurship: The Pursuit of Opportunities across National Borders*, 31–57

Liu, J., Li, J., Feng, L., Li, L., Tian, J., & Lee, K. (2014). Seeing Jesus in toast: Neural and behavioral correlates of face pareidolia. *Cortex*, 53, 60–77

Megginson, L. C. (1963). Lessons from Europe for American Business. *Southwestern Social Science Quarterly*, 44(1), 3–13

Navis, C., & Glynn, M. A. (2010). How new market categories emerge: Temporal dynamics of legitimacy, identity, and entrepreneurship in satellite radio, 1990–2005. *Administrative Science Quarterly*, 55(3), 439–471

Negro, G., Koçak, Ö., & Hsu, G. (2010). Research on categories in the sociology of organizations. In *Categories in Markets: Origins and Evolution* (Vol. 31, pp. 3–35). Emerald Group Publishing Limited

Nithyashri, J., & Kulanthaivel, G. (2012, December). Classification of human age based on Neural Network using FG-NET Aging database and Wavelets. In 2012 Fourth international conference on advanced computing (ICoAC) (pp. 1-5). IEEE.

Palmer, C. J., & Clifford, C. W. (2020). Face pareidolia recruits' mechanisms for detecting human social attention. *Psychological Science*, 31(8), 1001–1012

Paolella, L., & Durand, R. (2016). Category spanning, evaluation, and performance: Revised theory and test on the corporate law market. *Academy of Management Journal*, 59(1), 330–351

Pontikes, E. G. (2010). Two sides of the same coin: How category ambiguity affects multiple audience evaluations. In Proceedings of the Annual Meeting of the Academy of Management

Purcell, G., & Scheyvens, R. (2015). International business mentoring for development: The importance of local context and culture. *International Journal of Training and Development*, 19(3), 211–222

Rao, H., Monin, P., & Durand, R. (2005). Border crossing: Bricolage and the erosion of categorical boundaries in French gastronomy. *American Sociological Review*, 70(6), 968–991

Rogers, C. R. (1961). *On Becoming a Person: A Therapist's View of Psychotherapy.* Houghton Mifflin

Rosa, J. A., Porac, J. F., Runser-Spanjol, J., & Saxon, M. S. (1999). Sociocognitive dynamics in a product market. *Journal of Marketing*, 63(4_suppl1), 64–77

Rosa, J. A., & Spanjol, J. (2005). Micro-level product-market dynamics: Shared knowledge and its relationship to market development. *Journal of the Academy of Marketing Science*, 33(2), 197–216

Rosch, E., & Mervis, C. B. (1975). Family resemblances: Studies in the internal structure of categories. *Cognitive Psychology*, 7(4), 573–605

Saul, L. J. (1947). *Emotional Maturity; the Development and Dynamics of Personality.* Lippincott

Sibbritt, D. W., Byles, J. E., & Regan, C. (2007). Factors associated with decline in physical functional health in a cohort of older women. *Age and Ageing*, 36(4), 382–388

Stadler, C., Mayer, M., & Hautz, J. (2015). Few companies actually succeed at going global. *Harvard Business Review*

Statista. (n.d.). Cosmetics in the United States. Retrieved March 17, 2025, from https://www.statista.com/outlook/cmo/beauty-personal-care/cosmetics/united-states

Statista. (n.d.). Sun protection in the United States. Retrieved March 17, 2025, from https://www.statista.com/outlook/cmo/beauty-personal-care/skin-care/sun-protection/united-states

Statista. (n.d.). Vitamins and minerals in the United States. Retrieved March 17, 2025, from https://www.statista.com/outlook/hmo/otc-pharmaceuticals/vitamins-minerals/united-states

Shyamalan, M. N. (Director). (2013). *After Earth* [Film]. Columbia Pictures

Tatum, B. D. (2000). The complexity of identity: "Who am I?." *Readings for Diversity and Social Justice*, 2, 5–8

Williamson, O. E. (1979). Transaction-cost economics: The governance of contractual relations. *The Journal of Law and Economics*, 22(2), 233–261

Williamson, O. E. (1989). Transaction cost economics. *Handbook of Industrial Organization*, 1, 135–182

Zhang, M., Zhuang, C., & Gao, B. (2007). International market selection for agricultural product using fuzzy neural networks. In Fourth International Conference on Fuzzy Systems and Knowledge Discovery (FSKD 2007) (Vol. 2, pp. 503–507)

Zerubavel, E. (1999). *Social Mindscapes: An Invitation to Cognitive Sociology*. Harvard University Press

www.ingramcontent.com/pod-product-compliance
Lightning Source LLC
Chambersburg PA
CBHW081809200326
41597CB00023B/4196